ATTP 3-20.97

Dismounted Reconnaissance Troop

November 2010

Headquarters, Department of the Army

Published by Books Express Publishing
Books Express Publishing, 2011
ISBN 978-1-78039-949-2

Books Express publications are available from all good retail and online booksellers. For
publishing proposals and direct ordering please contact us at: info@books-express.com

Army Tactics Techniques and Procedures
No. 3-20.97

Headquarters
Department of the Army
Washington, DC., 16 November 2010

Dismounted Reconnaissance Troop

Contents

Figures

Tables

Preface

This Army Tactics, Techniques, and Procedures (ATTP) publication provides the doctrinal framework and tactical employment principles for the dismounted reconnaissance troop in the Infantry Brigade Combat Team's Reconnaissance Squadron. It is a companion to FM 3-21.10, *The Infantry Rifle Company*, and FM 3-20.971, *Reconnaissance and Cavalry Troop*, much of which applies to the dismounted reconnaissance troop and as such will not be repeated herein. This ATTP publication provides principles, tactics, techniques, and procedures for the employment of the dismounted reconnaissance troop throughout the spectrum of conflict.

In-depth coverage of major topics covered in FM 3-21.10, but limited in discussion here, includes preparation for war; troop-leading procedures; battle command and control; offensive and defensive operations; risk management and fratricide avoidance; operations in a chemical, biological, radiological, and nuclear environment; Army health service support; media considerations; pattern analysis; and situation understanding.

This ATTP publication applies to the Active Army, the Army National Guard/Army National Guard of the U.S., and U.S. Army Reserve, unless otherwise stated.

This publication is specifically directed toward the dismounted reconnaissance troop commander, executive officer, first sergeant, subordinate leaders, and all supporting units. It focuses on the actions of the dismounted troop as related to the reconnaissance squadron, and the employment capabilities of the troop relative to its sister motorized reconnaissance troops. Specific emphasis is given to section and platoon operations when necessary. For additional section and platoon reconnaissance operations, see FM 3-20.98, *Reconnaissance and Scout Platoon*.

This publication also--

- Provides doctrinal guidance for commanders, staffs, and leaders of the organizations, and personnel responsible for planning, preparing, executing, and assessing operations of the dismounted reconnaissance troop. It is also useful for military instructors, evaluators, training and doctrine developers, and Infantry commanders, officers, and noncommissioned officers.
- Updates existing doctrine based on current operations and higher doctrinal concepts and terminology, lessons learned from recent combat experiences, and training at the Joint Readiness Training Center.
- Reflects and supports Army operations doctrine as covered in FM 3-0, *Operations*; FM 3-90, *Tactics*; FM 3-90.6, *The Brigade Combat Team*; FM 3-20.96, *Reconnaissance and Cavalry Squadron*; and FM 3-20.971, *Reconnaissance and Cavalry Troop*. It is not a stand-alone reference for reconnaissance operations. It is intended to be used in conjunction with these and other existing doctrinal resources.

The proponent for this publication is the U.S. Army Training and Doctrine Command. The preparing agency is the U.S. Army Maneuver Center of Excellence. Comments and recommendations may be sent by any means: U.S. mail, e-mail, fax, or telephone, using or following the format of DA Form 2028, *Recommended Changes to Publications and Blank Forms*.

E-mail:	benn.catd.doctrine@conus.army.mil
Phone:	COM 706-545-7114 or DSN 835-7114
Fax:	COM 706-545-7500 or DSN 835-7500
U.S. Mail:	Commanding General, MCoE
	Doctrine and Collective Training Division
	Directorate of Training and Doctrine
	ATTN: ATZB-TDD
	Fort Benning, GA 31905-5593

Unless stated otherwise, masculine nouns and pronouns refer to both male and female genders.

This page intentionally left blank.

Chapter 1

Introduction

The dismounted reconnaissance troop (DRT) conducts reconnaissance, security, and surveillance operations. The DRT accomplishes its mission by providing timely, accurate, and relevant combat information across the full spectrum of operations. The troop supports the reconnaissance squadron's development of situational awareness (SA) and the commander's situational understanding (SU), by tracking the threat throughout the area of operations (AO). The troop is equipped and organized to satisfy the Infantry brigade combat team (IBCT) reconnaissance squadron commander's information requirements (IR) and to answer his critical information requirements (CCIR). In the AOs, the DRT, as part of the reconnaissance squadron, conducts reconnaissance, security, and surveillance operations, and collects information that enables the IBCT commander to focus lethal and nonlethal effects with precision. The troop also directs fires on specific targets provided in the commander's high-payoff target list (HPTL). Except as specifically directed, the DRT rarely engages the enemy with direct fire. When lethal fires are needed, the DRT most often employs indirect fire, close air support (CAS), or close combat attack (CCA) assets.

SECTION I – TEXT REFERENCES

1-1.   Table 1-1 consolidates the references to additional information.

Table 1-1. Guide for subjects referenced in text

Subject	References
Reconnaissance and Cavalry Troop	FM 3-20.971
Joint Operations	JP 3-0
Operations	FM 3-0
Mission Command: Command and Control of Army Forces	FM 6-0

SECTION II – DISMOUNTED RECONNAISSANCE TROOP

1-2.   The reconnaissance squadron is an IBCT asset that satisfies reconnaissance requirements within the brigade. The DRT conducts reconnaissance and security missions across the full spectrum of operations. The variables of mission, enemy, terrain, weather, troops, and support available; time available; and civil considerations (METT-TC) dictate how the missions will be conducted. However, the basic need for reconnaissance or security information remains a requirement for the IBCT throughout all operations. The DRT is suited to perform all civil support missions like any other troop or company.

1-3.   The DRT is the only dismounted troop of the three troops within the squadron. While each troop has essentially the same mission of reconnaissance and security, the DRT is most often used in missions or terrain where the nature of the operation is more closely suited for deliberate and stealthy reconnaissance. The DRT should be able to assume a motorized reconnaissance role given additional mobility assets. (For motorized troop operations refer to FM 3-20.971.)

OVERVIEW

1-4.   The DRT is organic to the reconnaissance squadron assigned to an IBCT. The reconnaissance squadron consists of a headquarters and headquarters troop (HHT), two motorized reconnaissance troops, and one DRT as shown in Figure 1-1. The DRT has approximately 80 personnel. Its mobility is largely accomplished by foot, with vehicles limited mainly to leadership and supply personnel.

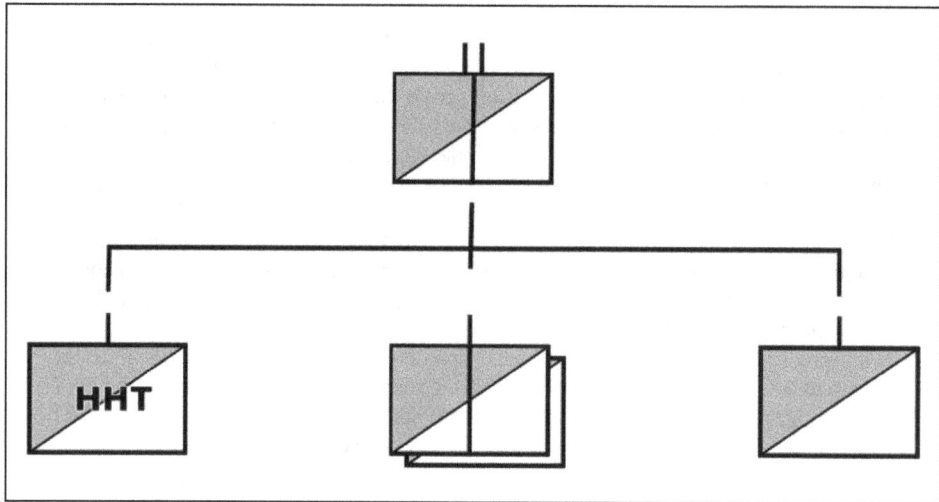

Figure 1-1. Reconnaissance squadron, IBCT

ROLE

1-5.   The DRT conducts close, deliberate, and stealthy reconnaissance to respond to the reconnaissance requirements of the IBCT reconnaissance squadron, and to help satisfy the CCIR. The IBCT commander develops his CCIRs and passes them to the commander of the reconnaissance squadron. The squadron commander in turn gives missions to his reconnaissance troops to assist in answering the IBCT CCIR.

1-6.   The squadron commander uses CCIR to facilitate timely decision making. The two key elements are friendly force information requirements and priority intelligence requirements (PIR) (Joint Publication [JP] 3-0). A CCIR is an information requirement identified by the commander as being critical to facilitating timely decision making and successful execution of military operations. The commander decides whether to designate an information requirement as a CCIR based on likely decisions and his visualization of the operation's course. A CCIR may support one or more decisions. During planning, the squadron staff recommends information requirements for the commander to designate as CCIRs.

RECONNAISSANCE

1-7.   The DRT, as well as other reconnaissance units, is used in reconnaissance to collect information about the AO, which will be used to develop intelligence. Knowledge of the AO is the precursor to all effective action. Acquiring information requires aggressive and continuous reconnaissance. Information collected from multiple sources and analyzed becomes intelligence that provides answers to information requests to validate the CCIR concerning the enemy, population, climate, weather, and terrain.

1-8.   Commanders and staffs continuously plan, task, and employ collection assets and forces. These assets and forces collect, process, and disseminate timely and accurate information, combat information, and intelligence to satisfy the CCIR and other intelligence requirements.

1-9.   Dismounted reconnaissance troop units should always ensure the information they gather and report is relevant. Relevant information is all information of importance to commanders and staffs needed for mission command and control (C2). To be relevant, information must be accurate, timely, usable, complete, precise, reliable, and secure. Relevant information provides the answers commanders and staffs need to conduct operations successfully. (FM 6-0 contains doctrine on relevant information and the cognitive hierarchy. The cognitive hierarchy describes how data becomes information, knowledge, and understanding.)

CAPABILITIES

1-10. The DRT has the following capabilities:

- Provides all-weather, continuous, accurate, and timely reconnaissance and security in complex, close, and urban terrain.
- Employs small unmanned aircraft systems (SUAS) to enhance reconnaissance efforts.
- Gathers information about multidimensional threats, both conventional and unconventional.
- Conducts stealthy reconnaissance and security operations.
- Rapidly assesses situations and directs combat power, reconnaissance, and security capabilities to meet PIR.
- Assists in answering a CCIR.
- Detects threat deception, decoys, and cover and concealment that otherwise would not be detected by single-capability surveillance means by employing integrated and synchronized reconnaissance.
- Supports targeting and target acquisition through available ground and aerial assets, including the fire support team (FIST) and SUASs.
- Rapidly develops the situation.
- Assists in shaping the AO by providing information or directing fires to disrupt the threat.
- Conducts reconnaissance of one zone, two routes, or six areas.
- Conducts up to 12 short-duration observation posts (OPs) for a period of less than 12 hours, or up to six long-duration OPs up to 24 hours, or up to six extended-duration OPs beyond 24 hours based on METT-TC variables.
- Conducts ground, water, and air insertion.
- Employs organic indirect fire support (FS) (60-mm mortar) to the troop.

LIMITATIONS

1-11. The DRT has the following limitations, which can be mitigated with careful employment or augmentation:

- Limited mounted capability, requiring augmentation of mobility platforms for rapid movement.
- Limited direct-fire standoff, lethality, and survivability.
- More time required to plan and employ.
- Dismounted tasks associated with zone, area, and route reconnaissance.
- Soldier load of dismounted troops.
- Force XXI battle command brigade and below (system) (FBCB2) only in the vehicles.
- May require augmentation to perform offense or defense missions.
- Requires augmentation from engineer assets to perform technical engineer tasks.
- Limited organic sustainment assets.

ORGANIZATION

1-12. Figure 1-2 depicts the organization of the DRT. The troop consists of a troop headquarters, a sniper squad, a mortar section, and two scout platoons. Each scout platoon has three scout sections consisting of two four-man scout teams each and a leader's vehicle carrying four personnel.

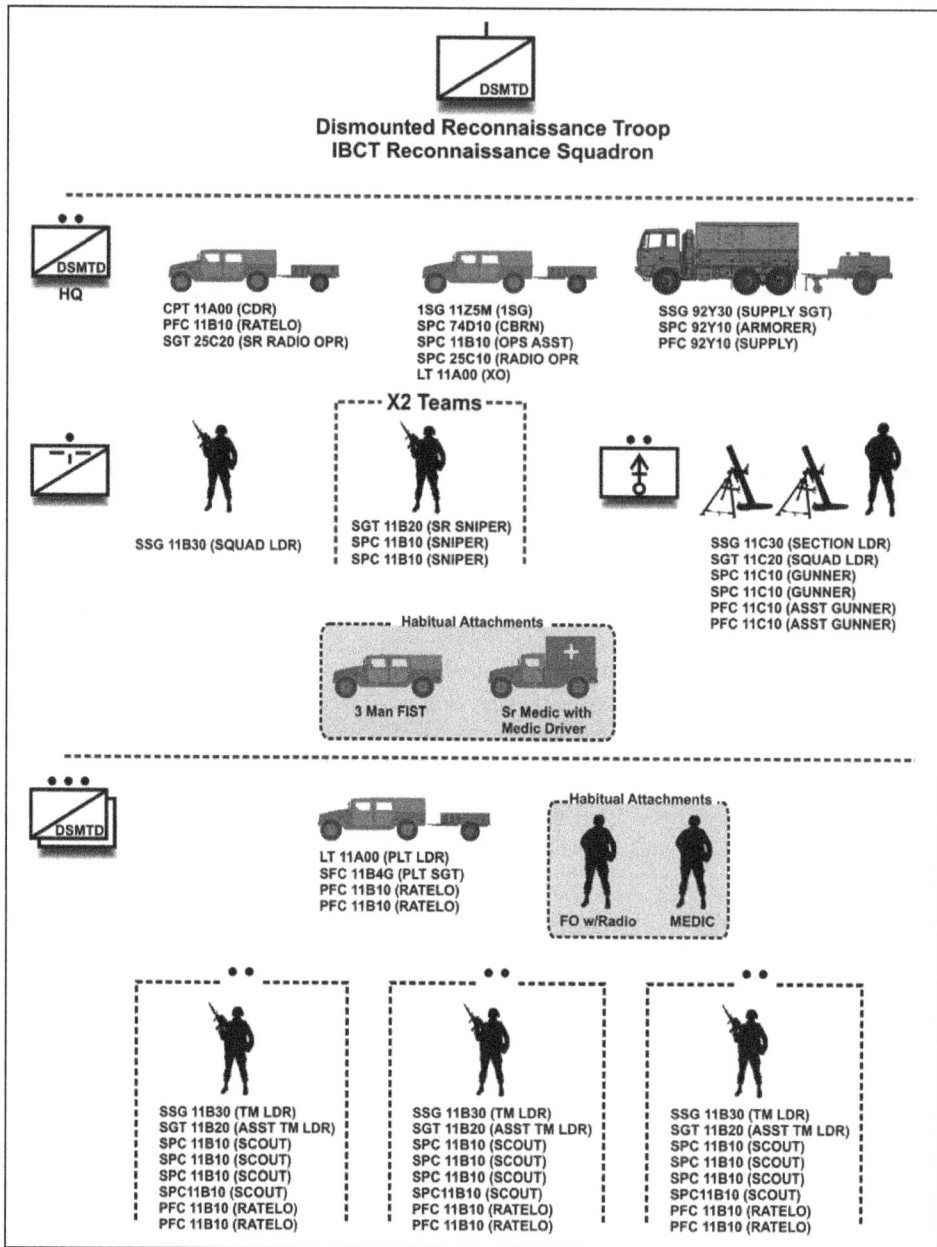

Figure 1-2. Dismounted reconnaissance troop

EQUIPMENT

1-13. The DRT is designed as a foot-mobile unit with few organic vehicles. The unit is equipped with weapon systems and equipment suited to dismounted reconnaissance and security operations. Most Soldiers within the unit are equipped with the M4 rifle. Currently, the other major equipment issued to the DRT includes:

- Troop headquarters.
  - 2–HMMWVs, with trailers.
  - 1–LMTV, with trailer.
  - 9–Inflatable boats with silenced motors.
  - 2–M249 SAW machine guns.
  - 1–.50 caliber machine gun.
  - 4–40-mm grenade launchers.
  - 1–SUAS.
  - 3–FBCB2 computers.
- Mortar section.
  - 2–60-mm mortars.
- Sniper squad.
  - 2–.50 caliber M107 sniper rifles.
  - 2–7.62-mm M110 sniper rifles.
  - 2–40-mm grenade launchers.
- Scout platoon headquarters (x2).
  - 1–HMMWV, with trailer.
  - 1–FBCB2 computer.
- Scout platoon (x2).
  - 6–M249 SAW machine guns.
  - 6–40-mm grenade launchers.
  - 3–Javelin command launch unit.

KEY PERSONNEL

1-14. A list of the key personnel within the DRT and members of the troop headquarters along with brief descriptions of their duties follow.

TROOP COMMANDER

1-15. The commander is responsible for the integration and synchronization of all reconnaissance assets and other enablers within the troop to accomplish the mission. The troop commander's responsibilities include the following:
- Serves as the subject matter expert in reconnaissance and security fundamentals and critical tasks.
- Accomplishes all missions assigned to the troop in accordance with (IAW) the higher commander's intent and scheme of maneuver.
- Plans and executes fires to support the troop's missions.
- Preserves the reconnaissance capability of the troop.

1-16. The commander can retain control of attachments at the troop level or task organize them to subordinate platoons. In some situations, the mission is best accomplished by delegating support and security of the attachment to a platoon leader (PL).

EXECUTIVE OFFICER

1-17. The executive officer (XO) is the troop's second in command, responsible for tracking and monitoring the tactical situation in the troop and squadron's AO. He receives, verifies, and consolidates digital and voice tactical reports from the platoons and forwards them to the squadron and to adjacent and following units. When FBCB2 use is limited, the XO ensures that voice radio reports convert into digital reports to generate friendly and threat SA. The XO's other duties include the following:

- Assists the commander in performing precombat inspections.
- Serves as officer in charge (OIC) of the troop command post (CP).
- Ensures all voice and digital communications are properly functioning.
- In conjunction with the first sergeant (1SG), plans and supervises the troop's sustainment effort.
- Assists in preparation of the operation order (OPORD), typically paragraph 4 (sustainment) and paragraph 5 (command and signal).
- Conducts coordination with higher, adjacent, and supporting units.
- As required, assists the commander in issuing orders to the troop headquarters and attachments.
- Conducts additional missions, as required. These may include serving as the OIC for a quartering party, leader of the detachment left in contact in a withdrawal, or liaison during a passage of lines.
- Assists the commander in preparations for follow-on missions.
- Assumes command of the troop, as required.

FIRST SERGEANT

1-18. The 1SG is the troop's senior noncommissioned officer (NCO), with the primary responsibility for training individual skills and sustaining the troop's ability to fight. He is the troop's primary sustainment operator. He helps the commander to plan, coordinate, and supervise all sustainment activities that support the tactical mission. He operates where the commander directs or where his duties require him.

1-19. The 1SG's specific duties include the following:
- Executes and supervises routine operations. This may include enforcing the tactical standing operating procedures (TACSOP); planning and coordinating training; coordinating and reporting personnel and administrative actions; and supervising supply, maintenance, communications, and field hygiene operations.
- Supervises, inspects, and observes all matters designated by the commander. For example, the 1SG may observe and report on a portion of the troop's AO.
- Assists in preparation of the OPORD plan, and rehearses and supervises key sustainment actions in support of the tactical mission. These activities include resupply of Class I, III, and V products and materials; maintenance and recovery; medical treatment and evacuation; and replacement/return-to-duty (RTD) processing.
- Assists and coordinates with the XO in all critical sustainment functions.
- As necessary, serves as quartering party non-commissioned OIC.
- Oversees training and ensures proficiency in individual and NCO skill, and battle drills contributing to small-unit collective skills that support the troop's mission-essential task list.
- In conjunction with the commander, establishes and maintains the foundation for troop discipline.

PLATOON LEADER

1-20. The PL is responsible to the troop commander for the discipline, training, and combat readiness of the reconnaissance platoon. He is proficient in the tactical employment of the platoon and the use of his digital equipment. He knows the capabilities and limitations of the platoon's personnel and equipment. He remains cognizant of all attached elements operating in his AO, and continually updates plans for their security and sustainment support as required.

1-21. The PL's additional responsibilities include the following:
- Accomplishes all missions assigned to the platoon IAW the troop commander's intent.
- Assists in synchronization and integration of reconnaissance assets and other enablers within the troop to accomplish the mission.
- Preserves the reconnaissance capability of the platoon, and informs the commander and XO of the tactical situation via frequency modulation (FM) and digitized contact and spot reports (SPOTREP).

PLATOON SERGEANT

1-22. The platoon sergeant (PSG) is the senior NCO in the platoon. He is responsible to the PL and the 1SG for the training of individual skills. His responsibilities include the following:

- Leads elements of the platoon as directed by the PL, and assumes command of the platoon in his absence.
- Assists the PL in maintaining discipline, conducting training, and exercising control.
- Supervises platoon sustainment, which includes supply and equipment maintenance.

SNIPER SQUAD LEADER

1-23. The sniper squad leader is responsible for employing the two sniper teams to ensure effective sniper support for the troop. His responsibilities include the following:

- Assists the troop commander in planning the employment of the sniper teams.
- Coordinates with the troop FIST.
- Controls the teams during tactical operations.
- Serves as the primary trainer for the sniper teams.

FIRE SUPPORT TEAM

1-24. The FIST is a habitually associated team attached from the fires support platoon in the squadron. The FIST consists of a fire support officer (FSO) and three personnel with high-mobility, multipurpose-wheeled vehicles at troop level, and a forward observer (FO) with a radio operator for each platoon.

1-25. The FIST vehicle also can serve as the alternate troop CP if necessary. The FSO has ready access to the higher-level SU, common operating picture (COP), and the radio systems necessary to replace the troop CP if it becomes damaged or destroyed. However, diverting the role of the FIST vehicle will impact the FIST's capability to provide responsive FS.

1-26. The FSO's additional responsibilities include the following:

- Advises the troop commander on the capabilities and current status of all available FS assets.
- Serves as the commander's primary advisor on the threat's indirect fire capabilities.
- Assists the commander in developing the OPORD to ensure full integration of fires.
- Recommends targets, fire support coordination measures (FSCM), and methods of engagement. Determines specific tasks and instructions required to conduct and control the fire plan.
- Develops an observation plan, with limited visibility contingencies, that supports the troop and squadron's missions.
- Requests critical friendly zones to assist counterbattery fires in response to threat artillery and/or mortar attacks and no fire areas (NFAs) around OPs, troop CP, sustainment areas, and forward reconnaissance units.
- Refines and integrates the troop target worksheet; submit the completed worksheet to the reconnaissance squadron's fires cell.
- Assists the commander to incorporate execution of the indirect fire and target acquisition plan into each rehearsal. This includes integrating indirect fire observers into the rehearsal plan.
- Alerts the commander if a request for fires against a target has been denied or shifts in priority of fires.
- Monitors the location and capabilities of friendly FS units and assists the commander in clearance of indirect fires.
- Tracks location of troop dismounted sections and OPs.

MORTAR SECTION LEADER

1-27. The mortar section leader provides responsive indirect fires to support the troop commander's concept of the operation. The section sergeant assists the commander with indirect mortar fire planning. He assists in establishing movement control, triggers for movement, triggers for shifting targets, and mortar caches. For a planning consideration, the mortar section normally maintains two-thirds maximum range of mortar fire forward of the reconnaissance elements. The section sergeant maintains discipline, conducts training, and exercises control over his mortar section. He supervises the section's sustainment, which includes supply and equipment maintenance. The mortar section sergeant's additional responsibilities include the following:

- Recommends employment techniques and positioning of the mortars to support the scheme of maneuver.
- Assists in developing the troop FS plan; determines the best type and amount of mortar ammunition to fire, based on the factors of METT-TC. This may include mission, types of rounds, terrain, and amount of rounds to be carried by Soldiers.
- Trains the section to ensure technical and tactical proficiency; cross-trains personnel within the section on key tasks to ensure continuous operations.
- Selects and reconnoiters new positions and routes for the section; controls the movements of the section.
- Keeps abreast of the threat situation and locations of friendly units to ensure the best use of ammunition and the safety of friendly troops.
- Supervises the execution of orders.
- Ensures that priority targets are covered at all times; establishes the amount and type of ammunition set aside for priority targets.
- Coordinates the fires and displacement of the mortar section with the actions of the troop CP and platoons.
- Anticipates needs and ensures that timely ammunition resupply, maintenance, and refuel requests are submitted to sustain combat operations.

COMMUNICATIONS SERGEANT

1-28. The communications sergeant assists in all aspects of tactical communications. His responsibilities include the following:

- Locates with the XO or 1SG per TACSOP and may operate the troop net control station (NCS).
- Receives and distributes signal operation instructions (SOI) and communications security (COMSEC) encryption keys.
- Ensures the troop receives the appropriate database for systems operating on the tactical internet.
- Ensures operators are properly trained in initialization and reinitialization of the systems and maintains the troop addressing and routing schemes.
- Troubleshoots troop digital communications equipment and ensures that necessary repairs are completed.

CHEMICAL, BIOLOGICAL, RADIOLOGICAL, AND NUCLEAR NCO

1-29. The chemical, biological, radiological, and nuclear (CBRN) NCO is responsible for troop CBRN defense activities. His responsibilities include the following:

- Supervises CBRN monitoring, detection, and decontamination operations.
- Assists in maintaining CBRN equipment and training CBRN equipment operators and decontamination teams.
- Operates from the troop CP and assists the XO in executing C2 operations. At this location, he advises the troop commander and XO on contamination avoidance measures and smoke, flame, and CBRN reconnaissance support requirements.
- Monitors reports of CBRN attacks and advises the commander on their impact.

SUPPLY SERGEANT

1-30. The supply sergeant receives transports and issues supplies and equipment to the troop. He works closely with the 1SG to accomplish these tasks. He leads the logistics package (LOGPAC) to the linkup point or, if the situation dictates, moves it forward to the troop's location.

ARMORER

1-31. The armorer performs organizational maintenance and repairs on the troop's small arms weapons. He evacuates weapons to the direct support maintenance unit, if required. Normally, he assists the supply sergeant in the brigade support area (BSA), but he may also operate forward with the troop CP to support continuous CP operations.

COMBAT MEDICS

1-32. Combat medics are attached to the troop and platoons from the squadron to provide emergency medical treatment for sick, injured, or wounded personnel. The senior medic and ambulance are normally at the troop CP under the supervision of the troop 1SG while the platoon medics are supervised by the PSG. Combat medics' responsibilities include the following:

- Provide medical guidance to troop leadership as required.
- Conduct triage for injured, wounded, or ill friendly and enemy personnel as they arrive at troop casualty collection points (CCPs) to ensure effective priority of treatment.
- Oversee sick call screening for the troop.
- Request and coordinate the evacuation of sick, injured, or wounded personnel under the direction of the 1SG.
- Assist in the training of troop personnel in basic first aid and of combat lifesavers (CLS) in enhanced first-aid procedures.
- Requisition Class VIII supplies from the squadron aid station (SAS).
- Recommend locations for troop CCPs. Provide guidance to the troop's CLS as required.
- Maintain SA of the tactical situation and coordinate Army health system support for health service support and force health protection (FHP) requirements.
- Advise the troop commander and 1SG on mass casualty operations.
- Keep the 1SG informed on the status of casualties and coordinate with him for additional Army health system requirements.

OTHER SYSTEMS

1-33. Various other systems used to gather information are also found throughout the IBCT. These include:

- Fire finder radars.
- Prophet Signal Intercept System.
- SUASs.
- CBRN reconnaissance teams.
- Engineer reconnaissance teams (ERT).

SECTION III – OPERATIONAL STRUCTURE

1-34. The DRT performs operations by integrating all available resources into a specific AO. These resources include personnel, systems, processes, missions, tasks, tactics, and techniques. The operational structure forms the overall operational environment (OE) within which the troop conducts missions.

1-35. The OE is a composite of the conditions, circumstances, and influences that affect the employment of the DRT and bear on tactical decisions. While they encompass all enemy, adversary, friendly, and neutral systems across the spectrum of conflict, they also include an understanding of the physical environment, the state of governance, technology, local resources, and the culture of the local population. It includes the physical environment, the information environment, and enemy, friendly, and neutral systems relevant to a specific operation (FM 3-0).

1-36. The OE includes physical areas, the information that shapes the OE as well as enemy, adversary, friendly, and neutral systems relevant to that joint operation. The OE for each campaign or major operation is different, and it evolves as each campaign or operation progresses. Army forces use operational variables to understand and analyze the broad environment in which they are conducting operations. They use mission variables to focus analysis on specific elements of the environment that apply to their mission.

PHYSICAL ENVIRONMENT

1-37. The physical environment consists of the air, land, sea, and space within the operational area. This environment is a key component in any military operation. The following factors affect the physical environment:

- Manmade structures, particularly urban areas.
- Climate and weather.
- Topography.
- Hydrology.
- Natural resources.
- Biological features and hazards.
- Other environmental conditions.

INFORMATION ENVIRONMENT

1-38. The information environment is the aggregate of individuals, organizations, and systems that collect, process, disseminate, or act on information. Throughout history, armies have operated in the information environment, using it for decision making and SU. In the information environment, the U.S. Army constantly strives to attain and maintain information superiority. "Information superiority" is the advantage gained from the ability to collect, process, and disseminate an uninterrupted flow of information while exploiting or denying an adversary's ability to do the same. Success in the physical environment does not guarantee success in the information environment. Company leadership must plan and direct operations to establish and maintain information superiority.

MISSION VARIABLES

1-39. At the operational level (corps and joint task force), an OE is evaluated by the operational variables of political, military, economic, social, information, infrastructure, physical environment, and time (PMESII-PT). Mission variables are those aspects of the OE that directly affect a mission. Leaders use the mission variables to synthesize tactical level information with local knowledge about conditions relevant to their mission. Upon receipt of a warning order (WARNO) or mission, leaders begin their initial mission analysis and start to visualize their desired end state. The categories of relevant information commanders use for mission analysis at the tactical level are the mission variables of METT-TC which are: mission, enemy, terrain and weather, troops and support available, time available, and civil considerations. Commanders and leaders view all the factors of METT-TC in terms of their impact on mission accomplishment. (For more information on the PMESII-PT variables, see FM 3-0.)

1-40. United States forces are currently engaged in, and will continue to be engaged in, a period of protracted confrontation among states, non-state, and individual actors increasingly willing to use violence to achieve their political and ideological ends. To be effective, the Soldier must understand the OE that shapes the conflict.

THREAT

1-41. Threats are nation-states, organizations, people, groups, conditions, or natural phenomena able to damage or destroy life, vital resources, or institutions. Threats may be described through a range of four major categories or challenges: traditional, irregular, catastrophic, and disruptive. While helpful in describing the threats the Army is likely to face, adversaries may use any or all of these challenges in combination to achieve the desired effect against the U.S. A good example of a threat that employs all four categories is North Korea: it has large conventional and irregular forces, is a nuclear threat, has been linked to clandestine arms, and exports drugs. The four major categories of threats are traditional, irregular, catastrophic, and disruptive.

TRADITIONAL

1-42. Traditional threats emerge from states employing recognized military capabilities and forces in understood forms of military competition and conflict. To counter these threats, U.S. forces would employ conventional weapons in primarily offensive and defensive operations.

IRREGULAR

1-43. Irregular threats are those posed by an opponent employing unconventional, asymmetric methods and means to counter traditional U.S. advantages. A weaker enemy often uses irregular warfare to exhaust the U.S. collective will through protracted conflict. Irregular warfare includes such means as terrorism, insurgency, and guerrilla warfare. United States forces are currently involved in countering irregular threats.

1-44. Threatening or extremist forces and organizations can be expected to use the environment and rapidly adapt. They will use the media, technology, and their position within a state's political, military, and social infrastructures to their advantage. Their operations combine conventional, unconventional, irregular, and criminal tactics. They focus on creating conditions of instability, seek to alienate legitimate forces from the population, and employ global networks to expand local operations. The threat employs advanced information operations and is bound by conventional limits on the use of violence.

1-45. Current and future conflicts are much more likely to be fought "among the people" instead of "around the people." This fundamentally alters the manner in which Soldiers can apply force to achieve success in a conflict. Enemies seek populations to hide in as protection against the proven attack and detection means of U.S. forces. Once secure within the population, these threat forces prepare and conduct attacks against communities and friendly forces while drawing resources from the population. Conflicts often take place in areas in which people are concentrated and require U.S. security dominance to extend across the population.

1-46. Some of the most effective tools that threat forces currently use against U.S. forces are improvised explosive devices (IEDs), mines, car bombs, unexploded ordnance (UXO), and suicide bombers. Infantrymen at all levels must know about these hazards. Additionally, they must know how to identify, avoid, and react to them properly. Newly assigned leaders and Soldiers should read everything they can find on current local threats. In addition, they should learn the unit's policies such as those found in the unit's TACSOP and in locally produced Soldier handbooks and leader guidebooks.

CATASTROPHIC

1-47. Catastrophic threats involve the acquisition, possession, and use of weapons of mass destruction. The proliferation of related technology has made this threat more likely than in the past.

DISRUPTIVE

1-48. Disruptive threats involve an enemy using new technologies that reduce U.S. advantages in key operational domains.

This page intentionally left blank.

Chapter 2

Command and Control

The essential task of the DRT commander is applying the art and science of war to C2 his troops in combat. He uses the elements of C2 and the components of the C2 system to initiate full-spectrum operations. The commander then influences and synchronizes these elements to impose his will on the situation and defeat the enemy. The commander exercises C2 in a dynamic AO where unexpected opportunities and threats rapidly present themselves.

SECTION I – TEXT REFERENCES

2-1. Table 2-1 consolidates the references to additional information.

Table 2-1. Guide for subjects referenced in text

Subject	References
Operations	FM 3-0
Reconnaissance and Cavalry Squadron	FM 3-20.96
The Operations Process	FM 5-0
Tactics	FM 3-90
Mission Command: Command and Control of Army Forces	FM 6-0
Intelligence Preparation of the Battlefield	FM 2-01.3
Multi-Service Tactics, Techniques, and Procedures for the High Frequency Automatic Link Establishment (HF-ALE) Radios	FM 6-02.74
Communications-Electronics Fundamentals: Wave Propagation, Transmission Lines, and Antennas	TC 9-64
Close Air Support	JP 3-09.3

SECTION II – OVERVIEW

2-2. Command and control is the exercise of authority and direction by a properly designated commander over assigned and attached forces in the accomplishment of a mission. Command also includes responsibility for health, welfare, morale, and discipline of assigned personnel. Command during operations requires understanding the complex, dynamic relationships among friendly forces, enemies, and the environment, including the populace. This understanding helps commanders visualize and describe their commander's intent and develop focused planning guidance. While command is a personal function, control involves the entire force. Control is the regulation of forces and warfighting functions to accomplish the mission IAW the commander's intent. It is fundamental to directing operations. (See FM 3-0.)

COMMAND AND CONTROL CHARACTERISTICS

2-3. Effective C2 has the following characteristics:
* Identifies and reacts to changes in the situation.
* Provides a continuous, interactive process of reciprocal influence among the commander, subordinate leaders, and available forces.
* Reduces chaos and uncertainty.

2-4. Command and control accomplishes the following:

- Gives purpose and direction to military operations.
- Integrates the efforts of subordinate and supporting forces, allowing separate activities to achieve coordinated effects.
- Determines force responsiveness and allocates resources.

2-5. Commanders at all levels exercise C2 for each mission through planning, preparation, execution, and assessment. (For further detail on C2 for reconnaissance commanders, see FM 3-20.96.)

COMMAND

2-6. Troop and PLs should be forward looking by seeing the terrain, the OE, and themselves. Effective commanders use integrated, information-age technologies, such as attached sensors, SUASs, and their associated tactics, techniques, and procedures to confirm and share a common operational picture that, in turn, fosters SA concerning the terrain, the threat, and themselves. This high-speed sharing of relevant information enables reconnaissance commanders to make better decisions faster than their opponents.

BATTLE COMMAND

2-7. Battle command is the art and science of understanding, visualizing, describing, directing, leading, and assessing forces to impose the commander's will on a hostile, thinking, and adaptive enemy. Through battle command the DRT commander ensures subordinates execute actions that are IAW the commander's intent. Commanders cannot perform these actions of leadership from the CP. They directly influence operations by their personal presence in the AOs, at the time and place of their choosing, and by skillful use of their C2 systems.

2-8. Understanding, visualizing, describing, directing, leading, and assessing are aspects of battle command common to all commanders. Command and control requires that commanders sort through and understand large amounts of information as they visualize the operation, describe their intent, and direct their subordinates.

MISSION COMMAND

2-9. Mission command is the conduct of military operations through decentralized execution based upon mission orders. Successful mission command—and effective mission accomplishment—results from subordinate leaders at all echelons exercising disciplined initiative within the commander's intent. It requires an environment of trust and mutual understanding.

ELEMENTS OF MISSION COMMAND

2-10. Mission command rests on the following four elements:

- **Commander's intent**. The commander's intent is a clear, concise statement of what the force must do and the conditions the force must meet to succeed with respect to the enemy, terrain, and desired endstate.
- **Individual initiative**. Individual initiative is the assumption of responsibility for deciding and initiating independent actions in the absence of orders when the concept of operations no longer applies, or when an unanticipated opportunity arises to achieve the commander's intent.
- **Mission orders**. The use of mission orders is a technique for completing combat orders that gives subordinates maximum freedom of planning and action in accomplishing missions. Mission orders state the task organization, mission of the force, commander's intent and concept of operations, subordinates' missions, and minimum essential coordinating instructions. A mission assigned to subordinates includes all the normal elements (who, what, when, where, and why), but the commander leaves the "how" of conducting the mission to subordinates.
- **Resource allocation**. Commanders allocate enough resources for subordinates to accomplish their missions. In the context of mission command, commanders consider information a

resource—comparable to more traditional ones, such as Soldiers and materiel—and share it through all levels of command.

EXERCISING MISSION COMMAND

2-11. Mission command concentrates on the objective of an operation, not on how to achieve it. It emphasizes timely decision making, understanding of the higher commander's intent, and the clear responsibility of subordinates to act within that intent to achieve the desired endstate. Establishing a climate of trust and mutual understanding that encourages subordinates to exercise initiative is the fundamental basis of mission command.

2-12. For the DRT commander, mission command is decentralized, informal, and flexible. Orders and plans are as brief and simple as possible, relying on implicit communication as well as on subordinates' ability to coordinate and the human capacity to understand with minimal information. By decentralizing decision-making authority, mission command increases tempo and improves subordinates' ability to act in fluid situations. Moreover, relying on implicit communication makes mission command less vulnerable to disruption of traditional means of communications. Moreover, relying on implicit communication makes mission command less vulnerable to degraded communications.

COMMAND AND CONTROL SYSTEM

2-13. A C2 system is the arrangement of personnel, information management, procedures, equipment, and facilities essential for the commander to conduct operations. Command and control consist of two components: the commander and his C2 system. The commander is the key individual in C2. He creates a positive command climate that instills and fosters trust and mutual understanding. He trains his subordinates in C2. Using his C2 system, the commander directs operations. The commander's most important role in C2 lies in combining the art of command with the science of control. The commander visualizes the AO, describes his vision to subordinates, directs actions to achieve results, and leads the troop to mission accomplishment. Under mission command, the commander drives the operations process. The commander establishes a command climate for his troop, prepares it for operations, directs it during operations, and continually assesses his subordinates. He uses influencing leadership actions, normally issuing broad guidance rather than detailed directions or orders. He limits his use of close personal supervision and intervenes in subordinates' actions only in exceptional cases. For the DRT commander, the C2 systems consist of troop CP, FBCB2, and radios.

2-14. An effective C2 system allows the commander to:
● Operate freely throughout the AO of operation to exercise C2.
● Delegate authority to subordinates to allow decentralized execution of operations.
● Synchronize actions throughout the AO.
● Focus on critical actions.

2-15. The troop commander exercises C2 based on an operations process that requires him to describe how the troop plans, prepares, and executes operations while continuously assessing the situation. These activities overlap and recur as circumstances demand.

Personnel

2-16. The C2 system begins with the troop CP personnel. Since combat involves Soldiers, no amount of technology can reduce the importance of the human dimension. Therefore, the commander bases his exercise of C2 on human characteristics more than on equipment and procedures. The commander establishes his CP with the C2 system and operates it based on his personality. He establishes a system to meet the demands he places on it, taking into account the abilities and personalities of his Soldiers and the capabilities of the troop's equipment.

Information Management

2-17. At the troop level, information management is the process of providing relevant information to the right person at the right time in a usable form to facilitate SA/SU and decision making. Its components are the information systems required to collect, process, store, display, and disseminate information. Information systems include computers and communications means, as well as policies and procedures for their use.

Procedures

2-18. Procedures are standard and detailed instructions on how to perform a specific task. They govern actions within a C2 system to make it more effective. Following procedures minimizes confusion, misunderstanding, and hesitancy as the commander makes frequent, rapid decisions to meet operational requirements.

2-19. At troop level the TACSOP is a set of instructions covering those features of operations that lend themselves to a standardized procedure without loss of effectiveness. Units base the TACSOP on doctrinal tactics, techniques, and procedures; the squadron's procedures; the commander's guidance; and experience. In general, the TACSOP apply to situations until the commanders change them. The TACSOP produce the following benefits:

- Simplified, brief combat orders.
- Enhanced mutual understanding and teamwork.
- Established synchronized battle drills.

2-20. A commander uses his TACSOP to reduce the number of instructions needed before, during, and after operations. The TACSOP details how to accomplish a mission or tactical task within a specific unit and standardize unit-level techniques and procedures to enhance flexibility and effectiveness. The TACSOP may also be adapted in a given location for a given threat. As the name implies, TACSOP standardize routine or recurring actions not needing the commander's personal involvement. They regulate operations within and among C2 system elements and allow internal and external elements to communicate with one another based on shared expectations. The TACSOP also serves as a starting point for new personnel to learn how the troop conducts operations.

Equipment and Facilities

2-21. Equipment and facilities provide sustainment resources and establish a work environment for the other elements of a C2 system. Facilities vary in size and complexity. At the troop level, a "facility" can be the commander's vehicle or the CP.

COMMAND POST

2-22. Troop CP personnel assist the commander in the coordination and supervision of the execution of plans, operations, and other activities. One of the primary functions of the CP is collecting combat information from the platoons and reporting significant enemy information gathered during their reconnaissance and security operations to the squadron main CP. Overall CP responsibilities are as follows:

- Assists the commander in C2.
- Maintains the current operations map. FBCB2 map chart tabs consisting of set map areas, static (notional) overlays, and CP (dynamic) overlays with associated CP filters:
    - OPNS/RECON–track and fight the reconnaissance/counterreconnaissance operation.
    - HIGHER OPS–track and fight the current operation.
    - CLR FIRES–clear artillery fires.
    - REAR–track sustainment activity in the AO.
- Maintains SA and COP by staying current regarding the following information:
    - Unit locations (scout teams; OPs; platoons; adjacent units; unit and squadron trains; and CP).
    - Unit status (maintenance; resupply; personnel).

- Artillery targets (list and overlay).
- Request for SUAS flight and airspace C2 coordination.
- Request CAS and CCA and monitor the missions.
- Obstacles (locations and overlay).
- Known/templated enemy locations.
- CCIR.
- Phases of the operation, with associated triggers and decisive points.
- Current mission statement and intent (own and higher).
- Serves as the troop's NCS.
- Reports information to squadron and adjacent units.
- Maintains a log of all incoming and outgoing messages on DA Form 1594 (Daily Staff Journal or Duty Officer's Log).
- Monitors and coordinates sustainment for the troop and attached elements.
- Answers all calls from the squadron unless directed specifically to the commander. Respond for the commander when he does not answer.
- Acts as a middleman for any calls directed within the troop and with the squadron headquarters.
- Conducts preventive, maintenance, checks, and services on all equipment.

CONTINUOUS OPERATIONS

2-23. The troop CP must be capable of operating on a 24-hour basis. During continuous operations, the CP normally operates in shifts. The importance of the XO as the troop's second in command must be accounted for when establishing shifts. The shifts should be established to provide a depth of experience throughout. The CP operates under the direction of the XO and is manned by the following:
- XO.
- Operations NCO.
- Communications NCO.
- CBRN NCO.
- Radio-telephone operators (RTO).

2-24. An example of CP shifts are as follows:
- Shift 1:
  - XO (may need to divide his time between both shifts).
  - Communications NCO.
  - RTO.
- Shift 2:
  - Operations NCO.
  - CBRN NCO.
  - RTO.

2-25. To ensure continuous operations, the CP personnel conduct a shift change briefing to update the incoming shift on the current status of the troop, the flank units, and the squadron. Both shifts review the significant activities during the previous shift to familiarize the oncoming shift with upcoming decisions and events. While the format for the brief is a matter of standard operating procedure (SOP), it should address the following:
- Task organization changes (FBCB2 task organization file in effect).
- Changes to mission (current fragmentary order [FRAGO] in effect).
- Current CCIR and answers to CCIR received during previous shift.
- Current enemy situation.
- Current friendly situation (two levels higher).
- Current platoon and attached element status for maintenance, resupply, and personnel.

- Platoon, section, and observation post (OP) locations, with associated NFAs if applicable.
- Significant activities (enemy and friendly) during previous shift.
- Activities scheduled during the next shift (timeline).
- Unresolved actions.
- Current communications status.
- CP priorities of work.
- Locations of:
  - Troop commander.
  - 1SG and trains.
  - Squadron/BCT commander.
  - Mortars.
  - FIST.
  - SUAS, including flight plans.
  - Human intelligence (HUMINT) elements operating in the troop AO.
  - Any attached enablers.

COMMAND POST POSITIONING

2-26. When planning an operation, the commander, XO, and operations NCO develop a plan that addresses the initial and subsequent positioning of the CP. The movement and positioning of the CP should be integrated into the troop plan and rehearsals. The CP is positioned where it can best balance the need for security and self-protection with the requirements to maintain both digital and radio voice communications. However, depending on the mission, there may be times when the CP is not supported by the troop commander's vehicle and FBCB2. During operations in noncontiguous AOs, the CP may be required to be in a centralized position. Conversely, during operations in contiguous AOs, the CP may be positioned well forward and prepared to move frequently in support of operations. Regardless, the CP should not be set up along likely enemy avenues of approach and must be ready to displace as necessary to ensure survivability and continuous communications.

2-27. The following general guidelines apply for planning the positioning of the CP:
- During reconnaissance or offensive operations, the CP should remain at least one terrain feature behind the troop reconnaissance elements, positioned to maintain communications with the platoons and the squadron tactical command post (TAC CP or main CP).
- During security or defensive operations, the CP should be positioned in sufficient depth to avoid contact with the threat while maintaining communications with the forward elements.

2-28. When conducting a reconnaissance for CP locations, consider towns and built-up areas, reverse slopes of hills, or a position that provides good communications. The proposed CP location must be located on firm and level ground with good drainage away from crossroads, hilltops, and other prominent terrain features. It must :
- Afford communications with higher and subordinate units.
- Provide cover and concealment.

ENHANCING COMMAND POST SECURITY

2-29. Command posts must secure themselves against a wide range of threats, including conventional attacks by mounted or dismounted forces, artillery and air attack, electronic attack, terrorist threats, or CBRN attacks, including weapons of mass destruction. The CP relies primarily on passive measures to avoid detection. It considers the following operation security (OPSEC) and information security (INFOSEC) measures when positioning the CP:
- Maintains noise and light discipline.
- Considers collocation of the mortar section in proximity to the DRT CP for mutual support and protection. The CP may also support displacement of the mortar section with vehicle support.
- Limits traffic into and out of the CP.

- Uses a listening post or OP or conduct local security patrols.
- Establishes fighting positions for CP personnel and maintain a 360-degree perimeter if time and recourses permit.
- Rehearses execution of the perimeter defense if time and recourses permit.
- Disseminates near and far recognition signals to all subordinate elements.
- Designates a rally point or an alternate CP location in the event of artillery or air attack.
- Positions vehicles in buildings - covered and concealed locations if possible.
- Ensures vehicle and equipment are camouflaged and generators are muffled.
- In stability operations, obtains a threat vulnerability assessment if the CP is occupying a permanent location or base camp/combat outpost.
- Considers operating the CP without vehicles during air assault operations or when operating in restrictive terrain.

DISPLACING THE COMMAND POST

2-30. While the CP normally controls operations from a static position, it may be forced to move during an operation. The troop's SOP should cover techniques for the handover of control during CP displacement. One technique is for the troop commander, while in his vehicle, to assume C2 functions while the XO displaces the CP to the next location.

2-31. The CP must conduct an operational update with the troop prior to displacement. All troop C2 elements (commander, XO, 1SG, and PLs) should eavesdrop on the command net while the CP displaces. During movement, messages to the CP should be minimized. This will require that the CP notify all stations of its planned displacement. It may also require a reconfiguration of FBCB2 auto-send and auto-forward functions to route messages to the next higher echelon during displacement.

2-32. Displacement of the CP while conducting operations without organic vehicles requires the same planning considerations as displacement with vehicles and careful attention to communications due to the lack of range with the dismounted radios and the lack of FBCB2.

CONTROL

2-33. Success in command is impossible without control. Within C2, control is the regulation of forces and WFF to accomplish the mission IAW the commander's intent. Control allows commanders to disseminate their intent, execute decisions, and adjust operations to reflect changing reality. It allows commanders to modify their vision to account for changing circumstances. Control also allows commanders to identify times and points at which new decisions will be required during preparation and execution.

ELEMENTS OF CONTROL

2-34. The elements of control are the following:
- **Information.** Information, in the general sense, is the meaning humans assign to data. It is the most important element of control and the commander's most important C2 resource. Intelligence is an important and distinct subset of relevant information and is integrated throughout C2.
- **Communication.** Communication is using any means or method to convey information of any kind from one person or place to another. Effective communication is essential to C2. Communication allows organizations to disseminate and share information vertically and horizontally among people, elements, and places.
- **Structure.** Structure is an organization that establishes relationships among its elements or a procedure that establishes relationships among its activities. Structure is employed by troop commanders to establish and maintain control.

2-35. In the broadest terms, control helps the troop commanders answer two fundamental questions:
- What is the actual situation compared with the desired endstate?
- Are adjustments to the plan necessary to reconcile the situation with the desired endstate?

SECTION III – PLANNING

2-36. Detailed planning at all levels helps ensure mission success and unit survival. The squadron and above use the military decision-making process (MDMP) to develop plans. The troop and platoons use troop-leading procedures (TLP). (See FM 5.0 for more details on TLP.) Planning time for any unit is usually short, especially for a reconnaissance troop, and commanders must provide sufficient time for their subordinates. The general guidance is the "1/3–2/3" rule: commanders take one-third of the allocated planning time and give their subordinates two-thirds. As a guideline, the length of time available determines whether the unit conducts deliberate or hasty planning as follows:

- Deliberate planning (24 to 48 hours available for planning).
- Hasty planning (less than 24 hours available for planning).

PARALLEL PLANNING AND SQUADRON WARNING ORDERS

2-37. The nature of reconnaissance operations requires the quick dissemination of orders, mutual trust between commanders and subordinates, and disciplined initiative. Reconnaissance units at all levels plan and operate with incomplete information. Additionally, reconnaissance leaders must be decisive, make plans quickly, pass whatever information is available to subordinates, and be responsive to change.

2-38. The type, amount, and timeliness of the information passed from squadron to troop headquarters directly impact the DRT leader's TLP. Parallel planning is critical. Reconnaissance units conducting reconnaissance pull cannot wait for complete orders from the squadron. Figure 2-1 illustrates the parallel sequences of the MDMP of the squadron with the TLP of the DRT. The figure indicates parallel planning conducted by the BCT, squadron, and troop. The solid arrows show where WARNOs or OPORDs and course of actions (COAs) trigger the initiation of TLP within a subordinate unit.

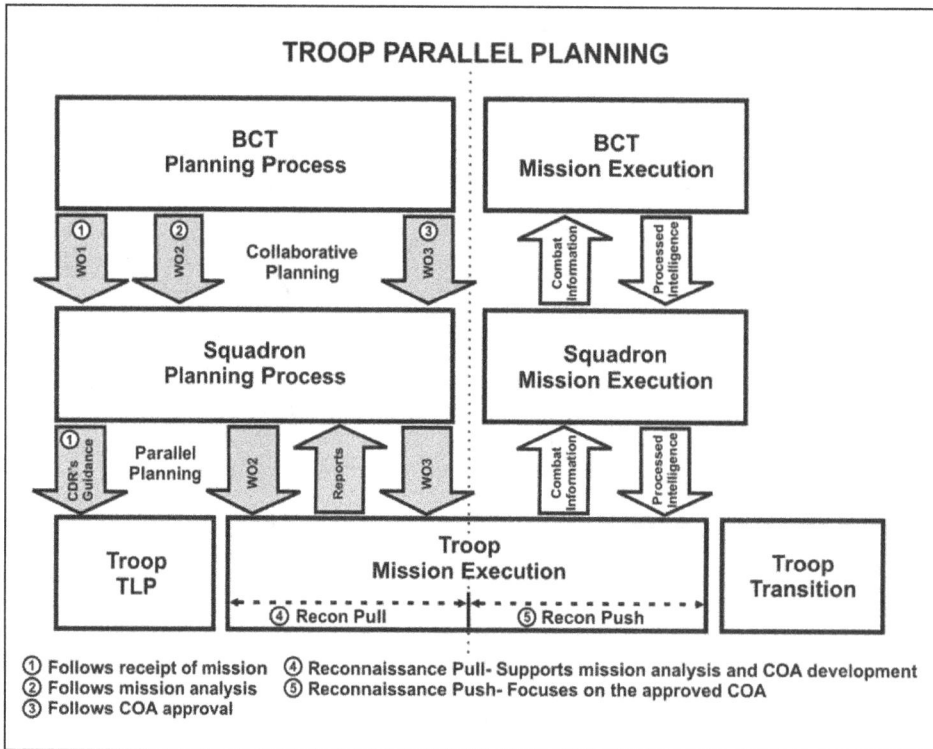

Figure 2-1. Troop parallel planning

2-39. Ideally, the squadron headquarters issues at least three WARNOs to the subordinate troops when conducting the MDMP. The troop commander should know what is contained in each WARNO, because it will be the basis for his WARNOs and his TLP. The three WARNOs are issued:

- **WARNO No. 1:** Upon receipt of mission.
- **WARNO No. 2:** Completion of mission analysis.
- **WARNO No. 3:** When the commander approves a COA.

2-40. However, the number of WARNOs is not fixed. Warning orders serve a function in planning similar to that of FRAGOs during execution. Commanders may issue a WARNO whenever they need to disseminate additional planning information or initiate necessary preparatory action, such as movement or reconnaissance.

2-41. The first WARNO (WARNO No. 1) normally contains minimal information. It alerts the troop commander that a new mission is pending. Warning order No. 1 normally contains the following information:

- The type of operation.
- The general location of the operation.
- The initial operational time line.
- Any movements to initiate.
- Any collaborative planning sessions directed by the commander.
- Reconnaissance and security plan and graphics.
- Initial information requirements or CCIR.

2-42. Warning order No. 2 is issued at the end of mission analysis and contains essential information for planning and directives to initiate movements and reconnaissance if reconnaissance pull is required by the IBCT. (See Chapter 3, Reconnaissance Operations, for discussion of reconnaissance pull and push.) Typically it includes:

- The approved unit mission statement.
- The commander's intent.
- Task organization changes.
- The unit AO (sketch, overlay, or some other description).
- The CCIR and essential elements of friendly information (EEFI).
- Risk guidance.
- Reconnaissance instructions.
- Reconnaissance planning guidance.
- Initial movement instructions.
- Security operations.
- Military deception guidance.
- Mobility, countermobility, and survivability (M/CM/S) guidance.
- Specific priorities.
- The updated operational time line.
- Guidance on collaborative events and rehearsals.

2-43. Warning order No. 3 is issued after COA approval and normally contains:

- Mission.
- Commander's intent.
- Updated CCIR and EEFI.
- Reconnaissance pull or reconnaissance push tasks (see Chapter 3).
- Concept of operations.
- Principal tasks assigned to subordinate units.
- Preparation and rehearsal instructions not included in SOPs.
- Final time line for the operations.

2-44. The DRT commander begins his TLP when he receives the initial WARNO or perceives a new mission. As each subsequent order arrives, leaders modify their assessments, update tentative plans, and continue to supervise and assess preparations. In some situations, security considerations or tempo may make it impractical for the squadron to issue the full sequence of WARNOs. However, with critical information in the released WARNO sequence, subordinate units should have enough information to begin planning and preparing for the operation. In other cases, the DRT commander may initiate TLP before receiving a WARNO based on existing plans and orders, such as contingency plans or be-prepared missions, and an understanding of the situation.

2-45. Parallel planning hinges on distributing information as it is received or developed. The DRT commander cannot complete his plan until he receives his mission. If each successive WARNO contains enough information, the squadron's final order will confirm what the troop commander has already analyzed and put into their tentative plan. In other cases, the squadron order may change or modify the troop's tasks enough that additional planning and reconnaissance is required.

TROOP-LEADING PROCEDURES

2-46. Troop-leading procedures provide leaders at troop level and below with a framework to develop plans and orders, and to prepare for operations. Troop-leading procedures are a dynamic process used by DRT leaders to analyze a mission, develop a plan, and prepare for an operation. These procedures enable leaders to maximize available planning time while developing effective plans and adequately preparing units for an operation. Some steps can be completed simultaneously while completing others. The standard Army planning process has five interrelated subprocesses: mission analysis, COA development, COA analysis, COA comparison, and COA selection. Risk management is also an integral part of operational planning in both MDMP and TLP. The MDMP is the process normally applied at squadron/battalion level and above to develop plans and orders where there is sufficient staff and time available to perform a detailed and thorough review and assessment IAW FM 5-0. In the MDMP process, formal COAs are developed and written orders are published. Troop-leading procedures are normally performed by leaders or commanders with no staff support and with limited time. Troop-leading procedures are similar methodologies used for planning the execution of the plans and orders developed through the MDMP. The key difference between the MDMP and TLP is the available time and staff resources to perform the process. Troop-leading procedures are as follows:

- Receive the mission.
- Issue the WARNO.
- Make a tentative plan.
- Initiate movement.
- Conduct reconnaissance.
- Complete the plan.
- Issue the order.
- Supervise and refine.

DISMOUNTED RECONNAISSANCE TROOP PLANNING CONSIDERATIONS

2-47. The following additional planning considerations can assist the DRT commander to maximize available planning time while developing effective plans and adequately preparing his unit for an operation.

MISSION ANALYSIS

2-48. To frame the tentative plan, the DRT commander performs troop mission analysis. This mission analysis follows the METT-TC format, continuing the initial assessment performed in the first TLP step.

2-49. In mission analysis, the DRT commander analyzes the reconnaissance squadron WARNO or OPORD to determine how the DRT contributes to the squadron's mission. In the analysis of the mission, he examines the following information.

Higher Headquarters Mission and Commander's Intent

2-50. The DRT commander determines the mission and commander's intent of his commander and the reconnaissance squadron. When these are unavailable, he makes decisions based on the information he has. When he receives the actual mission and commander's intent, he revises the plan, if necessary.

Reconnaissance Squadron's Concept of Operations

2-51. The DRT commander examines the concept of operations to determine how the troop's mission and tasks contribute to the reconnaissance squadron's success. He determines the details that will affect troop operations such as control measures and execution times.

Specified, Implied, and Essential Tasks

2-52. From WARNOs and OPORDs, the DRT commander extracts the specified and implied tasks assigned to the troop. He determines why each task was assigned to the unit to understand how it fits within the commander's intent and concept of operations. From the specified and implied tasks, he identifies essential tasks. These are the tasks that must be completed to accomplish the mission. Failure to complete an essential task results in mission failure.

Constraints and Limitations

2-53. The commander also identifies any constraints placed on the troop. Constraints can take the form of a requirement (for example, detach one platoon to an Infantry battalion) or a prohibition on action (for example, no reconnaissance forward of Line Bravo before H-hour). Limitations detail aspects of the mission that may be unfeasible (e.g., the DRT can only occupy a certain number of listening posts and OPs simultaneously). Limitations are based on the current capabilities of the unit.

Restated Mission

2-54. The product of the mission analysis is the restated mission. The restated mission is a simple, concise expression of the essential tasks the troop must accomplish and the purpose to be achieved. The DRT commander makes his assessment and constructs his mission statement. The mission statement states who (the unit), what (the task), when (either the critical time or on order), where (location), and why (the purpose of the operation).

ENEMY ANALYSIS

2-55. With the restated mission as the focus, the DRT commander continues the analysis with the threat. He needs to know about the threat's composition, disposition, strength, weaknesses, recent activities, ability to reinforce, and possible COAs. Much of this information comes from the squadron. Additional information comes from adjacent units and other leaders. Some information comes from the commander's experience. He determines how available information applies to troop operations. He also determines what he does not know about the threat, but should. He can then identify these intelligence gaps to the squadron or take action (such as sending out reconnaissance patrols) to obtain the necessary information.

TERRAIN ANALYSIS

2-56. Terrain profoundly influences operations. It is neutral and only favors the side that is more familiar with or better prepared to operate in it. There are two types, natural and man-made. Even though man-made structures dominate the terrain beneath them, natural terrain exerts a great influence.

2-57. The DRT commander considers terrain from both friendly and threat perspectives. The purpose is to identify likely enemy positions and routes so that the DRT commander can properly allocate his reconnaissance assets to accomplish the mission. A properly conducted terrain analysis provides the commander with:

- Probable enemy locations.
- Tentative observation points and areas to patrol.

- Areas to concentrate his reconnaissance efforts and areas where he can accept risk.
- Areas where he can infiltrate or hide the movement of his units.
- Tentative positions to establish patrol or operation bases.
- Locations for sustainment operations.

2-58. The elements of terrain analysis are observation and fields of fire, avenues of approach, key terrain, obstacles, and cover and concealment (OAKOC). Although they are remembered as five separate elements, the commander evaluates these military aspects of terrain together using the following considerations.

Observation and Fields of Fire

2-59. Observation is the condition of weather and terrain that permits a force to see friendly, threat, and neutral personnel and systems and key aspects of the environment (FM 6-0). The DRT commander analyzes the terrain to identify the tentative location for OPs or enemy positions. He can use the circular line of sight (LOS) FBCB2 tool to identify fields of observation and dead space. (The tool however, does not account for vegetation and man-made structures.)

Avenues of Approach

2-60. An avenue of approach is an air or ground route of an attacking force of a given size leading to its objective or key terrain in its path (FM 3-90). Generally, there are two types of avenues of approach the commander is concerned with: mounted and dismounted. Based on the mission and the threat, the commander can efficiently concentrate his reconnaissance assets to observe and report on likely avenues of approach.

Key Terrain

2-61. Key terrain is any locality or area of which seizure or retention affords a marked advantage to either combatant (FM 6-0). Since the enemy will try to retain it, key terrain is also a likely location for the troop to concentrate its reconnaissance effort.

Obstacles

2-62. Obstacles are any obstruction designed or employed to disrupt, fix, turn, or block the movement of an opposing force and to impose additional loss in personnel, time, and equipment on the opposing force. Obstacles can form bottlenecks that the enemy has to circumvent. They also are locations where the lightly armed DRT units can delay the enemy, if required.

Cover and Concealment

2-63. Cover is protection from the effects of fires (FM 6-0). Concealment is protection from observation and surveillance. The DRT commander considers cover and concealment from two perspectives:

- Areas where he can move and conceal his units.
- Areas where the enemy can hide his units.

WEATHER ANALYSIS

2-64. There are five military aspects of weather: visibility, winds, precipitation, cloud cover, and temperature/humidity (see FM 2-01.3). The consideration of their effects is an important part of the mission analysis. The squadron commander and staff provide forecasts and predictions on the effect of weather on operations. The DRT commander reviews the forecasts and conclusions available from the reconnaissance squadron and develops his own conclusions on the effects of weather on the mission. The effect of weather is often less severe and may provide an advantage for the DRT than on the operations of the motorized troops within the squadron. The dismounted troop can conduct operations under all but the most severe weather condition. The effects of weather on the DRT mission include:

- Infiltration and movement is less likely to be discovered during inclement weather.
- The enemy may be less alert due to extreme weather conditions.

- The local population is less likely to discover DRT units during extreme weather conditions.
- Movement may be reduced in inclement weather.
- Sustainment may be more difficult during inclement weather.
- Transportation support, especially aviation, may be reduced during inclement weather.

TROOP ANALYSIS–AVAILABLE ASSETS

2-65. Perhaps the most important aspect of mission analysis is determining the combat potential of one's own force. The DRT commander knows the status of his Soldiers' morale, their experience and training as well as the strengths and weaknesses of subordinate leaders. His assessment also includes understanding the full array of assets in support of the unit. Based on this, he can realistically determine whether he can accomplish the mission with the assets he has on hand. If he determines that he cannot, he requests additional support from the squadron or he must accept risk in allocating his resources to accomplish the mission. In either instance, the troop commander has to inform his commander of his additional requirements or his recommendations for modifying the mission.

TIME ANALYSIS

2-66. The commander not only appreciates how much time is available; he understands the time-space aspects of preparing, moving, operating, and sustaining. He views his own tasks and threat actions in relation to time. He knows how long it takes under such conditions to prepare for certain tasks (such as orders production, rehearsals, and subordinate element preparations). Most important, he monitors the time available. As events occur, he assesses their impact on the troop time line, which lists all events that affect the troop and its subordinate elements. He then updates the time lines for subordinates.

CIVIL CONSIDERATIONS

2-67. Civil considerations gauge the impact on military operations of man-made infrastructure, civilian institutions, and attitudes and activities of the civilian leaders, populations, and organizations within an AO (FM 6-0). Rarely are military operations conducted in uninhabited areas. Most of the time, units are surrounded by noncombatants, including residents of the AO, local officials, governmental agencies, and non-governmental organizations (NGOs). This is especially true during stability operations. Based on information from the squadron and his own knowledge and judgment, the DRT commander identifies civil considerations that affect the troop mission and analyzes them in terms of six factors (areas, structures, capabilities, organizations, people, and events):

- **Areas.** Areas include political boundaries, city districts, municipalities, trade routes, sociological and religious enclaves, agricultural and mining regions, and trade routes. Analysis may indicate areas in which friendly forces have an increased chance of encountering enemy elements.
- **Structures.** This category covers infrastructure (dams, bridges, power plants, warehouses, communications nodes) and religious or cultural areas (mosques, churches, libraries, schools, hospitals). Some structures may be identified as targets for military action; others may be precluded from targeting.
- **Capabilities.** Capabilities include sustenance, key civic services, and resources to support military operations. Populations with access to basic sustenance and services are usually not prone to support insurgent terrorist or criminal activity.
- **Organizations.** Organizations are the nonmilitary groups or institutions within the AO that influence and interact with the populace, military forces, and each other.
- **People.** This is the general term for nonmilitary personnel encountered by military forces whose actions and influence can affect the mission.
- **Events.** Events are the routine, cyclical, planned, or spontaneous activities that significantly affect organizations, people, and military operations. Events may arouse tremendous emotion in the population and affect support for U.S. forces.

Conduct Rehearsals

2-68. A crucial component of preparation is the rehearsal. Rehearsals allows the DRT commander to assess his subordinates' preparations and to identify areas that require closer supervision. The commander conducts rehearsals to:

- Practice essential tasks.
- Identify weaknesses or problems in the plan.
- Coordinate subordinate element actions.
- Improve understanding of the concept of operations.
- Foster confidence among Soldiers.

2-69. The DRT commander uses five types of rehearsals:

- Confirmation brief.
- Backbrief.
- Combined arms rehearsal.
- Support rehearsal.
- Battle drill or TACSOP rehearsal.

Confirmation Brief

2-70. Immediately after receiving the order, subordinate leaders brief the commander on the order they just received. They brief their understanding of the commander's intent, the specific tasks (and purposes) they have been assigned, and the relationship of their tasks to those of other elements conducting the operation. They repeat any important coordinating measures specified in the order. The confirmation brief is normally used in conjunction with other types of rehearsal.

Backbrief

2-71. The backbrief differs from the confirmation brief in that subordinate leaders are given time to complete their plan. Backbriefs require the fewest resources and are often the only option under time-constrained conditions. Subordinate leaders explain their actions to the commander from start to finish of the mission. Backbriefs are performed sequentially, with all leaders going over their tasks. When time is available, backbriefs can be combined with other types of rehearsals. Doing this lets all element leaders coordinate their plans before performing more elaborate drills. If possible, backbriefs are performed overlooking subordinates' AOs, after they have developed their own plans.

Combined Arms Rehearsal

2-72. A combined arms rehearsal requires considerable resources, but provides the most planning and training benefit. Depending on circumstances, the DRT may conduct a reduced force or full dress rehearsal.

Reduced Force Rehearsal

2-73. When circumstances prohibit a rehearsal with all members of the unit, DRT leaders and other key individuals may perform a reduced force rehearsal while most of their subordinates continue to prepare for the operation. Often, smaller scale replicas of terrain or buildings substitute for the actual AO. Dismounted reconnaissance troop leaders not only explain their plans, but also walk through their actions or move replicas across the rehearsal area or sand table. This is called a rock drill. It reinforces the backbrief given by subordinates because everyone can see the concept of operations and sequence of tasks.

Full Dress Rehearsal

2-74. The preferred rehearsal technique is a full dress rehearsal. The commander rehearses his subordinates on terrain similar to the AO, initially under favorable light conditions, and then in limited visibility. Small unit actions are repeated until executed to the commander's standard. Full dress rehearsals help Soldiers to clearly understand what is expected of them. It helps them gain confidence in their ability to accomplish the mission. Supporting elements meet key leaders and rehearse with them. The critical benefit is the opportunity to synchronize the operation.

Support Rehearsal

2-75. At any point during TLP, units may rehearse their support for an operation. The DRT XO or 1SG is normally responsible for these rehearsals and may participate in the squadron level support rehearsal. For the DRT, this typically involves coordination and procedure drills for fires, sustainment, or casualty evacuation (CASEVAC). Support rehearsals and combined arms rehearsals complement preparations for the operation. They may be conducted separately and then combined into full dress rehearsals.

Battle Drill or TACSOP Rehearsal

2-76. A battle drill is a collective action rapidly executed without applying a deliberate decision-making process. A battle drill or TACSOP rehearsal ensures that all participants understand a technique or a specific set of procedures. Throughout preparation, units rehearse battle drills and TACSOP actions. These rehearsals do not need a completed order from the squadron. The DRT commander places priority on those drills or actions that he anticipates will occur during the operation. For example, a reconnaissance platoon may rehearse a battle drill on reacting to an ambush while awaiting the movement order.

SECTION IV – COMMUNICATIONS

2-77. The reporting of combat information is fundamental to reconnaissance and security. This information is of interest to other maneuver units as well as to the IBCT and squadron staffs. It requires the widest dissemination possible by FM voice and digital systems. The DRT elements frequently operate over long distances, wide frontages, and extended depths far from the controlling headquarters. Communications must be redundant and long-range to meet these internal and external requirements. Because threat and friendly radar, radios, and lasers operate in the same electromagnetic spectrum, commanders must plan for interference. This may result from unintentional friendly interference, intentional threat jamming, equipment failure, atmospheric or terrain conditions, or nuclear blast electromagnetic pulse.

DIGITAL

2-78. The Army Battle Command System is a network of computer systems that allows for advanced reporting, orders and graphics sharing, and database management. The DRT digital systems include:
- FBCB2. Six systems in the troop are located in the key leaders' vehicles, allowing for receiving and inputting information into the FBCB2 system.
- Tactical internet consisting of single-channel ground/airborne radio system (SINCGARS) and enhanced position location reporting system (EPLARS) tactical radios.
- Global Command Support System.
- Digital message device.
- Lightweight mortar ballistic computer.
- Defense advanced GPS receiver.

2-79. Digitized information systems increase the complexity of C2 systems, but digital technologies provide more timely, accurate, and reliable information to the commander. This information allows the commander to make faster and better decisions. Digital C2 systems also support effective execution by reducing the human labor needed to organize information and by providing it in a usable form. Used correctly, their capabilities allow the commander to spend more time and energy on the art of command and the human dimensions of C2.

2-80. The dismounted elements of the DRT must transmit their information to an FBCB2 leader vehicle where it must then be placed into the system. Allowing for the population of the COP, leaders with FBCB2 in their vehicle lose this link when they dismount and must rely on other manned systems to input their information and receive information from FBCB2.

RADIO FREQUENCIES

2-81. Dismounted reconnaissance troop operations normally depend on radio as the primary means of communications for both voice and digital traffic. Net discipline and TACSOP procedures minimize needless traffic. To avoid detection by threat direction-finding equipment, reconnaissance units use all other means of communications to supplement the radio. Once in contact, the primary means will be FM voice. Radio communications include electromagnetic communications in FM, amplitude modulation, ultrahigh frequency (UHF), and very high frequency (VHF) spectrums.

2-82. Dismounted reconnaissance troop elements that can observe but cannot report what they see are a wasted resource. The ability to communicate is their first responsibility, and radios are their primary weapon. The DRT must be experts in the use of multiple radios systems and in the three primary military radio frequency spectrums: high frequency (HF), VHF, and UHF. Soldiers must be highly proficient in programming, troubleshooting, and maintaining many types of radios.

VERY HIGH FREQUENCY RADIOS

2-83. These are generally simple to use and provide reliable and clear, short-range tactical communications. The SINCGARS series of radios provide tactical units excellent communications that is easy to secure from enemy eavesdropping. Most of the common military radios operate within these frequencies.

ULTRA HIGH FREQUENCY RADIOS

2-84. These provide reliable tactical LOS, operational, and strategic communications. However, due to the high demand and to potential interoperability problems with other units, it is not always practical for reconnaissance units to use this spectrum. Military radios that operate within these frequencies include tactical satellite (TACSAT) radios.

2-85. A UHF TACSAT radio is a reliable communications system with unlimited range. Understandably, satellite channels are in high demand and are thus also in short supply. Because the priority for UHF TACSAT channels goes to division HQ and above, joint and special operations units and DRT units must usually share satellite channels. For this reason, the secure LOS radio systems remain the primary means of communication. When DRT units obtain satellite access, they must carefully manage it for airtime and message precedence.

NETWORKS

2-86. Troop tactical communications are mainly conducted using secure FM radios. As mentioned earlier, communications are critical to the success of DRT reconnaissance and security missions. The information gathered by DRT units must be transmitted to supported units in a timely manner for it to be transformed into intelligence and used by commanders to make tactical decisions.

2-87. Dismounted reconnaissance troop units most often operate as teams. As the organization states, two teams make a section, three sections make a platoon, and two platoons make up the troop. Transmission of information, such as that from a team surveillance site, is normally conducted over a platoon internal secure FM frequency. These transmissions are made from the surveillance site to the hide site. All teams within the platoon operate on the same net using specific time windows for each team for transmissions of reports. Alternate platoon frequencies are used for emergency transmissions.

2-88. Transmissions from the hide site are sent directly to the troop over the troop command net on a FM secure frequency. As with the teams, hide sites transmit during time windows using a troop alternate frequency for emergency transmissions. Platoon leaders monitor team transmissions from surveillance and hide sites. The troop in turn sends the information to the squadron.

TACTICAL TRANSMISSIONS

2-89. Information is normally transmitted over VHF secure FM radio systems. Transmissions are continually adjusted to reflect changing conditions and missions. Successful communications depends on team knowledge; the type of emission (voice or data); the transmitter power output; selection of the best possible antenna and antenna site; proper antenna construction; propagated frequencies; terrain and weather; and atmospheric conditions. The variable over which the unit has the most control is antennas. Training of team members on radio systems and antenna construction is essential to mission success (TC 9-64, FM 6-02.74).

BEYOND LINE OF SIGHT EQUIPMENT

2-90. Due to the frequency band they operate in, tactical VHF radios, like the SINCGARS, are LOS only. In addition to LOS communications, the DRT must also be able to communicate beyond line of sight (BLOS). High frequency and UHF bands may be used for BLOS communications by using the proper equipment. The DRT must be trained in the use of lower band HF and higher band UHF TACSAT systems to accomplish BLOS communications when necessary. High frequency systems allow for long range communications without the use of terrestrial or satellite relays. Tactical satellite radios must have LOS from the radio to the satellite, but allow for BLOS communications to a distant receiver that also has LOS to the satellite.

RETRANSMISSION

2-91. Retransmission can greatly extend the range of a radio LOS network. Traditionally, retransmission networks are used with two different frequencies or net identifications (IDs), called F1 to F2 retransmission. Some newer systems allow for retransmission using the same frequency or net identification (ID) called F1 to F1 retransmission. Most current radios support retransmission operations with the use of a retransmission cable. If the range between two networks is too great for ground wave radios, two LOS networks can be connected using TACSAT radios.

COMMERCIAL LINES

2-92. Commercial lines are used when approved by the squadron. Careful consideration must be given to securing commercial lines using devices like the secure telephone unit-III and limiting classified material sent over unsecured lines and on cell phones. Threat forces may rely heavily on local communications networks. If the squadron is forced to withdraw, it may consider cutting or removing existing wire lines, including commercial lines, so the threat cannot use them.

SOUND AND VISUAL

2-93. Sound and visual signals are covered in the SOI or the unit TACSOP. They include pyrotechnics, hand- and arm-, flag, metal-on-metal, sirens, rifle shot, whistles, and bells. TACSOP may establish signals not included in the SOI. The battlefield will have many sound and visual cues that become increasingly important in complex and urban terrain. Commanders and staff planners carefully determine how sound and visual signals will be used and authenticated.

MESSENGERS

2-94. Messengers can be used between CPs, trains, and higher and lower headquarters. The use of messengers from the DRT will be as fast as the messengers can walk unless they are provided other means of transportation.

This page intentionally left blank.

Chapter 3

Reconnaissance Operations

Focused reconnaissance enhances the ability of friendly units to operate inside the enemy's decision cycle and allows for commanders to retain the freedom of maneuver. Reconnaissance is the key to assisting the commander in determining an overall picture of the threat and which COA the threat will likely employ. It helps the squadron commander and staff to determine threat strong points and vulnerabilities and where intelligence gaps exist. Information collected by reconnaissance forces is processed into actionable intelligence by the squadron and IBCT staff allowing commanders to concentrate efforts in full-spectrum operations. This chapter discusses the fundamentals, planning, and execution of reconnaissance operations for the DRT.

SECTION I – TEXT REFERENCES

3-1.   Table 3-1 consolidates the references to additional information.

Table 3-1. Guide for subjects referenced in text

Subject	References
The Infantry Rifle Company	FM 3-21.10
Operations	FM 3-0
Reconnaissance and Scout Platoon	FM 3-20.98
Reconnaissance and Cavalry Squadron	FM 3-20.96
Combined Arms Operations in Urban Terrain	FM 3-06.11
Army Personnel Recovery	FM 3-50.1
Personnel Recovery	JP 3-50
Long-Range Surveillance Unit Operations	FM 3-55.93
Tactics	FM 3-90

SECTION II – RECONNAISSANCE OVERVIEW

3-2.   Reconnaissance and aggressive direct combat are mutually exclusive concepts. This is unequivocally true for lighter reconnaissance units, such as the DRT, which lack the protection of combat units. Reconnaissance units employed in a direct combat role (assaulting bunkers, seizing terrain, raiding buildings) are not conducting reconnaissance for the commander. Combat information will certainly result from such actions, but this is more than offset by what is lost in terms of vehicles destroyed, casualties incurred, and other reconnaissance missions neglected. Reconnaissance units are designed to gather information through reconnaissance. At times they may be required to conduct target acquisition or target interdiction within the capabilities of their particular unit.

DISMOUNTED RECONNAISSANCE TROOP MISSIONS

3-3.   The primary missions of the DRT, in support of squadron and brigade operations, include the following three forms of reconnaissance:
- Zone.
- Area.
- Route.

3-4. Table 3-2 shows a comparison of IBCT reconnaissance squadron motorized and DRT capabilities.

Table 3-2. DRT reconnaissance mission profiles

Reconnaissance Missions	IBCT Reconnaissance Squadron–Motorized Reconnaissance Troop	IBCT Reconnaissance Squadron–DRT
Zone Recon	F	P
Area Recon	F	F
Route Recon	F	P
F—Fully capable	P—Capable under permissive METT-TC	

FUNDAMENTALS

3-5. The IBCT, reconnaissance squadron, and DRT plan and perform successful reconnaissance operations according to the following seven fundamentals:

- Ensure continuous reconnaissance.
- Do not keep reconnaissance assets in reserve.
- Orient on the reconnaissance objective.
- Report all information rapidly and accurately.
- Retain freedom of maneuver.
- Gain and maintain enemy contact.
- Develop the situation rapidly.

RECONNAISSANCE PUSH

3-6. Reconnaissance push emphasizes development of a detailed plan to focus the reconnaissance effort on an evolving maneuver COA—or on several COAs—prior to the deployment of reconnaissance assets. The plan often encompasses several branches or COAs that will be triggered by decision points. These branches are understood by leaders at all levels and are well rehearsed. (Refer to FM 3-20.96 for further discussion of reconnaissance push.)

RECONNAISSANCE PULL

3-7. Reconnaissance pull is the technique wherein the IBCT commander defers committing to a specific plan or COA prior to deployment of reconnaissance elements. Reconnaissance is focused on collecting information on enemy strengths and weaknesses that will be critical in formulating the future plan or COA.

3-8. Reconnaissance pull emphasizes opportunity at the expense of a detailed, well-rehearsed plan. Upon discovering enemy strengths and weaknesses, the DRT as part of the reconnaissance squadron "pulls" the IBCT along the path of least resistance into positions of tactical advantage. When weaknesses are discovered during execution, a change in the scheme of maneuver can help the maneuver units to exploit opportunities. (Refer to FM 3-20.96.)

SECTION III – RECONNAISSANCE PLANNING CONSIDERATIONS

3-9. Planning at all levels helps ensure reconnaissance mission success and unit survival. Understanding the higher commander's intent for reconnaissance is critical throughout the process.

COMMANDER'S RECONNAISSANCE PLANNING GUIDANCE

3-10. The DRT commander develops his reconnaissance planning guidance based on the squadron commander's guidance and overall plan. An understanding of this guidance aids the troop commander in planning and executing the troop mission. The guidance enables him to clarify his own intent for his subordinate leaders. The commander's guidance consists of three areas:

- Focus of reconnaissance.
- Tempo of reconnaissance:
  - Stealthy or forceful.
  - Deliberate or rapid.
- Engagement criteria (if any), both lethal and nonlethal:
  - Aggressive.
  - Discreet.

FOCUS

3-11. The focus of the reconnaissance allows the DRT commander to determine which critical tasks he wants the troop to accomplish first. It narrows the troop's scope of operations to help get the information that is most important to squadron and brigade operations. It helps define where to concentrate information-gathering activities and allows the commander to select which critical tasks must be accomplished and with what asset(s). Reconnaissance focus must be linked to the tasks of answering the brigade and squadron CCIR, supporting targeting (lethal and nonlethal), and filling additional voids in information requirements. In small-scale contingency operations, the focus might be terrain-oriented or threat security force-oriented. In an environment involving stability operations, the focus might be on determining local populace sentiment or on identifying local paramilitary leaders. While all critical tasks have some degree of applicability in any given operation, certain ones are more important for specific missions and must be clearly articulated at each level.

3-12. The reconnaissance objectives of the troop must be focused on one or more of the following:

- Threat/enemy.
- Terrain.
- Infrastructure.
- Society.

Threat

3-13. It is critical to quickly identify and define the threat. The DRT is able to conduct reconnaissance against threats ranging from conventional military forces to poorly equipped and loosely organized local elements. To offset U.S. technical and tactical superiority, the threat will develop its own asymmetric warfighting methods that fit within its objectives, training, culture, and available equipment.

Civil Considerations

3-14. Gaining an awareness of how the local society affects military operations, as well as the impact of military operations on the society, is critical to the troop commander as he makes tactical decisions. Understanding how operations affect the society begins with collecting information on the size, location, composition, and temperament of the society. This process requires an understanding of cultural and human factors such as religion, ethnicity, language, and political and tribal organization.

Terrain

3-15. Terrain analysis is based on a focused reconnaissance of the AO. Reconnaissance identifies voids in terrain-related information requirements that a map or digital analysis cannot satisfy. The troop must see and understand the terrain as it affects friendly forces, threat forces, and civilian population. For the DRT to be effective with terrain-based analysis, the terrain should be restrictive or otherwise suited for the capabilities of the DRT. The leaders use the factors of OAKOC. (See FM 3-21.10 for a detailed discussion.)

Tempo

3-16. Tempo is defined in FM 3-0 as the relative speed and rhythm of military operations over time with respect to the enemy. The tempo of reconnaissance allows the troop commander to relate time requirements for the reconnaissance in relation to the squadron's mission and information requirements, as well as such factors as planning time, movement formations, and methods. The squadron commander visualizes the tempo of reconnaissance through the analysis of the following mission variables of METT-TC: mission, enemy, and time.

Stealthy, Forceful, Deliberate, and Rapid Reconnaissance

3-17. Through his intent, the commander defines when key reconnaissance tasks must be accomplished in relationship to the endstate for reconnaissance operations. This allows subordinate commanders and leaders to exercise individual initiative in determining how to meet the commander's intent. The tempo for reconnaissance may be described as stealthy.

3-18. The DRT conducts stealth reconnaissance with methodical, time-consuming operations that minimize chance enemy contact. It is conducted predominantly dismounted, although motorized reconnaissance may be involved as well.

3-19. Stealth is a consideration in all reconnaissance operations and must be strongly emphasized. Given DRTs lighter organization, stealth is even more essential. They can expect to operate over extended distances well before the execution of combat operations and must use stealth to gain information without alerting the enemy to the IBCTs intentions.

3-20. Forceful reconnaissance, the opposite of stealthy, involves predominantly mounted operations that are much faster paced and in which reconnaissance units are less concerned about being detected by the enemy. With augmentation of vehicles, the DRT could conduct forceful reconnaissance. The DRT may be assigned to conduct a security mission in support of the motorized troops' forceful reconnaissance. An example may be that the DRT conducts a screen to provide security to the motorized movement. Another example may be conducting area reconnaissance of restrictive terrain within the forceful reconnaissance AO.

3-21. Deliberate reconnaissance entails slow, detailed, broad-based operations in which the troop accomplishes several tasks. The DRT is suited for deliberate reconnaissance, but must be within the DRT's overall dismounted tempo.

3-22. Rapid reconnaissance, the opposite of deliberate, focuses the troops on a few key pieces of information required by the squadron commander.

3-23. The troop commander's guidance for tempo also covers specific execution information to include:
- Planning timelines.
- Tasks to subordinate units.
- Specific information requirements.
- Latest time information is of value.
- Movement techniques.
- Reconnaissance methods (mounted, dismounted, aerial, sensor).
- Tactical risk.

ENGAGEMENT CRITERIA

3-24. Engagement criteria establish which targets the troop is expected to engage—under what circumstances—using either direct or indirect fires—and which ones they are expected to hand over to a maneuver element. The commander develops his engagement criteria based on established rules of engagement (ROE) and his analysis of the METT-TC variables.

3-25. The commander issues planning guidance to define the engagement criteria as well as specific execution information which may include:

- Engagement criteria.
- Guidance on actions on contact.
- Bypass criteria.
- Reconnaissance handover (RHO) criteria.
- Priority of fires.
- ROE and or rules for the use of force.
- FSCMs: Weapons and control status.
- Information engagement (IE) guidance:
    - Aggressive reconnaissance implies liberal engagement criteria.
    - Discreet reconnaissance is conducted with restrictive engagement criteria. The DRT can conduct discreet reconnaissance based on its ability to conduct dismounted stealth reconnaissance.

OPERATIONAL CONSIDERATIONS

3-26. For the DRT, each mission varies by type, focus, tempo, engagement criteria, size, environment, duration, and complexity as well as other factors. So, there are no correct tactics or techniques for employing reconnaissance elements in an AO. Employment of reconnaissance elements also varies drastically based on terrain. Units may be able to cover a larger area while establishing OPs in open or flat terrain as opposed to mountainous or wooded terrain and may find it extremely difficult in an urban environment.

HIDE SITES AND OPS

3-27. Hide sites and OPs are used to assist in conducting the reconnaissance or surveillance mission. A hide site is a temporary grouping of operations, communications, and support personnel formed to conduct a specific operation or mission such as an OP. Observation posts are most often a camouflaged site used to observe the objective.

3-28. Hide sites are also used by DRT Scouts for specific activities such as eating or resting. Dismounted reconnaissance troop members may rotate between the hide and OPs during the course of the operation. The OP often has communication with the hide site through secure FM and contains supplies, OP rotation personnel, and longer-range communications equipment used for the transfer of information sent from OP personnel. Team members run the team's communications equipment directly from the hide site. If communications is lost between the two positions, they perform a linkup to determine the nature of the problem.

3-29. In preparation for a surveillance operation, team leaders reconnoiter and select positions for the OPs and hide sites. Where to establish the positions depends on his METT-TC analysis conducted during the planning phase and his continued analysis once he is in the vicinity of the objective.

Mission Duration

3-30. Reconnaissance missions are also characterized by the duration of the mission. The duration of the mission may be short, long, or extended as described below.

Short Duration

3-31. Short-duration missions are established quickly at a designated time and maintained for less than 12 hours. The DRT can maximize the number of personnel on the ground for a short period of time and man up to 12 OPs.

Long Duration

3-32. Long-duration missions are maintained for more than 12 hours but less than 24 hours. The number of personnel decreases because platoons must manage a deliberate rotation schedule. The DRT can establish up to six long-duration OPs.

Extended Duration

3-33. Extended-duration missions are maintained for longer than 24 hours. Units may have to coordinate for supplies, augmentation, and other support needed based on mission variables. This may include Class IV materials or additional engineer support, obstacles, dedicated quick-reaction forces (QRF), and other support that allows the unit or OPs to operate for an indefinite period of time.

INTEGRATION OF SENSORS

3-34. Current and emerging sensor technology enables reconnaissance units to detect and identify targets at increased distances. Sensors provide the troop with early warning and help limit exposure to threat reconnaissance and acquisition systems. This capability provides the troop with maximum standoff range and allows the commander to make timely decisions.

3-35. Despite the continual evolution of sophisticated sensors and collection assets, SA will not be perfect. This is true in periods of limited visibility or adverse weather. Uncertainty will always be present in the AO. Thus, the scout remains the most important information-gathering asset in the IBCT. The commander must fully integrate the troop's personnel and organic sensors in a complementary manner.

3-36. The primary sensor system organic to the DRT is a SUAS. The troop may also receive additional support from squadron and higher echelon assets.

3-37. The squadron staff and troop commander use a variety of reconnaissance management methods such as cueing, mixing, redundancy, and task organization. (See Table 3-3.) They do this in an attempt to use limited assets most effectively and to collect the most critical information with the fewest assets as quickly as possible. (For detailed information on reconnaissance management refer to FM 3-90.)

Table 3-3. DRT reconnaissance management

Cueing	The integration of one or more types of reconnaissance or surveillance systems to provide information that directs follow-on collection of more detailed information by another system.
Mixing	Using two or more different assets to collect against the same information requirement.
Redundancy	Using two or more like assets to collect against the same information requirement.
Task Organization	The placing of additional assets under the control of the DRT.

SMALL UNMANNED AIRCRAFT SYSTEM

3-38. Small unmanned aircraft system operations support the DRT commander as he plans, coordinates, and executes operations, providing reconnaissance capabilities to enhance his SA. An Army SUAS can also perform acquisition, detection, designation, and battle damage assessment (BDA) to improve targeting. The troop has an organic SUAS, but can also have direct access to real time or near real time feeds from additional SUAS support provided by the squadron, IBCT, or a higher headquarter.

Missions

3-39. Small unmanned aircraft systems are capable of locating and recognizing threats forces, moving vehicles, weapon systems, and other targets that contrast with their surroundings. In addition, SUASs are capable of locating and confirming the position of friendly forces and the presence of noncombatant civilians. Small unmanned aircraft systems can support ground units in the following missions:
- Reconnaissance.
- Surveillance.

- Target acquisition.
- BDA.

Capabilities

3-40. Small unmanned aircraft systems bring numerous capabilities to the DRT, providing near real time reconnaissance, surveillance, and target acquisition. They can be employed throughout the AO. Employed as a team, SUASs, and manned systems provide excellent reconnaissance and security capabilities. Small unmanned aircraft systems provide the following additional capabilities (see Chapter 7, Enablers, Other Intelligence Assets, for details on the SUASs.):

- Support target acquisition of threat forces.
- Assist area surveillance.
- Locate threat elements and help determine their composition, disposition, and activity.
- Maintain contact with threat forces from initial contact through BDA.
- Provide target coordinates with enough accuracy to enable immediate target handover, as well as first-round fire-for-effect engagements.
- Provide or enhance multispectral sensor coverage of the AO.
- Provide information to manned systems, thus increasing survivability and cueing.
- Reduce or eliminate exposure time of manned systems in high-risk environments.
- Provide an extended three-dimensional vantage, both in distance and time, at critical decision points in difficult terrain.
- Perform decoy, demonstration, feint, and deception operations.
- Support mission duration beyond the capability of manned reconnaissance. Provide digital connectivity, allowing for rapid dissemination of information.

Limitations

3-41. Small unmanned aircraft systems are an excellent force multiplier, especially employed as part of an overall collection plan that takes advantage of their capabilities. At the same time, they have limited effectiveness in locating threat forces that are well covered or concealed. The SUASs are not well suited for wide-area surveillance. Other limitations include the following:

- Vulnerability to enemy fire.
- Significant audio signature.
- Weather restrictions (such as cloud cover and turbulence).
- Requirement to maintain LOS to ground control stations.
- Limited frequencies for SUAS control.
- Air space C2 issues.
- Limited sensor field of view.
- Limited detection capability in areas of heavy vegetation.
- Unique supply requirements.
- Assembly area survivability.
- Launch and recovery criteria.
- Weather conditions.

Small Unmanned Aircraft System Planning Considerations

3-42. Planning for SUAS operations should include the following:

- Deconflict with the squadron S2/S3 and fires support element request for SUAS missions.
- Unit AO.
- Mission statement.
- Time window for the SUAS mission.
- Reconnaissance objective.

- PIR and information requirement.
- Line of departure (LD) or line of contact (LC).
- Initial named area of interests (NAIs).
- Routes to the AO.
- Restricted operations area and/or restricted overflight zone, IBCT air coordination.
- Coordinating altitudes.
- Ingress route (azimuth, distance, time).
- Egress route (azimuth, distance, time).
- Entry control points.
- Holding points.
- Emergency recovery point (including route).
- Control point location.

Air Ground Reconnaissance Handover

3-43. When the SUAS makes contact, particularly during reconnaissance operations, the operator will update digital systems and hand over the contact to ground Scouts via FM radio as quickly as possible. Rapid RHO (See Section V of this chapter for more information on RHO) allows the SUAS to avoid threat air defense weapons and also helps to maintain the tempo of the operation.

3-44. During the handover, SUASs assist in providing direction to the ground element charged with establishing contact with the threat. They maintain contact with the threat until ground units are in position and have also established sensor or visual contact.

3-45. The first actions in the RHO process are a SPOTREP and a situation report (SITREP) from the SUAS operator to the ground element. These reports are sent by FM voice, followed by digital systems reports. Next, the SUAS reconnoiters the area for secure positions for the ground element, identifying tentative hide, overwatch, and OP positions and likely mounted and dismounted routes into the area.

3-46. The ground element moves to initial hide positions along the route selected by the commander based on SUAS-collected information. The DRT element then moves to establish sensor or visual contact with the threat. Once this contact is established, the DRT element sends a SPOTREP to the SUAS operator via FM, followed by digital systems reports. When the operator confirms that the DRT element can observe threat elements and has a clear picture of the situation, handover is complete. The SUAS can be committed to a follow-on mission in support of the troop.

SECTION IV – FORMS

3-47. There are four forms of reconnaissance: zone, area, route, and reconnaissance in force. Zone, area, and route reconnaissance are normally conducted with a multidimensional focus that includes such factors as society, infrastructure, threat, and terrain. During a zone, area or route reconnaissance, units often have to collect specific data on the terrain and terrain features. To assist in collection and classification, FM 3-20.98 gives a thorough explanation of collection of essential field data including, for example, classification of streams, bridges, and slopes. Below is a brief definition of each form of reconnaissance. (For further details on these forms, see FM 3-20.96.)

ZONE RECONNAISSANCE

3-48. Zone reconnaissance is a form of reconnaissance that involves a directed effort to obtain detailed information on all routes, obstacles, terrain, and enemy forces within a zone defined by boundaries. (See FM 3-90.)

3-49. The DRT can conduct one zone reconnaissance within the squadron's zone reconnaissance area. The DRT is limited by their movement capabilities, understanding they will not be able to cover as large an area as a motorized unit in the same amount of time. However, the IBCT battalions are also moving at a dismounted pace. The zone reconnaissance by the DRT may be limited to restrictive terrain most suited to their capabilities or threat-based zone, which utilizes the DRT's stealth capability. A zone reconnaissance most often takes more time to execute than any other reconnaissance mission because the target area is larger and the initial intelligence preparation of the battlespace (IPB) usually generates many unanswered questions. The squadron commander must ensure that he gives adequate time to the DRT to accomplish the mission. If the time available is not adequate, he seeks additional time, reinforcements, or systems to assist in the reconnaissance effort. If necessary, the squadron commander may allow troop commanders to accelerate the reconnaissance effort and accept a degree of risk by reducing the number of critical tasks to be accomplished. The DRT may also conduct a screen to a flank or portion of the zone reconnaissance area to provide security for motorized troops and conduct an accelerated zone reconnaissance.

PLANNING CONSIDERATIONS

3-50. Dismounted reconnaissance troop zone reconnaissance is organized with subordinate platoons operating abreast of each another within a portion of the zone as designated by graphic control measures (GCM). (See Figure 3-1.) The DRT commander expects significant threat forces to be found within the zone. He may have assets allocated from the IBCT, such as aviation forces, to deal with the anticipated threat. If reconnaissance elements will likely encounter significant obstacles or mobility impediments, they may also be augmented with combat engineers.

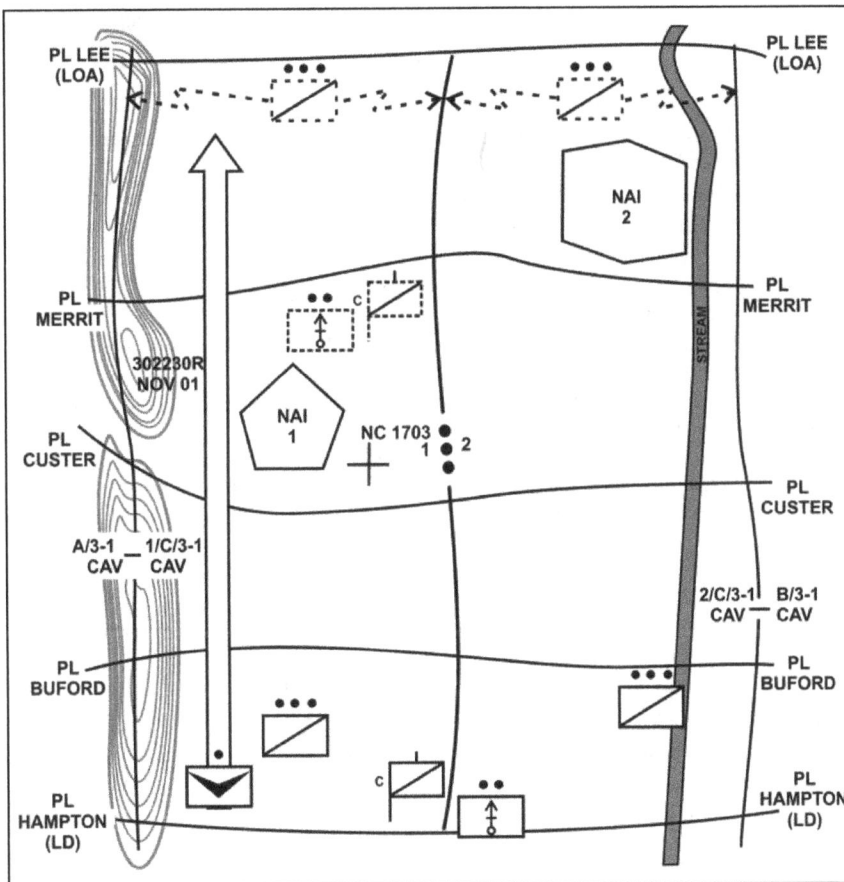

Figure 3-1. Example of a DRT zone reconnaissance

3-51. The DRT commander considers the following when planning for a zone reconnaissance mission:
- Friendly force considerations, including the following:
  - Mission of adjacent and follow-on forces.
  - Reconnaissance objectives of the reconnaissance squadron and follow-on forces.
  - CCIR of the squadron and follow-on forces.
  - Higher commander's reconnaissance focus, tempo, and engagement criteria, including considerations for adjusting tempo and engagement criteria during reconnaissance.
  - Missions of collection assets, such as Prophet, operating within the troop's AO but not under troop control.
  - Capabilities and limitations of other collection elements, such as ground sensors that are attached to or controlled by the DRT.
- The enemy situation, including the following:
  - Type and capabilities of likely enemy weapon systems, night vision devices (NVDs) and related systems, and surveillance radar.
  - Special equipment, such as body armor, ground sensors, and signal intercept, if applicable.
  - The reconnaissance squadron's enemy COAs, including a situation template (SITTEMP) depicting composition, known and template dispositions, and potential engagement areas (EAs).
- Terrain and weather considerations, including the following:
  - Effects on effective ranges of weapon systems and NVDs.
  - Effects on SUASs and other aviation assets for reconnaissance, transport, resupply, FS, and medical evacuation (MEDEVAC) or CASEVAC.
  - Effects on cross-country mobility.
  - Effects on civil functions and services.
- Civil considerations, including the following:
  - Locations, functions, and jurisdictions of government agencies and offices, political party headquarters, and NGOs.
  - Composition and dispositions of regional/local military, paramilitary, and law enforcement organizations.
  - Locations of police stations, armories or barracks, encampments, weapons holding areas, and staging areas.
  - Factions, key leaders, locations, composition, and dispositions of known friendly, neutral, and belligerent elements. Considerations include recent trends in public opinion, intensity levels of current and past disturbances, and if applicable, effects of use of lethal force against civilians.
  - If applicable, description and capabilities of uniforms, insignia, vehicles, markings, and equipment, including weapons and NVDs.
  - Locations of power generation/transformer facilities, water treatment plants, and food distribution points.
  - Locations of communications networks and media outlets.

3-52. The DRT commander addresses the following:
- Key reconnaissance tasks that must be accomplished during the zone reconnaissance.
- Purpose for reconnaissance in relation to the squadron's reconnaissance objective.
- Endstate for reconnaissance.

3-53. The DRT commander develops a concept of the operation that describes, at a minimum, the following:
- Focus and tempo for reconnaissance, including changes to tempo based on anticipated contact or other requirements.
- Reconnaissance of the zone to answer the applicable information requirement, including the following:

- Determines if platoons should conduct zone, area, or route reconnaissance, or any combination of the three to enable the DRT to complete its zone reconnaissance.
- Identifies platoon and other subordinate element tasks, including reconnaissance, security, and follow and support, as required.
- Determines task organization and subordinate unit AOs based on critical tasks and other METT-TC factors.
- Integrates reconnaissance methods such as sensor, aerial, and dismounted reconnaissance.
- Determines deployment method, and select movement techniques that support the tempo.
- If necessary, identifies infiltration route(s) against a higher threat.
- If necessary, determines requirements for short- and long-duration surveillance of NAIs.
- If necessary, integrates urban assessment and information requirement.
- Plan for establishing a screen upon reaching the limit of advance (LOA).
- Synchronizing target acquisition assignments with reconnaissance tasks, covering the following:
  - Target description, location (known or templated), and method of engagement.
  - Desired target effect and purpose for effect.
  - Criteria to change from target surveillance to designation (illumination).
- Integration of other elements or assets into the reconnaissance effort, including the following:
  - SUAS and Army aviation assets, such as attack reconnaissance units, to reconnoiter routes, infiltration lanes, or key and restricted terrain within the AO.
  - Ground sensors to orient on NAIs in advance of the platoons or on avenues of approach or routes on the flanks of the platoons' reconnaissance.
  - Ground sensors, which are emplaced on flank avenues of approach or routes leading into the troop AO.
  - Engineers to assist with classification of bridges, overpasses, culverts, fords, routes, obstacles, infrastructure, environment, and other classifications related to area damage control in the designated zone.
- Locations and criteria for RHO and target handover, covering the following:
  - Accepting handover from or transferring responsibility to another element.
  - Conducting handover within the troop by subordinate elements.
- Priorities of fire and use of fires to maintain maximum range forward of the reconnaissance and scout platoons, including the following:
  - Establishing mortar firing points so the mortar section is in position to support the troop at critical times.
  - Splitting the mortar section or keeping the two guns together.
  - Considering colocating the mortar section with the troop CP for security and displacing the mortar section with CP vehicles.
  - Using trigger points to enable the mortar section to effectively cover the platoons as they bound forward in the AO.
- Bypass and engagement criteria during reconnaissance.
- If necessary, instructions for forward passage of lines.
- Commitment criteria and actions of the squadron's reaction force or reserve in support of the troop's infiltration, movement, and reconnaissance.
- Graphic control measures that support the concept of the operation, including the following:
  - Boundaries identifying the DRT's AO, platoon AOs, LD, and LOA.
  - Routes or lanes and designated start points (SP), release points (RP), and rally points for each route.
  - Phase lines, checkpoints, and contact points for coordination with other elements.

3-54. Terrain index reference system or grid index reference system points to assist in C2. Sustainment considerations include the following:
- Sustainment priorities.

- Security requirements and techniques for combat trains or supporting sustainment elements.
- Movement and positioning of trains and sustainment supply points.
- Resupply, including emergency resupply and caches, covering the following:
  - Caches for Class I, III, IV, and VIII and other mission-specific items such as batteries.
  - Drop points away from the platoon vehicle hide position and OPs.
- Casualty consolidation and evacuation.
- Equipment and supply destruction criteria. Communications considerations include the following:
  - Positioning of the DRT commander, XO, or CP and, if necessary, retrans to maintain communications with the reconnaissance squadron and other designated elements.
  - Method and techniques for communications between CP vehicles, platoon CP vehicles and dismounted elements.
  - Responsibilities and procedures for integrating supporting analog platoon elements into the troop digital network.

3-55. Critical tasks of the zone reconnaissance include:

- Find and report all enemy forces within the zone.
- Clear all enemy forces in the designated AO within the capabilities of the unit conducting the reconnaissance.
- Determine the trafficability of all the terrain within the zone, including built-up areas.
- Locate and determine the extent of all contaminated areas in the zone.
- Evaluate and classify all bridges, defiles, overpasses, underpasses, and culverts in the zone.
- Locate any fords, crossing sites, or bypasses for existing and reinforcing obstacles (including built-up areas) in the zone.
- Locate all obstacles and create lanes as specified in execution orders.
- Report the above information to the commander directing the zone reconnaissance, to include providing a sketch map or overlay.

AREA RECONNAISSANCE

3-56. An area reconnaissance is a form of reconnaissance that focuses on obtaining detailed information about terrain or enemy activity within a prescribed area. This area may include a town, a ridgeline, woods, an airhead, or any other feature critical to operations. The area may consist of a single point, such as a bridge or an installation. Areas are normally smaller than zones and are not unusually contiguous to other friendly areas targeted for reconnaissance. Because the area is smaller, reconnaissance moves faster than a zone reconnaissance. (See FM 3-90.)

ORGANIZATION OF THE DISMOUNTED RECONNAISSANCE TROOP

3-57. The DRT conducting an area reconnaissance organizes according to the size, geography, physical infrastructure, and social dynamics of the area to be reconnoitered. The troop can conduct decentralized reconnaissance in multiple areas simultaneously, either by maneuvering elements through the areas or by establishing stationary OPs.

GRAPHIC CONTROL MEASURES

3-58. Area reconnaissance may be controlled using an LD, lateral boundaries, and an LOA. Within the area, the troop commander can further divide the AO with additional lateral boundaries to define platoon AOs. Phase lines and contact points can be designated to coordinate the movement of elements operating abreast. Critical terrain features or recognizable landmarks can be designated as checkpoints. Fire support coordination measures can be included. The example in Figure 3-2 shows a DRT conducting area reconnaissance of an area subdivided into smaller AOs, with a SUAS conducting a forward screen.

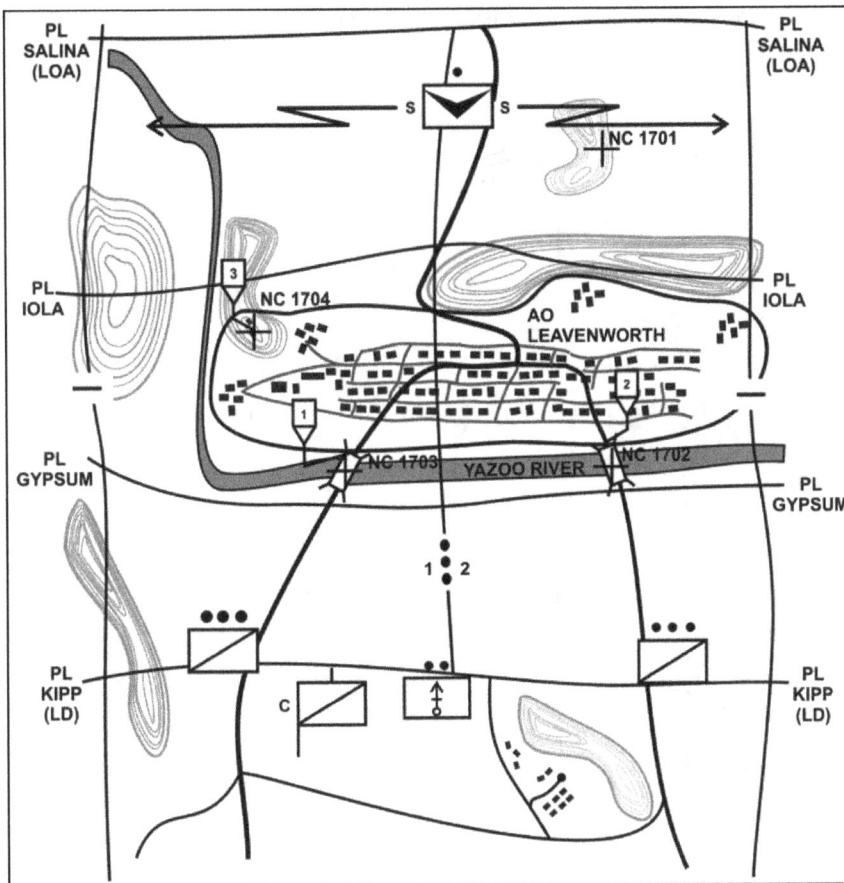

Figure 3-2. Example of a DRT conducting area reconnaissance

CRITICAL TASKS

3-59. The tasks accomplished as part of an area reconnaissance are basically the same as those for a zone reconnaissance, though the scope of tasks will differ. In addition, an area reconnaissance is normally conducted on a smaller scale than a zone reconnaissance.

EXAMPLE OF A DISMOUNTED RECONNAISSANCE TROOP AREA RECONNAISSANCE

3-60. As with the zone reconnaissance, the DRT commander ensures that the troop has all known information and intelligence pertaining to the AO. The reconnaissance squadron may designate troop infiltration lanes. The troop commander determines the infiltration method and sequence. At times, the commander may be required to identify the infiltration lanes. If so, he conducts reconnaissance during his troop-leading procedures to identify and select infiltration lanes. He coordinates for support from other collection assets available to the squadron or IBCT to assist with this reconnaissance. Information from signal intelligence and imagery intelligence can assist the DRT commander in developing and completing his scheme of maneuver during troop-leading procedures. He uses imagery intelligence, along with a detailed map reconnaissance, in determining how terrain supports movement. The commander views the terrain not only from the perspective of how it supports his mission success, but also from the enemy's perspective. He should focus measurement and signature intelligence assets on restricted terrain or high-speed avenues of approach to provide early warning of potential enemy movements. Small unmanned aircraft systems can support infiltration and reconnaissance to provide early warning and reconnaissance of areas that are inaccessible to the ground troop. Figure 3-3 illustrates an example of a DRT conducting area reconnaissance of designated NAIs.

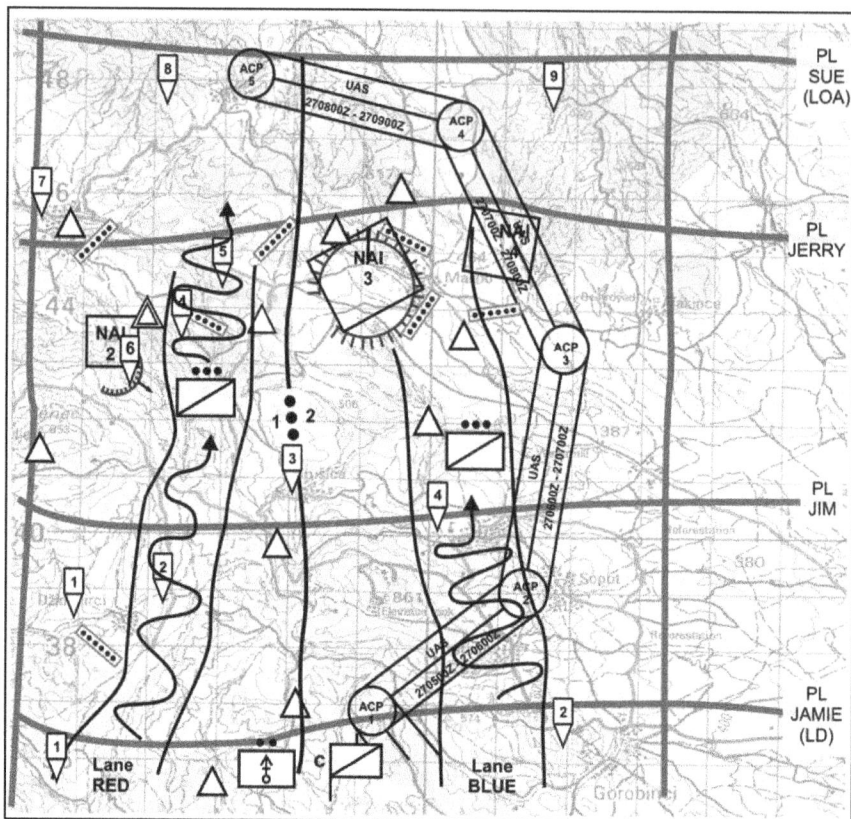

Figure 3-3. Example of a DRT conducting an area reconnaissance of designated NAIs

3-61. The DRT commander considers the following as he develops his area reconnaissance plan during troop-leading procedures: (For a detailed list of additional considerations under each category, refer to the discussion of zone reconnaissance earlier in this chapter.)

- Friendly forces.
- The enemy situation.
- Terrain and weather.
- Civil issues.
- If applicable, an urban operations (UO) sketch that portrays key terrain, including the following:
  - Safe havens.
  - Hospitals.
  - Police stations, armories, and similar sites.
  - Embassies.
  - Power generation, communications, and water treatment facilities.
  - Restricted or protected areas designated by the ROE.
  - Hazardous areas, including above- or below-ground natural gas or other fuel storage; construction sites; intersections and bridges; and known hostile, belligerent, or criminal areas.

- Major terrain and man-made features, such as parks, industrial complexes, airports, and buildings that mask or interfere with communications or GPS.
- Avenues of approach, including main thoroughfares or improved road surfaces, escape and evasion routes or corridors, and subterranean routes and access.

3-62. The DRT commander addresses the following:

- Key reconnaissance tasks that must be accomplished during the area reconnaissance.
- Purpose for the reconnaissance in relation to the reconnaissance objective of the squadron.
- Endstate for reconnaissance.

3-63. The commander develops a concept of the operation that describes, as a minimum, the following (this outline lists items specific to the area reconnaissance; for a detailed list of additional considerations under each category, refer to the discussion of zone reconnaissance earlier in this chapter):

- Focus and tempo for reconnaissance.
- Movement to the areas to be reconnoitered, including techniques and formations, if applicable. Considerations include the following:
  - Selects movement techniques that support the tempo and avoiding known enemy forces outside the areas to be reconnoitered.
  - Selects the route(s) and establishing a march order on each route.
  - Identifies infiltration route(s) against a higher threat and establishing an order of march.
  - Identifies concealed locations to position vehicles prior to conducting the reconnaissance.
  - Identifies vehicle positions that ensure connectivity with higher and lower communications (FBCB2).
- Reconnaissance of the designated areas to answer the applicable information requirement.
- Synchronizing target acquisition assignments with reconnaissance tasks.
- Integration of other elements or assets into the reconnaissance effort, including SUAS and Army aviation assets, Prophet, ground sensors, and engineers.
- Locations and criteria for RHO and target handover.
- Priorities of fire and use of fires to maintain maximum range of the forward platoon.
- Bypass and engagement criteria during both movement to and reconnaissance of designated areas.
- Commitment criteria and actions of the reconnaissance squadron's reaction force or reserve in support of the troop's infiltration, movement, and reconnaissance.
- Graphic control measures that support the concept of the operation, including the following:
  - Boundaries identifying the troop's AO, platoon AOs, and the LD.
  - Areas to be reconnoitered with a given AO.

3-64. Sustainment considerations for the area reconnaissance are the same as those for zone reconnaissance, as outlined earlier in this chapter.

3-65. Communications considerations for the area reconnaissance are the same as those for zone reconnaissance, as outlined earlier in this chapter.

ROUTE RECONNAISSANCE

3-66. Route reconnaissance is a form of reconnaissance that focuses along a specific line of communication, such as a road, railway, or cross-country mobility corridor. (See FM 3-90.)

3-67. The DRT is capable of conducting two simultaneous route reconnaissances. Routes for the IBCT may include avenues of approach and direction of attack for the Infantry battalions along with vehicle routes. Vehicle route reconnaissance is best suited for the motorized troops of the squadron but the DRT, given the time, can also conduct a dismounted route reconnaissance.

ORGANIZATION OF FORCES

3-68. If augmented with vehicles for each platoon, the DRT can conduct reconnaissance of two vehicle routes. The integration of ground, air, and other assets can facilitate a faster and more detailed route reconnaissance.

GRAPHIC CONTROL MEASURES

3-69. The DRT commander places lateral boundaries on both sides of the route that allow reconnaissance of all terrain from which the enemy could influence the route. He designates an LD perpendicular to the route short of the SP and places an LOA far enough beyond the route's RP to include any terrain from which the enemy could influence the route. The commander also establishes coordination points or contact points to enable proper flank coordination. If air reconnaissance is employed, an air LOA is normally established to provide greater depth and to take advantage of the aircrafts' elevated observation platform and long-range acquisition capability. The SP and RP define that section of the route on which the unit collects detailed information. Phase lines and checkpoints are added to maintain coordination, control movement, or designate critical points. Fire control measures and FSCMs help the unit to coordinate fires as necessary. All GCMs are placed along or on recognizable terrain features. If possible, they are identifiable from both the ground and the air to assist in air-ground coordination. (See Figure 3-4 for an example of GCMs of route reconnaissance by a DRT.)

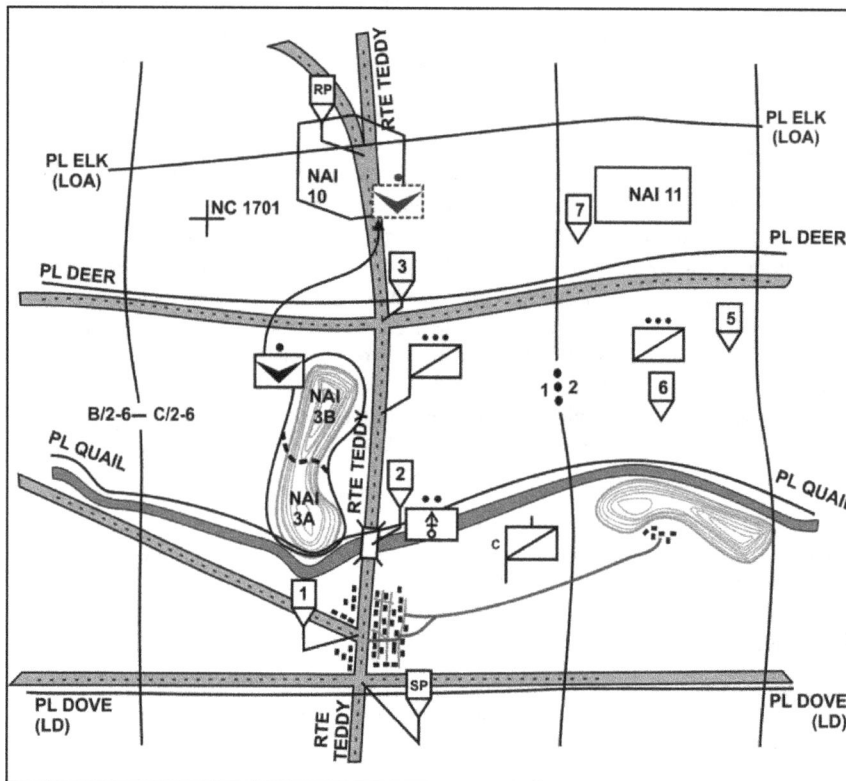

Figure 3-4. Example of graphic control measures of route reconnaissance by a DRT

CRITICAL TASKS

3-70. Based on time factors and the commander's intent, The DRT commander may direct the platoons to reconnoiter for specific information. He directs the following critical tasks in a route reconnaissance:

- Finds, reports, and clears all enemy forces, within capabilities, that can influence movement along the route.
- Determines the trafficability of the route; can it support the friendly force?
- Reconnoiters all terrain that the enemy can use to dominate movement along the route, such as check points, ambush sites, pickup zones, landing zones (LZs), and drop zones (DZs).
- Reconnoiters all built-up areas, contaminated areas, and lateral routes along the route.
- Evaluates and classifies all bridges, defiles, overpasses, and underpasses.
- Locates all obstacles and create lanes as specified in the execution order.
- Reports the above route information to the headquarters initiating the route reconnaissance mission, to include providing a sketch map or overlay. (See FM 3-90.)
- Locates mines, obstacles, and barriers.
- Locates bypasses around built-up areas, obstacles, and contaminated areas.
- Determines the type and volume of traffic on the route.
- Updates route information.

EXAMPLE OF ROUTE RECONNAISSANCE

3-71. The reconnaissance squadron specifies the route, including the SP, RP, and other critical points along the route. It establishes Air space C2 measures, specifies the reconnaissance start time, and designates a completion time. Using the provided IPB and imagery, the DRT commander analyzes the terrain to gain an appreciation of the danger areas within his AO and the nature of the potential enemy. He determines how much terrain on each flank of the route is to be reconnoitered. Squadron constraints or restrictions may also influence how much terrain is reconnoitered. The troop commander coordinates to ensure support from other collection assets available to the squadron and the IBCT both prior to and during reconnaissance. The commander may also direct a platoon to conduct a route reconnaissance as a specific task in another mission. Figure 3-5 illustrates a DRT conducting route reconnaissance.

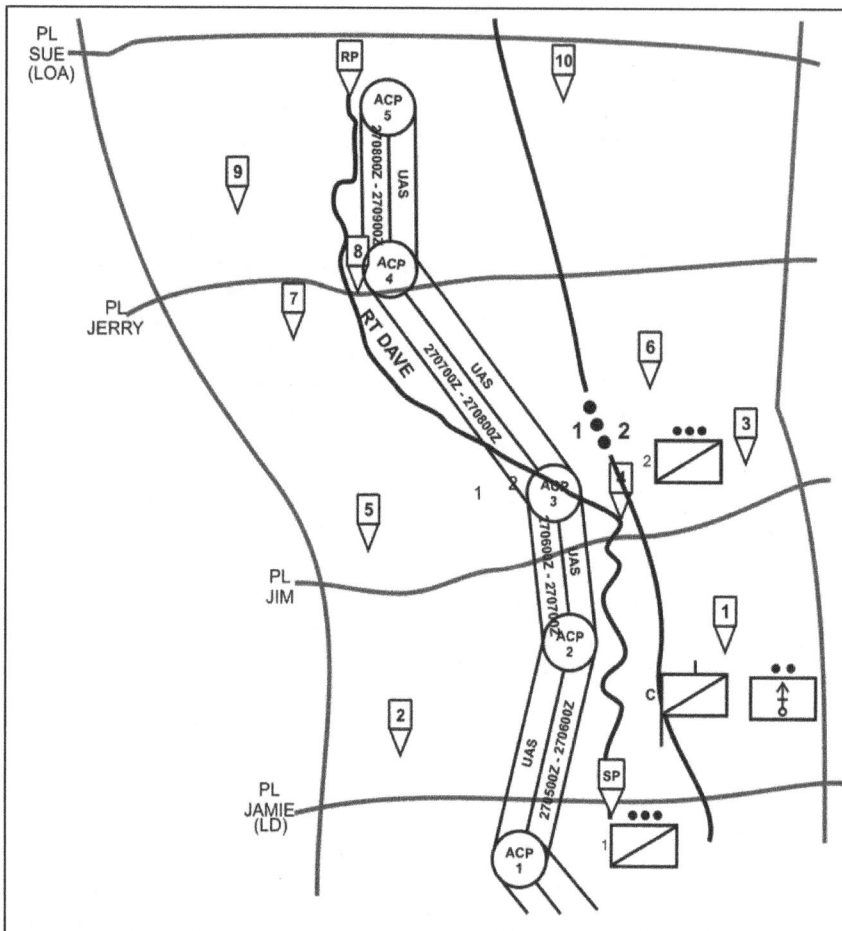

Figure 3-5. Example of a DRT conducting route reconnaissance

3-72. The DRT normally performs a tactical foot march to the LD and deploys to execute reconnaissance of the route unless transportation has been arranged. Based on the amount and quality of intelligence known about the enemy, the commander determines how much security is required for the move to the LD. The commander also considers the effect his final disposition of forces will have on the troop's follow-on mission. The DRT commander considers the following as he develops his route reconnaissance plan during troop-leading procedures. (For a detailed list of considerations under each category, refer to the discussion of zone reconnaissance earlier in this chapter.)

- Friendly force considerations, including the following:
  - Missions of other elements that support troop reconnaissance, such as Prophet or SUAS.
  - Missions of other elements operating within the troop AO but not under troop control.
- The enemy situation, including the following:
  - Types and capabilities of likely enemy weapons systems, NVDs and related systems, and communications systems.
  - The squadron's enemy COAs, including a SITTEMP depicting composition, known and template dispositions, and potential EAs. Potential enemy COAs include ambushes along the route in close or restricted terrain or tied to obstacles along the route and attack by long-range direct or indirect fires from dominating terrain along the route.

- Terrain and weather considerations, including the following:
    - Effects on SUAS and other aviation assets for reconnaissance, CASEVAC, or fire support.
    - Effects on civilian traffic flow.
- Civil considerations, including the following:
    - Local government jurisdictions that encompass the route.
    - Relief agencies and other NGOs using the route.
    - Dislocated civilians using the route.

3-73. The DRT commander develops his intent to address the following:
- Key reconnaissance tasks that must be accomplished during the route reconnaissance.
- Purpose for reconnaissance in relation to the squadron's reconnaissance objective.
- Endstate for reconnaissance.

3-74. The DRT commander develops a concept of the operation that describes, as a minimum, the following: (This outline lists items specific to the route reconnaissance; for a detailed list of additional considerations under each category, refer to the discussion of zone reconnaissance earlier in this chapter.)
- Focus and tempo for reconnaissance.
- Reconnaissance of the route to answer the applicable information requirement, including the following:
    - Identifies requirements to reconnoiter and classify the route or designated portions of the route.
    - Identifies requirements to conduct an area reconnaissance of designated terrain on the flanks of the route.
    - Selects movement techniques that support the tempo.
    - Specifies actions at built-up areas and actions on contact with enemy forces or civilians.
- Transition to follow-on mission after completing the reconnaissance or reaching the LOA.
- If necessary, synchronization of target acquisition assignments with reconnaissance tasks.
- Integration of other elements or assets into the reconnaissance effort, including SUAS and Army aviation assets, Prophet, ground sensors, engineers, and CBRN reconnaissance elements (to reconnoiter for contamination and bypasses).
- Locations and criteria for RHO.
- Priorities of fire and use of fires to maintain maximum indirect fire range forward of the platoons.
- Bypass and engagement criteria for elements conducting the route reconnaissance.
- Commitment criteria and actions of the reconnaissance squadron's reaction force or reserve in support of the DRT's infiltration, movement, and reconnaissance.
- Graphic control measures that support the concept of the operation, including the following:
    - Boundaries identifying the troop's AO and subordinate element boundaries lateral to the route to support reconnaissance on the flanks.
    - Routes, including SPs, RPs, and checkpoints for other critical points.
    - Phase lines and contact points for coordination with other elements.
    - LOA.

3-75. Considerations for sustainment and communications during the route reconnaissance are the same as those for zone reconnaissance, as outlined earlier in this chapter.

RECONNAISSANCE IN FORCE

3-76. A reconnaissance in force is a deliberate combat operation designed to discover or test the enemy's strength, dispositions, and reaction, or to obtain other information. A commander uses a reconnaissance in force when the enemy is known to be operating within an area, and the commander cannot obtain adequate intelligence by other means. A unit may also conduct a reconnaissance in force in restrictive terrain where the enemy is likely to ambush smaller reconnaissance forces. A reconnaissance in force is an aggressive reconnaissance, conducted as an offensive operation in pursuit of clearly stated CCIRs. The overall goal of a reconnaissance in force is to determine enemy weaknesses that can be exploited. It differs from other reconnaissance operations because it is usually conducted only to gain information about the enemy, and not the terrain. Neither the DRT nor the squadron is equipped to conduct a reconnaissance in force. The squadron requires significant augmentation with combat elements to conduct a reconnaissance in force. The DRT may conduct a screen, area, or zone reconnaissance in support of a larger unit conducting a reconnaissance in force.

SECTION V – RECONNAISSANCE HANDOVER

3-77. Reconnaissance handover is the process of planning, preparing, and executing transfer of responsibility and information from one element to another to facilitate continued observation or surveillance of enemy contact or an assigned area. Reconnaissance handover may cover an area/zone—such as an AO, named area of interest (NAI), or target area of interest (TAI)—or enemy elements. It may involve visual, electronic, digital, or analog observation and information sources (or any combination of these). It is usually associated with a designated RHO coordination point or a phase line designated as a reconnaissance handover line.

3-78. Reconnaissance handover shares several critical tasks with battle handover (BHO), including relief in place, linkup, and passage of lines. Unlike BHO, however, it does not imply direct fire contact.

3-79. This task provides the information connection, overlapping communications, and commander's reconnaissance focus (commander's focus may differ for each echelon) required when planning and executing layered reconnaissance operations with multiple assets.

PLANNING

3-80. Responsibility for planning and coordinating RHO normally passes from squadron to the DRT. Planning may take place before operations, or it may be conducted during operations as part of a change of mission. When planning is conducted before an operation, the developing reconnaissance and security plan is analyzed to determine which elements may be required to conduct RHO and where the handover may take place. Once this is determined, locations or criteria for RHO are coordinated with squadron headquarters as applicable. Abbreviated planning steps are as follows:

- Coordinate for redundant surveillance to assist in maintaining enemy contact during RHO.
- Coordinate location and criteria for RHO with the squadron.
- Coordinate a communications plan between squadron elements.
- Coordinate indirect fires and exchange FS information.
- Exchange plans.
- Identify and coordinate for target handover, as necessary.
- Coordinate GCM to facilitate RHO.
- Select contact points or linkup points to collocate troop CPs.
- Coordinate transfer and acceptance of C2 between units.
- Plan for integration of non-digital elements.

PREPARATION

3-81. The DRT begins coordination as RHO requirements between units are identified. The commander finds handover criteria in the squadron order. Coordination includes establishment of a communications plan between the units as necessary. The communications plan includes radio frequencies, net IDs, enhanced position location reporting system (EPLRS) needlines, host files required to conduct the linkup (if units are from different maneuver control systems), and COMSEC variables for communications. Recognition signals are established or confirmed to prevent fratricide.

3-82. The troop exchanges information requirements to understand how it may answer or support the adjacent or follow-on unit's information requirements while remaining focused on the squadron or IBCT requirements. This understanding can assist in the transfer of vital information collected by the troop to the squadron/battalion during critical moments, such as identifying a security element along the squadron/battalion axis of advance that is not included in the IBCT's PIR.

3-83. If necessary, the troop coordinates indirect fires and FSCMs, critical friendly zones, preplanned targets, final protective fires (FPF), and obscuration missions. This includes criteria for preplanned RHO and/or high-payoff target (HPT) handover.

3-84. Coordination is conducted to identify the transfer or acceptance of C2 of elements between units as necessary. An example is for the troop to leave a scout section in contact with an enemy security element while the rest of the troop continues reconnaissance farther into the AO. As the IBCT shifts the handoff between the units, the follow-on unit may accept C2 of the troop's scout section until one of its scout sections is able to relieve the troop's section in observing the enemy element. Additionally, the squadron may issue on-order missions to other collection assets to assist in the handover. An example of this is a SUAS tasked to establish and maintain contact with a moving force while RHO of the force is being conducted from the troop to a follow-on unit. As RHO becomes imminent and final coordination begins, this level of coordination supports the RHO by allowing the SUAS maximum time on station and ensuring redundant observation during handover.

3-85. Rehearsals are of paramount importance before executing any plan. During rehearsals, elements involved in the RHO confirm and practice coordination to ensure clarity and understanding.

EXECUTION

3-86. The DRT may conduct RHO with follow-on or security (stationary) forces, accept RHO from a forward force, or provide C2 for handover between subordinate elements.

3-87. The requirement to maintain liaison and exchange information becomes more important as the distance closes between the forces executing RHO. Units may establish liaison by collocating their commanders, XOs, or CPs, if applicable. The follow-on unit may attach a scout section to the troop to facilitate C2 and handover. Every effort is made to establish face-to-face liaison. If this is not possible, units must establish a reliable digital or voice linkup to exchange critical information.

3-88. If face-to-face linkup is made, units complete final coordination and exchange information, then confirm that RHO is complete based on the specified criteria. If a target is being handed over, the criteria require the accepting unit to acquire the target before handover is complete. The unit that is handing over responsibility may then be required to support the unit accepting handover by executing responsibilities of the stationary unit while conducting a forward passage of lines or relief in place. If follow-on forces are conducting an attack, the unit handing over the reconnaissance may facilitate the attack by conducting reconnaissance pull, executing targeting, and employing previously coordinated indirect fires. Figures 3-6 through 3-8 depict an example of RHO from an IBCT DRT conducting zone reconnaissance to the scout platoon of an attacking Infantry battalion.

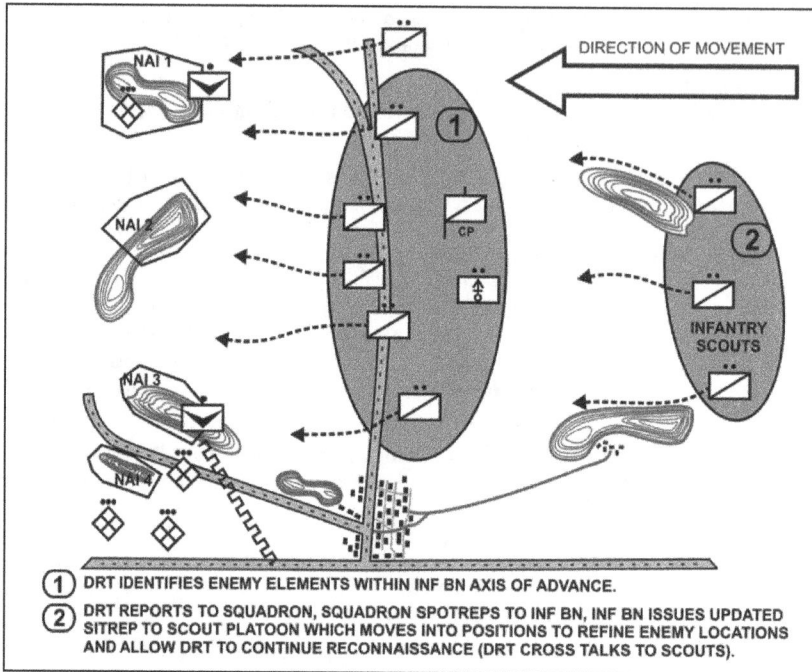

Figure 3-6. Example of reconnaissance handover (phase one)

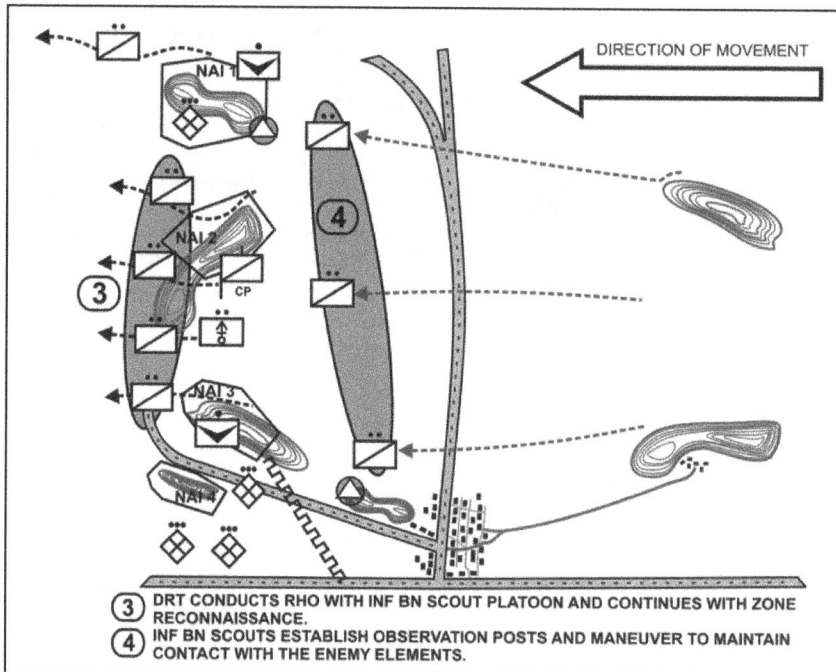

Figure 3-7. Example of reconnaissance handover (phase two)

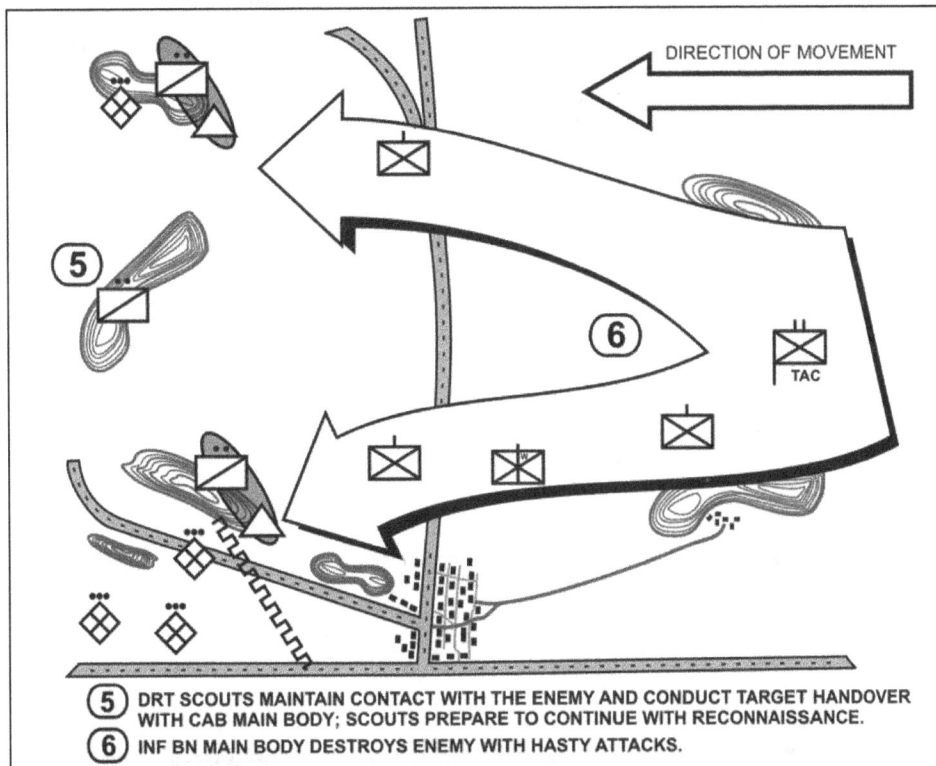

⑤ DRT SCOUTS MAINTAIN CONTACT WITH THE ENEMY AND CONDUCT TARGET HANDOVER
WITH CAB MAIN BODY; SCOUTS PREPARE TO CONTINUE WITH RECONNAISSANCE.
⑥ INF BN MAIN BODY DESTROYS ENEMY WITH HASTY ATTACKS.

Figure 3-8. Example of reconnaissance handover (phase three)

SECTION VI – CONDUCT RECONNAISSANCE IN URBAN AREAS

3-89. Understanding the urban environment is essential for conducting effective reconnaissance and security missions. Urban environments confront commanders with a unique combination of difficulties resulting from an intricate topography and a high population density. The geography's complexity stems from man-made features and supporting infrastructure superimposed on the natural terrain. Civilians may be near or intermingled with friendly and enemy combatants. This factor, and the human dimension it represents, is potentially the most important and perplexing for commanders and their staffs to understand and evaluate. (For detailed urban reconnaissance information, refer to FM 3-06.11, Combined Arms Operations in Urban Terrain and FM 3.06, Urban Operations.)

URBAN TERRAIN

3-90. Although complex and often difficult to penetrate with available reconnaissance assets, the terrain is the most recognizable aspect of an urban area. A true understanding of urban terrain requires the troop's leaders and Soldiers to comprehend its multidimensional nature. A proper analysis must consider both natural and man-made features.

3-91. Man-made features significantly affect military systems and units, and thus tactics and operations. Buildings, streets, and other infrastructure occur in a variety of patterns, forms, and sizes. The infinite ways in which these elements can intertwine make it difficult to describe a "typical" urban area, but it is possible to use a careful analysis of this framework to gain an understanding of complex urban terrain.

MULTIDIMENSIONAL ASPECT OF RECONNAISSANCE

3-92. Because of its composition and capabilities, the troop is ideally suited to conduct the multidimensional aspects of reconnaissance in urban areas. To do this successfully, however, leaders and Soldiers must understand the situation at regional, local, and neighborhood levels during stability operations. They can then develop a sense for their AO similar to the awareness of a "police officer on the beat" in any given community policing program. Scouts must learn how the urban area operates and how to identify sources of power or influence. Examples of this information include the following:

- Formal and informal political power structure.
- Police, secret police, and intelligence agencies.
- Criminal organizations.
- Military and paramilitary structures.
- Key terrain.
- Sensitivities of the populace.

CONSIDERATIONS

3-93. Considerations for UO include:

- Conduct aggressive reconnaissance operations.
- Understand the human dimension.
- Distinguish between noncombatants from combatants.
- Avoid the attrition approach.
- Control what is essential.
- Maximize effects without unnecessary collateral damage.
- Conduct close combat.
- Conduct transition control.

SECTION VII – ACTIONS ON CONTACT

3-94. Actions on contact include knowing the forms of contact, knowing the steps for conducting actions on contact, and understanding the time required to conduct actions on contact. The DRT analyzes the threat throughout the TLP to identify likely contact situations that may occur during an operation. Intelligence reports from the squadron help to clarify the threat's COAs and likelihood of contact. Through planning and rehearsals conducted during TLP, and through the use of the IPB, the DRT commander develops and refines his COAs to deal with probable threat contact or actions. The IPB helps prepare the commander for contact to include threat composition and actions. This in turn assists the commander in formulating his COA and reaction to contact with threat elements. Troop actions must be in concert with the current ROE and any engagement/disengagement criteria set forth in a higher OPORD. Dismounted reconnaissance troop elements must understand what actions are appropriate to include self-defense measures.

FORMS OF CONTACT

3-95. Contact occurs when elements of the troop encounter any situation that requires an active or passive response to the threat. These situations may entail one or more of the following eight forms of contact:

- Visual contact or observation.
- Physical contact (direct fire) with a threat force.
- Indirect fire contact.
- Contact with threat obstacles or those of unknown origin.
- Contact with threat or unknown aircraft.
- Situations involving CBRN hazards.
- Situations involving electronic warfare tactics.

- Nonhostile contact. This new category covers contact with personnel or elements that do not pose an immediate lethal threat to friendly forces. Some examples are:
    - Civilians (belligerent or nonhostile).
    - Factions.

PLANNING CONSIDERATIONS

3-96. During the mission planning, leaders evaluate a number of factors to determine their impact on the unit's actions on contact. For example, the troop needs to consider how the likelihood of contact will affect its choice of movement techniques and formations. Through this analysis, the leaders can begin preparing their unit for actions on contact; for example, they may outline procedures for the transition to more secure movement techniques or cue surveillance assets before contact is initiated.

3-97. Leaders also understand that properly executed actions on contact require time at both platoon and troop levels. For example, to fully develop the situation, a platoon or troop may have to execute extensive lateral movement or call for and adjust indirect fires. Each of these activities requires time. The troop must balance the time required for subordinate elements to conduct effective actions on contact with the need for higher elements to maintain tempo and momentum. In terms of slowing the tempo of an operation, the loss of a platoon or team is normally much more costly to future operations than the additional time required to allow the subordinate element to properly develop the situation.

INITIAL CONTACT

3-98. Dismounted reconnaissance troop units must be prepared to execute actions on contact during the conduct of reconnaissance missions. Whether the platoon remains undetected or is identified by threat forces, it must first take actions to protect itself, find out what it is up against, and decide on a COA. To properly execute actions on contact, the platoon must take action consistent with the fundamentals of reconnaissance:

- Ensures continuous reconnaissance.
- Does not keep reconnaissance assets in reserve.
- Orients on the reconnaissance objective.
- Reports all information rapidly and accurately.
- Retains freedom of maneuver.
- Gains and maintains enemy contact.
- Develops the situation.

FIVE STEPS OF ACTIONS ON CONTACT

3-99. When contact is made, the unit executes actions on contact, designated by TACSOP, to maintain freedom of maneuver and avoid becoming decisively engaged. It takes the five steps of actions on contact:

- Deploys and reports.
- Evaluates and develops the situation.
- Chooses a COA.
- Executes the COA.
- Recommends a COA to the higher commander.

3-100. The steps that make up actions on contact must be thoroughly trained and rehearsed so that the unit can react instinctively as a team whenever it encounters threat forces. These actions apply to all DRT scout platoons, sections, and teams.

STEP 1 – DEPLOY AND REPORT

3-101. When a scout makes contact with the threat, he reacts according to the circumstances of the contact. The unit that makes initial visual contact with the threat deploys to covered terrain that affords good observation and fields of fire. If the Scouts receive fire from the threat, they return fire, but only with the intent of breaking direct fire contact.

3-102. The scout or element in contact sends a contact report to the PL and follows as soon as possible with a SPOTREP using the SALUTE format (size, activity, location, unit identification, time, and equipment). If the scout or element in contact is unable to report or cannot report quickly, another team in the section must report.

3-103. Scouts that are not in contact temporarily halt in covered terrain, monitor the incoming reports, and plot the situation on their maps. Once they determine that they cannot be influenced by the threat or are not needed to support the element in contact, they continue their mission with the PL's approval. The PL or PSG relays the contact report to the commander, followed as soon as possible by a SPOTREP and updates.

STEP 2 – EVALUATE AND DEVELOP THE SITUATION

3-104. The Scouts next concentrate on defining what they are up against. If they have not sent a SPOTREP to this point, they initially focus on getting enough information to send one. If they have not been detected by the threat and time is available, the Scouts reconnoiter the threat position, emphasizing stealth and the use of additional assets such as SUASs. If the threat is aware of their presence, the Scouts conduct reconnaissance to get detailed information on threat dispositions.

3-105. When direct fire contact occurs, the reconnaissance or scout platoon employs indirect and direct fires to suppress or fix the threat while maneuvering to get information. The Scouts attempt to confirm or determine threat size, composition, activity, orientation, and weapon system locations. Once the Scouts determine what they are up against, the PL updates the SPOTREP.

STEP 3 – CHOOSE A COURSE OF ACTION AND MANEUVER THE FORCE

3-106. Developing the situation is a critical step in choosing the correct COA and providing an accurate, timely report to the commander. Once the DRT commander has enough information to make a decision, he selects a COA that is within the capabilities of the troop; that allows the DRT to continue the reconnaissance as quickly as possible; and that supports the commander's concept of the operation. He considers various possible COAs, based on well-developed tactics, techniques or procedures, and battle drills, to react appropriately to the types of contact the platoon may encounter. At a minimum, the platoon must rehearse and be ready to execute these potential COAs:

- Disengage from threat or contact.
- Maintain contact and bypass.
- Maintain contact to support an attack on an inferior force.
- Conduct an attack against an inferior force.
- Conduct a hasty defense.
- Conduct RHO.
- Conduct BHO, if applicable.

3-107. Once the platoon in contact has developed the situation and the DRT commander has enough information to make a decision, he selects a COA. He ensures that the COA is within the capabilities of the troop, that it allows the platoons to continue the reconnaissance as quickly as possible, and that it supports the squadron commander's concept of the operation. The DRT commander should consider all available COAs. Once he decides on a COA, he recommends the action to the squadron commander, providing information on how the DRT COA will affect the squadron's situation. (For further details on each of these COAs, see FM 3-20.98.)

STEP 4 – EXECUTE THE COURSE OF ACTION

3-108. If the DRT commander has anticipated the threat situation the platoon is reporting, he will already have addressed the contingency in the OPORD and given guidance on which COA the platoon should execute. In such a case, the PL can evaluate the situation, choose the predetermined COA consistent with the commander's intent or concept, and execute it without further guidance. The DRT commander keeps the squadron commander informed of what he is doing as he executes the COA.

STEPS 5 – RECOMMEND A COURSE OF ACTION TO THE HIGHER COMMANDER

3-109. Once the DRT commander selects a COA, keeping in mind his squadron commander's intent, he reports it to his commander, who has the option of disapproving it based on its impact on his mission. To avoid delay, unit TACSOP may provide automatic approval of certain actions.

Chapter 4

Security Operations

Security operations are undertaken by a commander to allow for early and accurate warning of enemy action, time, maneuver space for the protected force to react to the threat, and effective use of the protected force. By the nature of their design, reconnaissance units are inherently involved in security in some capacity regardless of the specific mission they are conducting. Reconnaissance efforts assist in providing information that enhances the security of maneuver forces. Reconnaissance units are also given missions that are intended to specifically provide security for other forces. These missions are most often given to motorized reconnaissance units due to their mobility and increased firepower. Dismounted reconnaissance units may also execute limited security missions as part of a larger security operation. The DRT is well suited for security operations involving severely restricted and urban terrain where their unique capabilities offer an advantage over a motorized reconnaissance unit.

SECTION I – TEXT REFERENCES

4-1.   Table 4-1 consolidates the references to additional information.

Table 4-1. Guide for subjects referenced in text

Subject	References
Reconnaissance and Cavalry Squadron	FM 3-20.96
Combined Arms Improvised Explosive Device Defeat Operations	FM 3-90.119
Reconnaissance and Cavalry Troop	FM 3-20.971
Tactics	FM 3-90

SECTION II – OVERVIEW

SECURITY PLANNING GUIDANCE

4-2.   Effective DRT security operations require the reconnaissance squadron commander's guidance, defined in terms of:

- Focus.
- Tempo.
- Engagement/displacement criteria.

4-3.   This guidance answers basic questions the troop commander needs to know to plan and execute his mission and in turn provide his own guidance to subordinate leaders. (Refer to FM 3-20.96 for more detailed information.)

Note. The commander can specify different guidance for each phase of a security operation and can adjust the components of his guidance at any point in the operation.

FOCUS

4-4. Security missions focus on the elements to be protected that may include the higher unit, fires sections, critical assets, the population, etc. The focus of the security operation allows the troop commander to determine the specific critical tasks, and the priority, that need to be accomplished. Security operations are terrain or friendly unit-oriented. The focus should be what the troop is to protect and why, or what the expected results of the security are. Examples of focus include the following:

- Local society or population to protect them from the threat/enemy.
- Infrastructure.
- Terrain.

4-5. Named areas of interest (NAIs) provide a method of focusing the troop effort; they link most likely threat activities to terrain where those activities may occur. Using the NAIs as a guide, DRT PLs can position their assets to provide the most effective observation; for example, they can emplace OPs to observe primary threat avenues of approach and employ ground-based sensors for secondary approaches.

TEMPO

4-6. The tempo of the DRT conducting security missions allows the troop commander to establish associated time requirements that drive certain aspects of the security plan, including OPs, SUAS rotation, and augmentation assets necessary to execute the mission. Tempo can relate to depth, especially in screening missions where time is needed to properly deploy assets into position to achieve the required depth. Tempo may dictate whether DRT units employ short-, long-, or extended-duration OPs.

ENGAGEMENT/DISPLACEMENT CRITERIA

4-7. Engagement criteria establish the conditions under which the troop is expected to engage the enemy. The DRT troop commander's understanding of the squadron commander's expectations, coupled with his knowledge of the enemy's most likely COA, allow him to determine the troop's engagement criteria.

4-8. Displacement to subsequent positions is normally event-driven. The approach of an identified and specified threat element, detection by a threat force, relief by a friendly unit, or movement of the protected force may dictate the displacement of the DRT. Collapsing of a screen, executed well by the DRT platoons, provides security and maintains contact for the troop and squadron as it displaces. The protected force commander normally does not place time requirements on the duration of a screen unless the intent is to provide a higher level of security to the protected force or to provide a tentative time frame for subordinate unit planning.

TROOP'S ROLE IN SECURITY

4-9. The DRT performs security missions to provide the protected unit with early and accurate warning. This prevents the IBCT main body from being surprised and preserves the combat power of the unit for decisive employment. Critical information includes the size, composition, location, direction, and rate of movement of the enemy. Terrain information focuses on obstacles, avenues of approach, and key terrain features that affect movement. The intent is to provide information that gives the commander reaction time and the maneuver space necessary to effectively fight the enemy.

4-10. Current trends stress the likelihood of conducting operations in noncontiguous, extended AOs, possibly creating significant gaps between IBCT units. Despite continual evolution of sophisticated sensors and collection assets, SA will never be perfect. This is true especially in periods of limited visibility or adverse weather. Uncertainty will always be present in the AO. Accordingly, the troop will be prepared to conduct security missions.

SURVEILLANCE AND COUNTERRECONNAISSANCE

4-11. Surveillance may be continuous in all security operations. By conducting surveillance, the reconnaissance troop provides information to the commander to prevent surprise, provide reaction time, and allow him to make decisions for maneuver and fires. The organization, training, and equipment capabilities of the troop allow it to provide continuous security.

4-12. Counterreconnaissance is also a crucial component of security operations. Counterreconnaissance is the sum of all actions taken to defeat enemy reconnaissance efforts. The focus of counterreconnaissance is on denying the enemy any information about friendly operations. It is accomplished by deceiving, defeating, or destroying enemy reconnaissance efforts.

SECTION III – FUNDAMENTALS OF SECURITY OPERATIONS

4-13. The fundamentals of security operations, which are covered in detail in FM 3-90 and FM 3-20.96, are the following:
- Provide reaction time and maneuver space.
- Orient on the force, area, or facility to be protected.
- Perform continuous reconnaissance.
- Maintain enemy contact.

SECTION IV – FORMS OF SECURITY

4-14. Security operations are categorized in terms of the degree of security provided and the amount of combat power required. The DRT is not organized or equipped to execute much of the security mission by itself. It may, however, participate in some larger squadron security missions as a member of a robust combined arms force. Commanders at all levels must consider METT-TC when employing their units in a security role. The five forms of security operations are screen, guard, cover, area, and local. Route and convoy security mission are subsets of area missions. Table 4-2 shows the comparisons of security missions' capabilities of the DRT and the motorized troops of the IBCT Reconnaissance Squadron.

Table 4-2. DRT security mission profiles

Security Missions	IBCT Reconnaissance Squadron - Motorized Reconnaissance Troop	IBCT Reconnaissance Squadron - DRT
Screen	F	P
Area Security	R	R
Local Security	F	F
Route Security	F	P
Convoy Security	F	R
F–Fully capable R–Capable when reinforced P–Capable under permissive METT-TC		

SCREEN

4-15. A screen is a form of security that provides early warning to the protected force. A screening force is a security element which primarily observes, identifies, and reports information. A screening force only fights in self-protection (see FM 3-90). Although it provides the least amount of protection of any security mission, a screen is appropriate when operations have created extended flanks, when gaps between forces exist and cannot be secured in force, or when early warning is needed over gaps that are not considered critical enough to require security in greater strength. A commander normally assigns reconnaissance units this mission when he needs time to respond to an unexpected enemy attack and cannot afford to commit other forces to the task.

4-16. The DRT can screen the front, flanks, and rear of a stationary force, and to the flanks or rear of a moving force. A screen is established by emplacing a series of OPs, augmented with patrols to ensure continuous surveillance of dead space and avenues of approach. The DRT normally fights only in self-defense. However, based on the commander's intent and unit capabilities, the DRT can disrupt, defeat, and destroy threat elements within its capabilities.

4-17. The DRT may be required to conduct a moving flank screen or to screen the rear of the protected force as it attacks. As the protected force moves, the troop occupies a series of successive screens. Movement is regulated by the requirement to maintain the time and distance factors desired by the protected force commander. Screening operations are not performed forward of a moving force (see FM 3-90).

4-18. Critical tasks for the screen are the following:

- Allow no enemy ground element to pass through the screen undetected and unreported.
- Maintain continuous surveillance of all avenues of approach larger than a designated size into the area under all visibility conditions.
- Destroy or repel all enemy reconnaissance patrols within its capabilities.
- Locate the lead elements of each enemy advance guard and determine its direction of movement in a defensive screen.
- Maintain contact with enemy forces and report any activity in the AO.
- Maintain contact with the main body and any security forces operating on its flanks.
- Impede and harass the enemy within its capabilities while displacing.

DEPTH

4-19. Depth is critical in a screen. The term "screen line" is descriptive only of the forward trace along which security is provided. It allows for threat contact to be passed from one element to another without displacing. Depth allows the troop to accomplish the following:

- Prevent the threat from identifying and penetrating the screen.
- Prevent gaps in the screen from occurring when OPs are displaced, suppressed, neutralized, or destroyed.
- Facilitate the destruction of threat elements without compromising critical OPs.
- Maintain contact with threat elements without compromising OPs.

4-20. Depth is achieved primarily by positioning OPs and SUASs particularly along avenues of approach. The mortar section and attached elements positioned behind the screen line establish local security and provide support. The degree to which depth can be attained is a function of many factors, which include the following:

- Higher commander's intent and concept as expressed in the OPORD.
- Graphical trace of the screen line (may be the LOA or other screen line).
- Engagement criteria.
- Destruction criteria.
- Cueing, mixing and redundancy of assets as described earlier in Chapter 3.
- Displacement/disengagement criteria.
- Width of the troop AO.
- Depth of the troop AO.
- Terrain and avenues of approach it will support.
- Attachments and detachments.

PLANNING CONSIDERATIONS

4-21. A DRT executing a screen requires the following minimum guidance:

- Focus, tempo, and engagement criteria.
- General trace of the screen and time it will be established.
- Width of the screened AO.
- Force to be screened.
- Rear boundary of the screening force.
- Possible follow-on missions.

- Fire support plan of the squadron and protected force.
- Other available support, such as Army aviation.

4-22. Given the commander's guidance, the DRT commander then considers:
- Location of the screen.
- Movement/maneuver to occupy the screen.
- Passage lanes and passage points.
- Assigned AOs for platoons.
- Air-ground integration.
- Surveillance and acquisition assets.
- Fires planning.
- Mobility/countermobility/survivability.
- Positioning of C2 nodes with or without vehicles.
- Sustainment.
- Control of displacement to subsequent positions.

4-23. Displacement of screen elements is event-driven. While displacing, the screen continues to maintain contact and provide security. The following factors may dictate displacement:
- Approach of an identified and specified threat element.
- Detection by a threat force.
- Relief by a friendly unit.
- Movement of the protected force.

PLANNING CONSIDERATIONS FOR STATIONARY SCREEN

4-24. The DRT can conduct a stationary screen for a stationary or moving protected force. To ensure the DRT can plan for and perform all the key tasks of a screen, the squadron provides the troop commander with the information covered in the following discussion.

Augmentation

4-25. Augmentation covers any additional assets the troop receives to conduct the mission. Augmentation from the squadron or IBCT can include the following:
- Antiarmor, from a weapons company.
- Engineer platoon.
- Additional sniper squads.
- Additional reconnaissance assets.
- Air and missile defense, aviation, and sustainment assets.

General Trace of the Screen and Time the Screen Must be Established

4-26. A phase line placed along identifiable terrain graphically indicates the trace. Consideration should be given to the amount of early warning required, range of indirect fires, desired protected force maneuver space, and fields of observation. In a screen forward of the IBCT, this phase line represents the forward line of own troops (FLOT). A coordinated fire line, which does not need to be on identifiable terrain, may be placed beyond the FLOT to minimize the need for additional coordination for indirect fires. Placing screening forces beyond the trace line requires approval of the squadron. Any forces positioned beyond the trace should be protected by FSCMs, such as NFAs or restrictive fire areas.

Width of Screened Area of Operations

4-27. The troop may be assigned a wide frontage in excess of its capabilities. If the troop is required to screen beyond its capabilities, the commander requests additional assets to accomplish the tasks assigned. Careful consideration must be given when assigning ground-based and aerial sensor systems their own terrain, since the ability to execute the mission can be affected by weather, station time, and terrain. Sensors complement ground forces and provide extended depth, some width, and increased flexibility to the operation.

Rear Boundary of the Screening Force

4-28. The rear limit of the DRT is depicted as a boundary. Responsibility for the area between the protected force and the DRT rear boundary lies with the protected force. This boundary reflects time and space requirements, clearly delineates terrain responsibilities, and provides depth required by the troop. The boundary can also serve as an RHO line to control the passage of responsibility for the threat to the protected force.

Counterreconnaissance and Engagement Criteria

4-29. A thorough understanding of the composition of threat reconnaissance elements enables the DRT to accurately determine likely reconnaissance avenues of approach and how best to acquire them. This drives the task organization and positioning of forces. The reconnaissance squadron's IPB focuses on identifying the type and quantity of threat reconnaissance and security forces, as well as their potential avenues of approach. The troop commander or XO works with the squadron staff during mission analysis to identify these avenues of approach. The higher commander's guidance specifically defines the troop's engagement and destruction criteria for counterreconnaissance.

Movement to Occupy the Screen

4-30. Time and threat situation determine the method of occupying the screen. There are three primary methods available to occupy the screen.

Zone reconnaissance

4-31. If the situation is vague or more information is required on the terrain between the protected force and the screen line and time is available, the DRT conducts a zone reconnaissance to the designated screen line. This method is time-consuming, but provides the most security. It identifies any threat in the AO and familiarizes the troop with the terrain.

Infiltration

4-32. If the threat situation is vague, or the threat is known to be in the AO, and the intent is not to make contact with the threat prior to occupying the screen, the DRT infiltrates to get to the screen line. Infiltration provides the optimum level of stealth, but is also time-consuming and less secure for the DRT because it offers less flexibility in massing combat power.

Tactical Foot March

4-33. If there is an accurate picture of the threat situation or time is short, the troop may conduct a tactical foot march to an RP behind the templated screen and deploy from there to the screen line.

Control of Displacement to Subsequent Positions

4-34. The squadron headquarters uses phase lines and other GCMs to control the operation and orient the screen; it also defines the event criteria triggering displacement. Since displacement to subsequent positions is event-driven, phase lines serve to guide the DRT commander's planning and orientation for displacement to subsequent screen lines during the execution of the screen mission.

Possible Follow-on Missions

4-35. To facilitate planning and future operations, the troop's next likely mission is defined with enough information to allow the commander to begin planning and preparing for it. Providing this information also helps define the endstate of the screen mission.

4-36. When the DRT receives a security mission, its AO is usually identified by lateral boundaries with a FLOT or LOA (PL BIRD) and a rear boundary (PL DOG) specified. (See Figure 4-1, stationary screen.) The threat boundary may also be the designated RHO line. The reconnaissance squadron includes A2C measures to facilitate aerial reconnaissance within or beyond the troop's AO.

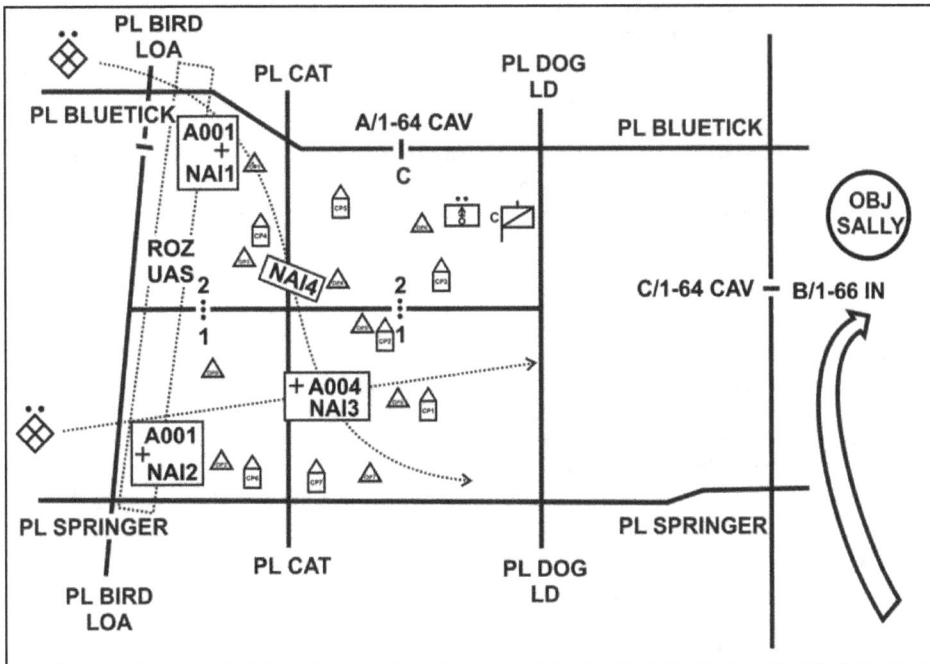

Figure 4-1. Stationary screen

4-37. Based on the squadron or protected force guidance, the DRT commander develops his plan during TLP, considering the following:

- Friendly force considerations, including:
  - Protected force's mission, commander's intent, and CCIR.
  - Mission of adjacent forces and coordination points for them.
  - Higher commander's reconnaissance focus, tempo, engagement criteria, and security destruction and displacement criteria.
  - Missions of other reconnaissance elements, such as a Prophet operating within the troop AO or in support of the troop, but not under troop control.
  - Capabilities and limitations of other reconnaissance elements that are attached to or controlled by the troop.
- Terrain and weather considerations, including effects on effective ranges of weapon systems, laser designators, and NVDs.
- Effects on SUASs and other aviation assets for reconnaissance, transport, resupply, fires, or CASEVAC/MEDEVAC.
- Effects on cross-country mobility.
- The threat situation, including:
  - Type and capabilities of likely threat weapon systems.
  - Special equipment, such as ground sensor systems, signal intercept, and surveillance radar.
  - Squadron guidance on threat COAs, including a SITEMP that depicts composition, dispositions, and likely axis of advance.

- ■ Reconnaissance focus, composition, and purpose.
- ■ Objective of threat reconnaissance efforts.
- ■ Threat reconnaissance COAs and avenues of approach, including mounted and dismounted infiltration routes.
- ■ Possible air insertion of LZs.
- ● Civil considerations that may affect the mission, such as:
  - ■ Composition and disposition of military, paramilitary, and law enforcement organizations.
  - ■ Locations of police stations, armories or barracks, encampments, weapons holding areas, and staging areas.
  - ■ If applicable, description and capabilities of uniforms, insignia, vehicles, markings, and equipment, including weapons and NVDs.
  - ■ Locations of communications networks and media outlets.

4-38. The DRT commander develops his intent, addressing the following:

- ■ Key reconnaissance and security tasks that must be accomplished during the screen.
- ■ Purpose for the screen in relation to the protected force's mission.
- ■ Endstate for the screen.

4-39. The DRT commander develops a mission statement that includes the screen location, start time, duration, orientation, and follow-on missions. He also develops a concept of the operation that describes, as a minimum, the following aspects of the operation:

- ● Moves to the initial screen line.
  - ■ Understands that time and enemy situation determine the method of occupying the screen.
  - ■ If applicable, conducts infiltration to avoid threat forces and establish the screen.
  - ■ If applicable, conducts a tactical foot march to the screen line.
  - ■ Establishes the screen.
  - ■ If necessary, determines changes to task organization and subordinate unit AOs reconnaissance based on tasks and METT-TC factors.
  - ■ Determines primary screen orientation for platoons and primary OPs, as necessary.
  - ■ Identifies method to gain contact with threat reconnaissance and other designated threat forces.
  - ■ Identifies engagement criteria as necessary.
  - ■ Identifies method of displacement to subsequent screen lines while maintaining contact with the threat.
  - ■ If applicable, identifies initial locations for attached maneuver forces, such as an Infantry platoon, that provide flexible response against threat reconnaissance throughout the troop AO.
  - ■ If necessary, determines requirements for short- and long-duration surveillance of NAIs.
  - ■ If necessary, determines patrol requirements between or in support of OPs.
- ● Specifies GCMs that support the concept of the operation, including the following:
  - ■ Boundaries identifying the DRT's AOs, LD, and initial and subsequent screen lines.
  - ■ SPs, RPs, and rally points for each route.
  - ■ Phase lines, checkpoints, and contact points for coordination with other units.
  - ■ RHO lines.
  - ■ Terrain index reference system or grid index reference system to assist C2.

4-40. The commander defines and establishes procedures for the communications architecture, including reporting flow and C2 responsibilities that cover the following:

- ● Position of commander, XO, or CP, and if necessary, retrans to maintain communications with the squadrons headquarters and other designated elements.
- ● Method and techniques for communications between all elements.

- Requirements and procedures for establishing digital connectivity and communications with supporting assets.
- Communications plan for RHO or target handover.
- FBCB2 friendly SA display to assist in clearing fires if DRT vehicles are part of the screen.
- Coordination with maneuver elements to operate on the same FM nets.
- Tailored message address groups to ensure proper message routing.
- Internet protocol (IP) addresses of all IBCT aid stations to assist location of and navigation to the nearest aid station.
- Conducting rehearsals of the stationary screen to include:
  - Inspections of personnel and equipment.
  - Movement and movement formations.
  - Occupation of OPs and CP.
  - Actions on contact.
  - Engagements based on engagement criteria.
  - Setup and take down sensor fields.
  - Establish communications.
- Establishing the screen, including how to:
  - Conduct reconnaissance of the screen AO that uses cueing, mixing, and redundancy to integrate troop and other assets into the security effort to gain and maintain contact throughout the depth of the AO.
  - Position OPs in depth and focused on NAIs.
  - Employ SUAS and Army aviation assets, such as attack reconnaissance units to reconnoiter routes, infiltrate lanes or key and restricted terrain forward, or to the flanks of the troop AO.
  - Orient other reconnaissance assets on NAIs located on avenues of approach or routes forward or to the flanks of the troop screen line.
  - Emplace ground sensors on flank avenues of approach or routes leading into the troop AO.
  - Employ CBRN reconnaissance teams to reconnoiter templated attacks and bypasses.
- Defeating or destroying threat reconnaissance IAW troop capabilities and engagement criteria, including how to:

  - Position reconnaissance elements as far forward as possible to gain contact with threat reconnaissance.
  - Position or coordinate attached maneuver elements to allow flexible response and maximum response time and mobility in defeating or destroying threat reconnaissance without compromising the locations of OPs or reconnaissance elements.
  - Array and position all assets with flexibility to refine or adjust dispositions throughout the operation.
  - Coordinate and position elements to accept handover based on cues from higher reconnaissance assets.
  - Mix troop elements and assets to provide depth and redundancy within the AO, using sensors to make first contact or to cover less likely or restricted reconnaissance avenues of approach.
- Synchronizing target acquisition tasks with security and reconnaissance tasks, specifying the following:
  - Target description, location (known or templated), and method of engagement.
  - Desired target effect and purpose for effect.
  - Criteria to change from target surveillance to designation.
  - Fires synchronization to suppress stationary elements or destroy high-value targets with precision-guided munitions as required.

- Troop mortars positioning to effectively support the indirect fire plan, considering colocation of the mortars with the DRT CP post.
- Establishment of fire priorities, and employing fires to maintain maximum range forward of the reconnaissance platoons.
- Incorporation of hasty obstacles with restricted terrain to halt or slow threat reconnaissance elements and enable effective indirect fire engagement.
- Linking of surveillance tasking to triggers.
- Covering both mounted and dismounted avenues of approach.
- Establishing locations and criteria for RHO and target handover, covering the following:
  - Accepting handover from or transferring responsibility to another element.
  - Conducting handover within the troop by subordinate elements.

4-41. The commander conducts ongoing sustainment operations using procedures that prevent the threat from detecting reconnaissance and maneuver element locations, specifying the following:
- Priorities for sustainment. Considerations include the following:
  - Troop reconnaissance elements should be prepared to operate for as long as possible (24 to 72 hours) without resupply.
  - Forward movement of resupply vehicles is restricted.
  - Reconnaissance and maneuver elements are rotated to resupply points in the rear of the troop AO.
- Security requirements and techniques for troop trains or supporting elements.
- Movement and positioning of trains and sustainment supply points.
- Resupply operations, including emergency resupply and caches that specify the following:
  - Caches for mission-specific items.
  - Drop points away from hide positions and OPs.
- Casualty consolidation and evacuation plan that addresses the location of all aid stations and methods for ground and air evacuation.
- Vehicle recovery, including secured collection points and maintenance procedures.
- Equipment and supply destruction criteria.

MOVING SCREEN

4-42. The planning considerations discussed above for a stationary screen also apply to a moving screen. However, emphasis can shift since the main body is moving. The DRT can conduct a moving flank screen to the flank or rear of a moving force by itself or as part of the squadron or IBCT. Screening the rear of a moving force is essentially the same as that for a stationary screen. As the protected force moves, the troop occupies a series of successive screen lines. Movement is regulated by the requirement to maintain the time and distance factors directed by the main body commander. Small unmanned aircraft systems or sensors can support the screen during the maneuver of reconnaissance platoons or sections. They can also work to extend the areas of coverage.

4-43. The moving flank screen poses additional considerations. The width of the screen AO is not as important as maintaining orientation on the force being protected and maintaining continuous observation of the threat avenues of approach that might affect the protected force's maneuver. The DRT screens forward of the lead combat element in the main body or to the rear of the protected elements, exclusive of front and rear security forces. The trains move with the troop or can travel with the squadron or Infantry battalion trains.

Occupying the Screen

4-44. There are three basic techniques for occupying a flank screen of a moving force. Employment of a specific technique, or combination of techniques, is determined by the threat situation (and the knowledge available on the threat), the squadron commander's intent, and the speed at which the protected force is moving. The three techniques are as follows:

- **First technique.** The troop crosses the LD separately from the protected force and conducts a tactical foot march within an AO parallel to the force. It then deploys from an RP to the initial screen positions and orientation. Platoons occupy OPs as they reach them. Small unmanned aircraft systems can reconnoiter forward of the troop or assist in maintaining contact with the protected force. Sensors can occupy OPs and provide long-range surveillance of threat avenues of approach. This is the fastest but least secure technique. This technique is appropriate when the protected force is moving very quickly, the LD is not the LC, or earlier intelligence indicates threat contact is not likely in the area through which the DRT is moving.
- **Second technique.** The DRT crosses the LD separately from the protected force and conducts a zone reconnaissance within an AO parallel to the force. Screen positions are occupied when they are reached. This technique is slower, but provides better security to the DRT and the protected force. It is appropriate when the protected force is moving slower, the LD is not the LC, or earlier intelligence indicates threat contact is possible in the troop AO.
- **Third technique.** The DRT crosses the LD with the protected force and conducts a zone reconnaissance out to the screen. This technique provides the most security for the troop and the protected force, but requires more time. It is appropriate when the protected force is moving slowly, the LD is the LC, or the threat situation is vague or expected.

4-45. In all three techniques, the DRT must maintain contact with the protected force, reorient the screen in relation to the protected force's maneuver, and conduct reconnaissance and screen in two directions (forward of the troop and to the flank).

Repositioning the Screen

4-46. Movement along the screen is determined by the speed of the protected force, distance to the objective, and the threat situation. Troop movement centers on a designated route of advance. This route is parallel to the axis of advance of the protected force and is large enough to accommodate rapid movement of the troop and to facilitate occupation of the screen. The route must be kept clear to ensure rapid movement of the troop's enablers, sustainment, and C2 assets. Sustainment elements should remain off the main route unless moving or traveling on alternate routes in depth.

4-47. Three basic techniques of movement used by both ground and aerial reconnaissance assets are the following: (See Table 4-3 for a summary of each technique.)
- Continuous marching.
- Bounding by platoons (alternate and successive).
- Bounding by OPs (alternate and successive).

Table 4-3. Screen movement techniques

METHOD	CONSIDERATIONS	ADVANTAGES	DISADVANTAGES
Continuous Marching.	Main body movement is very fast. Perform as route reconnaissance. Contact not likely. Air screen active on flank.	Fast. Maintains unit integrity.	Least secure.
Alternate Bounds by Platoon.	Main body movement is faster. Bound rear to front by platoons. Contact possible.	Fast. Allows good surveillance. Maintains unit integrity.	May leave temporary gaps.
Successive Bounds by Platoon.	Main body movement is slow. Bound simultaneously or in succession by platoon or troop. Contact possible.	Most secure. Allows maximum surveillance. Maintains unit integrity.	Slowest method. Less secure during simultaneous move. May leave temporary gaps.
Bounds by OPs (Alternate and Successive).	Main body movement is faster. Contact possible. Execute bounds from rear to front.	Very secure. Allows maximum surveillance.	Slow. Disrupts unit integrity.

Continuous Marching

4-48. Continuous marching is appropriate when the protected force is moving quickly and contact is not likely. It is the least secure movement technique. Reconnaissance platoons deploy in platoon column formation with their reconnaissance and security orientation to the flank. The remaining troop elements, organic or attached, deploy in depth between the screen line and the protected force. Small unmanned aircraft systems can be deployed forward of the troop route of march or forward of the screen. The trace of the screen is essentially the route of advance for the reconnaissance platoons in column. The remainder of the troop moves along a designated route or axis of advance. (See Figure 4-2.)

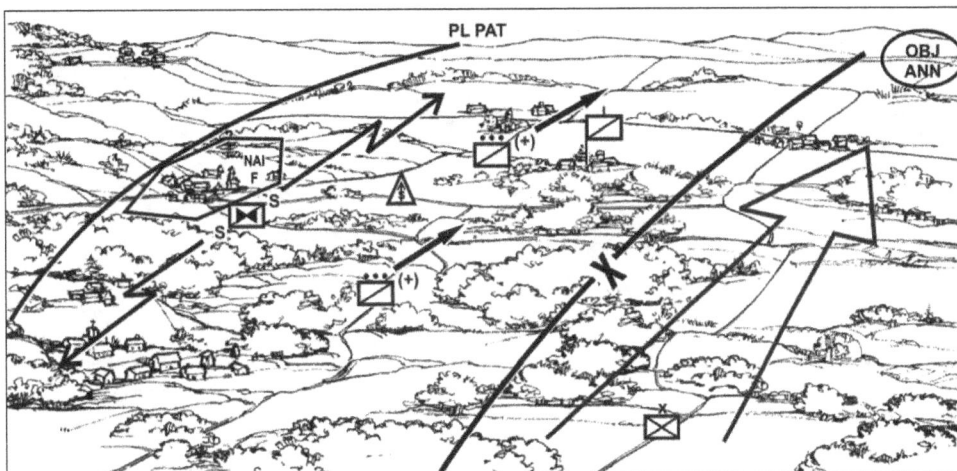

Figure 4-2. Example of a DRT repositioning the screen by continuous marching

Bounding

4-49. Reconnaissance units use bounding techniques while conducting a screen in order to maintain protection of a moving maneuver force. Bounds may be alternating or successive. Dismounted reconnaissance troop platoons using bounding techniques will often bound by OPs in order to maintain the screen while keeping up with the protected force. While not often employed by dismounted reconnaissance units, motorized units may bound by larger units such as platoons.

Bounding by OPs

4-50. This technique is appropriate when the main body is moving slowly, contact is possible, and maximum security is required. Bounding OPs alternately will disrupt the integrity of the platoons as OPs bound to their next position. Bounding OPs successively is easier for the platoons to control.

4-51. The troop initially deploys platoons abreast. Each platoon then either alternately bounds its rearmost OP around or to the rear of the forward OP to assume a new position along the screen line (see Figure 4-3) or has its OPs bound successively along the screen line (see Figure 4-4). The number of OPs on the screen line at any given time can be reduced as two or more may be bounding at any given time. The protected force's rate of advance determines this. Ground-based sensors and SUASs can be employed to mitigate the challenges encountered when bounding OPs.

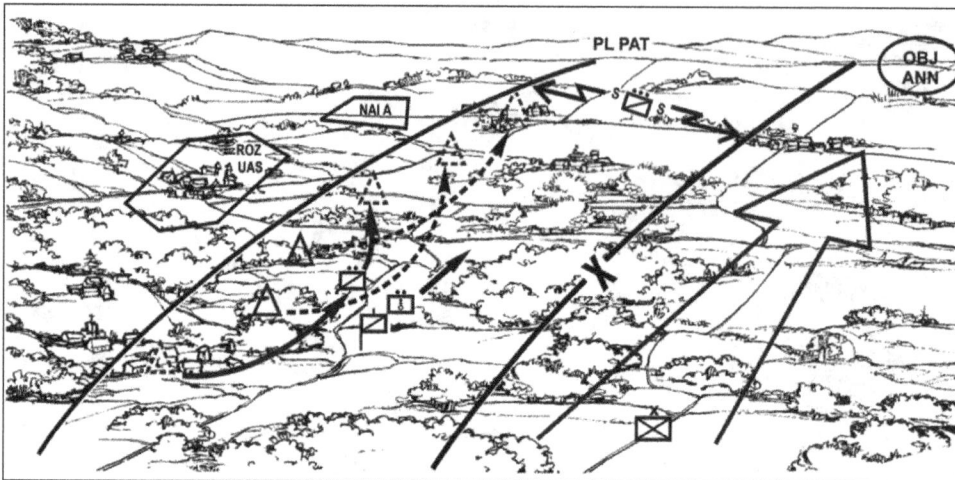

Figure 4-3. Example of a DRT moving with one platoon alternately bounding OPs

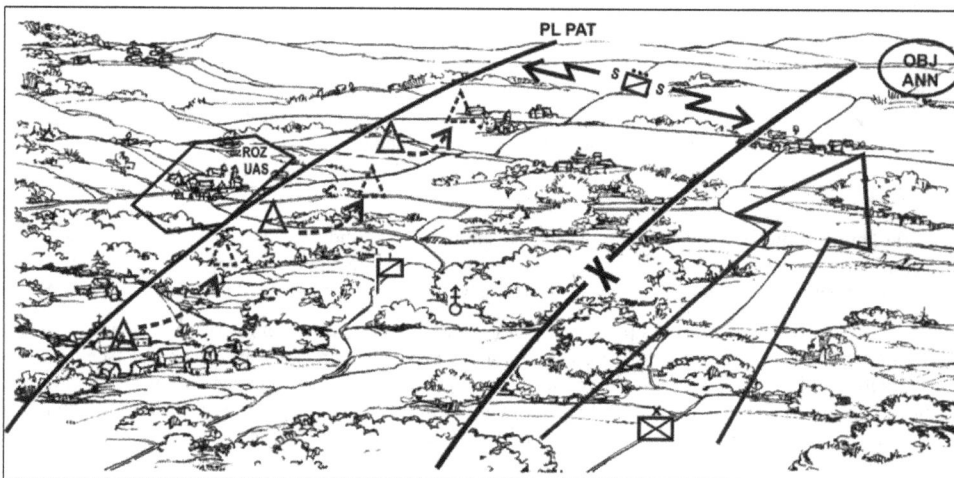

Figure 4-4. Example of a DRT moving with one platoon successively bounding its OPs

LIMITED VISIBILITY

4-52. When limited visibility conditions occur, as they often do during screen missions, squadron and DRT commanders must adapt the screen to these conditions. The screen can never be left with gaps when aircraft cannot fly or Scouts cannot observe. The troop takes the following actions to guard against gaps:

- Adjusts ground OPs.
- Employs night and thermal observation devices.
- Increases the use of surveillance devices and ground-based sensors if available.
- Places trip flares and OPs along dismounted avenues of approach.
- Conducts patrols between OPs.

4-53. Depth in the screen facilitates acquisition of threat forces that may elude forward elements. Patrols are closely coordinated to prevent misidentification and fratricide. As mentioned earlier, C2 measures are paramount in limited visibility conditions. Elements without digital tracking capabilities must establish effective communications to maintain a high state of SA of friendly unit positions. This must be done without compromising friendly unit locations to threat forces. Sound and light discipline at night prevents compromise and bypass of OPs by threat reconnaissance forces. Additional OPs can be established as listening posts to take advantage of the extended distance sound travels at night. Indirect illumination is also planned and used as necessary.

GUARD

4-54. The DRT does not have the capability to execute a guard mission. They may, however, participate in a guard mission to the limit of their capabilities. If participating in a guard mission with a larger fighting force, DRT units will normally participate in screening operations for the guard force. Screening operations for a guard force are conducted similarly to those of a screen for any other maneuver force. (See FM 3-90 and FM 3-20.96 for more information on guard.)

4-55. A guard is a form of security operations whose primary task is to protect the main body by fighting to gain time while also observing and reporting information and preventing threat ground observation of and direct fire against the main body. It differs from the screen in that the guard force, which normally operates within the range of the main body's indirect fire weapons, fights the threat when necessary to gain time and allow freedom of maneuver for the protected force. The guard force prevents threat ground observation of and direct fire against the main body by reconnoitering, attacking, defending, and delaying.

COVER

4-56. As with a guard force, the DRT does not have the capabilities to execute a cover mission. They may participate in a covering force mission to the limit of their capabilities. Similarly to their participation in a guard mission, if participating in a covering force, DRT units will normally participate in screening operations. (See FM 3-90 for more information on cover.)

4-57. A cover is a form of security operation whose primary task is to protect the main body by fighting to gain time while also observing and reporting information and preventing threat ground observation of and direct fire against the main body. A cover prevents threat indirect fires, direct observation, and direct fires against the main body by reconnoitering, attacking, defending, and delaying. A covering force accomplishes all the tasks of screening and guard forces. Unlike a screening or guard force, however, the covering force is a self-contained element capable of operating independently of the main body. A covering force, or portions of it, often become decisively engaged with threat forces. Therefore, the covering force must have substantial combat power to engage the threat and still accomplish its mission.

AREA SECURITY

4-58. Area security is defined as a security mission conducted to protect friendly forces, installations, routes, and actions within a specified area. It includes the reconnaissance and security of the area specified for protection, including personnel, airfields (as well as terrain around airfields from which surface-to-air missiles can be launched), unit convoys, facilities, main supply routes (MSRs), lines of communications (LOCs), terrain features, towns, equipment, and critical points. (See Figure 4-5.) Area security is conducted to deny the threat the ability to influence friendly actions in a specific area or to deny the threat use of an area for its own purposes. It may entail occupying and establishing a 360-degree perimeter around the area being secured or taking actions to destroy threat forces already present. Area security operations may require the execution of a wide variety of supporting operations and tasks; therefore, the troop may require augmentation when it is assigned to perform area security.

DISMOUNTED RECONNAISSANCE TROOP TASKS

4-59. The DRT can execute the following tasks when conducting area security operations:
- Zone, area, and route reconnaissance.
- Screen.
- Offensive and defensive tasks (within capabilities).

- Convoy security (within capabilities).
- Route security.
- High-value asset security.
- Fixed site security.
- Checkpoint security.
- Downed aircraft recovery team security.

AREA SECURITY PROCEDURES

4-60. When conducting an area security mission, the DRT prevents threat ground reconnaissance elements from directly observing friendly activities within the area being secured. It prevents (within capabilities) threat ground maneuver forces from penetrating the defensive perimeters. The commander has his subordinate platoons employ a variety of techniques such as OPs, BPs, ambushes, and combat outposts to accomplish this security mission. A reserve or QRF enables him to react to unforeseen contingencies. Using the intelligence acquisition capability available to the squadron and IBCT, the DRT can execute ambushes and preemptive strikes with greater precision.

4-61. METT-TC determines required augmentation for the DRT. Particular consideration is given to the need for aviation, maneuver forces, engineers, and artillery. Early warning of threat activity is paramount in area security missions and provides the commander with time and space to react to threats. Proper planning, coupled with patrols and aerial reconnaissance, is critical to successful operations, especially in securing fixed sites. Failure to conduct continuous reconnaissance can create a vulnerable seam within which the threat can execute an infiltration or attack.

4-62. A perimeter or combat outpost is established when a unit must secure an area where the defense is not tied into an adjacent unit. Combat outpost vary in shape and distribution of assets based on the results of IPB and METT- TC. A most probable direction of attack may require extra "weighting" of that portion of the perimeter to defeat attack or infiltration. METT-TC variables may require that one platoon mans the combat outpost while the other platoon conducts other security missions. The platoon should rotate between COP defense/maintenance/sleep/rest and the other mission on a random schedule.

4-63. The combat outpost is typically divided into platoon AOs with boundaries and contact points if the DRT has no other missions to conduct. A screen is established, integrating OPs, ground-based sensors, SUASs, HUMINT, and patrols. Organic or attached (a section from a weapons company), antiarmor weapon systems are emplaced to orient on high-speed avenues of approach. Ground-based sensors and SUASs provide overlapping reconnaissance capabilities at extended distances from the perimeter.

4-64. Most circumstances will not permit establishment of defined, neat perimeters. When a perimeter is not feasible, the troop secures the area by establishing a presence and conducting reconnaissance operations throughout the area. Platoons can establish perimeters around base camps, critical infrastructure, and high-value assets, while other units conduct operations to establish presence, provide security, and assist stability operations. The troop can also position reaction forces or disperse its reserve between several secured perimeters. Other missions or tasks in support of area security may include the following:

- Screens along zones of separation or other designated areas.
- Route security of critical LOCs.
- Checkpoint operations to monitor or control movement.
- Patrolling between secured perimeters.
- Demonstrations to maintain an observable presence.

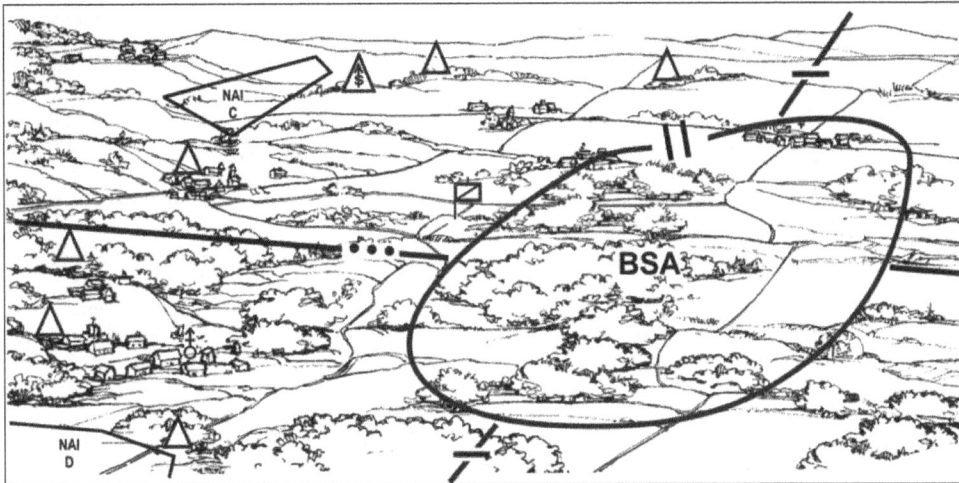

Figure 4-5. Example of a DRT conducting area security

4-65. Route security is a subset of area security. The purpose of route security is to prevent a threat from attacking, destroying, seizing, containing, impeding, or harassing traffic along the route. It also prevents the threat from interdicting traffic by emplacing obstacles on or destroying portions of the route. Route security operations are defensive in nature and, unlike screen operations, are terrain oriented.

4-66. Threat forces will try to sever supply routes and LOCs by various methods. Roads, waterways, and railways may be mined or have IEDs emplaced along them; ambush sites can be located adjacent to the route being secured; or bridges and tunnels can be destroyed by demolitions. Because of the nature of this mission, very long routes may be extremely difficult to secure; however, measures can be enforced to reduce the effect of threat forces.

SECURITY FORCE TASKS

4-67. A route security force operates on and to the flanks of a designated route. To accomplish the route security mission, the DRT performs the following functions:

- Conducts dismounted reconnaissance of the route and key locations along it to ensure the route is trafficable. Mounted reconnaissance if augmented with vehicles.
- Conducts route clearance (task organized with attached engineers and other elements as required) at designated irregular intervals to prevent emplacement of threat mines and other explosive hazards along the route. (See FM 3-90.119.)
- Identifies sections of the route to search suspected threat locations.
- Establishes roadblocks/checkpoints along the route and lateral routes to stop and search vehicles and persons on the route and those entering the route. This may require augmentation from other units, such as an Infantry platoon.
- Occupies key locations and terrain along or near the route.
- Conducts ground and aerial reconnaissance/surveillance to maintain route security.
- Establishes OPs (covert/overt) or ambushes at critical points to watch for threat activity.
- Employs snipers to overwatch route for unusual activity, such as personnel attempting to plant an IED.

ROUTE SECURITY METHODS

4-68. The following discussion highlights two methods that the DRT can use in executing route security depending on the nature of the threat, purpose of the security mission, and characteristics of the route. The methods are as follows:

- **First method.** The squadron or troop conducts route reconnaissance at irregular intervals to avoid developing a pattern that the threat may exploit. The troop reconnoiters the route, including conducting zone reconnaissance to either flank. Organic or attached SUASs or supporting aviation assets can reconnoiter in advance of ground troops or assist in screening the flanks. In addition to conducting reconnaissance, troop elements may escort engineers conducting route clearance, improvement, or maintenance; clearing terrain at potential ambush sites; and repairing damage caused by threat actions. Augmentation of tactical vehicles will greatly enhance the execution of this method by the DRT. The motorized troops are better suited to conduct this method of route security.

- **Second method.** This method entails using an economy of force technique to protect only critical lengths or locations along the route. The squadron or DRT establishes mutually supporting combat outposts and provides security between them. Combat outposts are established at critical choke points to prevent sabotage and to defend against or respond to attacks to interdict the route between outposts. Based on METT-TC, a DRT can establish one or two combat outposts, and a squadron can typically establish up to six. The route outside the reach of the combat outpost is not secured or, normally, patrolled. A squadron provides route security by combining this method at two locations or critical choke points with route reconnaissance along the rest of the route using the combination of motorized and dismounted troops. Combat outposts include FS assets, troop mortars, or howitzer sections capable of massing fires in support of both the combat outposts and the operations between them. Patrols are conducted at irregular intervals between the combat outposts based on threat trends and recent activities. Patrols are organized with sufficient combat power to destroy near ambushes and to survive initial threat contact from far ambushes. Each combat outpost maintains a reaction force within their capabilities to respond to threat activity or reinforce patrols.

ROUTE SECURITY PROCEDURES

4-69. Artillery or mortars are deployed into fixed firing positions, moved between position areas for artillery, or collocated in base camps or combat outposts. However FS assets are controlled and deployed, some should be available to all reconnaissance elements along the route, with the capability to mass at critical positions or into areas of most frequent threat activity. Fire plans should consist of priority targets to support convoy or patrol movement and FPF to support checkpoints or combat outposts. Targets should be registered whenever possible.

4-70. Patrols are conducted at irregular intervals along the route based on threat trends and recent activities. Threat forces emplace IEDs, mines, and demolitions; create craters or abatises, or establish ambushes or roadblocks to interdict or destroy traffic. Air, mounted, and dismounted patrols facilitate detection of threat forces before emplacing obstacles or execute ambushes. Patrols are organized with sufficient forces to reconnoiter off-route ambush sites and with enough combat power to survive initial threat contact. Based on threat capabilities and the patrol's purpose, reconnaissance patrols should be augmented with engineers, Infantry, military police, and other assets to increase combat capability. Other techniques to defeat threat attempts to interdict the route or ambush convoys include the following:

- Deceptive "mock" convoys under escort to determine threat reactions. The DRT must be augmented or cross attached to elements with motorized troops.
- Ambushes along known or suspected dismounted approaches to the route.
- Registered indirect fires triggered by sensor cues followed by patrols.
- Combat patrols conducting reconnaissance by fire at irregular intervals during limited visibility, prior to sunrise, or in advance of critical convoys to detect and destroy ambushes.

4-71. Although SUASs cannot secure the route, they can assist in observing the route by conducting aerial reconnaissance, effectively covering large areas in a short time on a continuous basis. Small unmanned aircraft systems can also assist in providing surveillance depth to the screen securing the route. Ground sensors can be used in surveillance of key avenues of approach or areas that do not require continuous surveillance by Scouts. This reduces the manpower and sustainment demands on the DRT's resources.

CONVOY SECURITY METHODS

4-72. Convoy security is a subset of area security. To conduct convoy security, the DRT must be augmented tactical vehicles. Convoy security missions are conducted when insufficient friendly forces are available to continuously secure LOCs in an AO. They may also be conducted in conjunction with route security operations. A convoy security force operates to the front, flanks, and rear of a convoy element moving along a designated route. Convoy security missions are offensive in nature and orient on the force being protected. All convoy security elements fall under the control of the protected convoy commander. Once threat contact is made, the convoy commander continues to maneuver the convoy out of the area while the security force commander maneuvers elements to defeat or destroy the threat. (For details on conducting convoy security, see FM 3-20.971, Reconnaissance and Calvary Troop.)

CRITICAL TASKS

4-73. A convoy security mission has certain critical tasks that guide planning and execution. To protect a convoy, the security force must accomplish the following:

- Reconnoiter the route the convoy will travel.
- Clear the route of obstacles or positions from which the threat could influence movement along the route.
- Provide early warning and prevent the threat from impeding, harassing, containing, seizing, or destroying the convoy.

ORGANIZATION

4-74. The DRT organizes its convoy security force into three or four elements:

- **Reconnaissance element.** The reconnaissance element performs tasks associated with zone and route reconnaissance forward of the convoy. It may perform duties of the screen element.
- **Screen element.** The screen element provides early warning and security to the convoy's flanks and rear. It may also perform duties of the reconnaissance element. If the troop is required to employ a screen element, the commander may have to request additional augmentation from the squadron or supported higher headquarters.
- **Escort element.** The escort element provides close-in protection to the convoy. It may also provide a reaction force to assist in repelling or destroying threat contact.
- **Reaction force.** The reaction force provides firepower and support to assist the other elements in developing the situation or conducting a hasty attack. It may also perform duties of the escort element.

LOCAL SECURITY

4-75. Local security includes any measure taken by the DRT against threat actions. The requirement for maintaining local security is inherent in all operations. The DRT most often provides its own local security and may also be tasked to provide local security for another unit. It includes finding any threat forces in the immediate vicinity and knowing as much as possible about threat intentions. Local security prevents surprise and is important to maintaining the initiative. Figure 4-6 shows an example of the DRT providing local security for another unit.

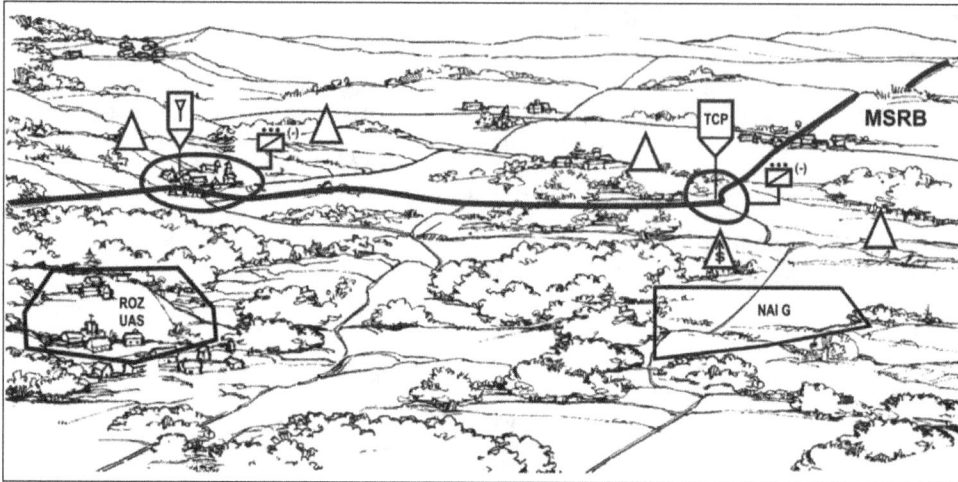

Figure 4-6. Example of a DRT conducting local security along an MSR

4-76. The troop provides local security by:

- Using OPs and patrols.
- Establishing specific levels of alert within the troop.
- Conducting stand-to.
- Using effective camouflage.
- Employing strict movement control.
- Enforcing OPSEC.
- Enforcing noise and light discipline.
- Employing proper communications procedures.

Chapter 5

Stability Operations

Stability operations are conducted outside the U.S. to maintain or reestablish a safe and secure environment. They also provide essential governmental services, emergency infrastructure reconstruction, and humanitarian relief. During stability operations, the DRT conducts reconnaissance, security, and economy-of-force missions similar to those conducted during offensive and defensive operations. The DRT may also be required to accomplish non-reconnaissance-related missions such as conducting negotiations with local leaders, defending a base, and manning checkpoints and observation points.

SECTION I – TEXT REFERENCES

5-1. Table 5-1 consolidates the references to additional information.

Table 5-1. Guide for subjects referenced in text

Subject	References
Reconnaissance and Cavalry Squadron	FM 3-20.96
Stability Operations	FM 3-07

SECTION II – OVERVIEW

5-2. Stability operations are a part of full-spectrum operations and typically occur in conjunction with either offensive or defensive operations in foreign countries. They may be the decisive operation within a phase of a campaign or major combat operation. Although military forces may initially take the lead in conducting stability operations for success, the goal is to transition to where the host nation or other instruments of power predominate.

PURPOSE

5-3. The five purposes for stability operations are:
- Provide a secure environment.
- Secure land areas.
- Meet the critical needs of the populace.
- Gain support for host nation government.
- Shape the environment for interagency and host nation success.

PRIMARY TASKS

5-4. Army forces perform five primary stability tasks that are neither discrete nor mutually exclusive. Brief descriptions of these tasks follow:
- **Establish civil security.** Army forces protect the populace from external and internal threats.
- **Establish civil control.** Army forces regulate selected behavior and activities of individuals and groups.
- **Restore essential services.** Army forces establish or restore the most basic services and protect them until a civil authority or the host nation can provide them.

- **Provide governance support.** Stability operations establish conditions that enable actions by civilian and host nation agencies to succeed.
- **Provide economic support and infrastructure development.** This support helps the host nation develop capability and capacity in these areas.

SECTION III – RULES OF ENGAGEMENT

5-5. In all operations, effective command guidance and a detailed understanding of the ROE are critical. The ROE are not limited to stability operations. Even in general war, U.S. Soldiers may have limitations on the type and extent of weapons they can employ.

5-6. The ROE are directives that explain the circumstances and limitations under which U.S. forces initiate and continue combat engagement with forces encountered. These rules reflect the requirements of the laws of war, operational concerns, and political considerations when the OE shifts from peace to conflict and back to peace.

5-7. The ROE must be briefed and trained to the lowest level. They should be established for, disseminated to, and thoroughly understood by every Soldier in the unit. Commanders must assume that the belligerents they encounter also understand the ROE. These unfriendly elements will attempt to use their understanding of the ROE to their own advantage and to the disadvantage of friendly forces.

SECTION IV – DISMOUNTED RECONNAISSANCE TROOP MISSIONS

5-8. Stability operations are complex and demanding. The DRT in a stability operation must maintain their reconnaissance abilities as well as master new skills. In this section, the term "enemy forces" refers to guerillas, terrorists, or insurgent forces that generally try to blend into the local populations and engage in asymmetric warfare.

RECONNAISSANCE MISSIONS

5-9. As part of stability operations, the troop conducts reconnaissance either to complement concurrent operations or as a separate mission as directed by the higher commander. Reconnaissance is planned and executed to support the stability goals of establishing civil security, establishing civil control, and reconstructing or restoring essential services and governance. (Refer to FM 3-20.96 for further discussion.) Examples of tasks the DRT conducts during reconnaissance in stability operations include:

- Within capabilities, conducts HUMINT operations, such as determining civilian demographics, tribal affiliations, key leaders, and required essential services.
- Conducts liaison/negotiation.
- Executes checkpoints and/or conduct patrols.
- Conducts tactical questioning.

5-10. The DRT's capabilities are optimized when given an area reconnaissance mission in restricted terrain with limited vehicular mobility. In this type of terrain, the DRT establishes checkpoints and OPs, conducts patrols, and accomplishes other reconnaissance tasks. It also conducts area reconnaissance missions in urban areas. The dismounted nature of DRT operations are also an advantage in urban stability operations.

5-11. Given an area reconnaissance mission, the DRT usually establishes a CP and assigns AOs to each of its platoons. The commander also considers:

- Assigning a QRF mission to a designated platoon or an on-call mission for the platoon not in contact.
- If the mission is lengthy, establishing a platoon rotation of reconnaissance, base security, and QRF.
- Assigning elements of a platoon to provide security for the CP and troop base, which may include the mortar section and FIST team.
- Retaining the sniper teams under company control or attached to a platoon.

SECURITY FORCE ASSISTANCE

5-12. As part of the reconnaissance squadron, the DRT may be involved in security force assistance while conducting stability operations. Security force assistance is the unified action to generate, employ, and sustain local, host nation, or regional security forces in support of a legitimate authority. Some aspects of security force assistance operations include:

- Joint effort of military and other governmental agencies.
- Training of military, police, border security, and other paramilitary organizations.
- Training that includes conventional combat, combating internal threats, or serving as multinational partners or peacekeepers in other areas.

5-13. The DRT may be assigned to three general types of security assistance operations: partnering, augmenting, or advising.

PARTNERING

5-14. Partnering attaches U.S. units at various levels with foreign units to leverage the strengths of both U.S. and foreign security forces. A partnering unit shares responsibility for a host nation's AO and supports its partner host nation's operations. Partnering activities for the DRT may include combined planning, training, and operations. Partnering troops may have to provide advisor teams as well as support maneuver units.

AUGMENTING

5-15. Augmenting is an arrangement in which the host nation provides individuals or elements to combine with U.S. units or U.S. individuals or elements combine with the host nation. Augmenting immerses host nation personnel in a U.S. environment to provide language and cultural awareness to the U.S. unit. Augmentation improves the interdependence and interoperability of U.S. and foreign security forces. Augmentation can occur at many levels and in many different forms. For example, a DRT squad can be augmented with host nation individuals or the troop can be augmented with a host nation platoon. Similarly, augmentation can be of short duration for a specific operation or of a longer duration for an enduring mission.

ADVISING

5-16. Advising is the use of influence to teach, coach, and advise while working by, with, and through the host nation. Advising is the primary type of security force assistance and is the most efficient means of helping a host nation to become an effective and legitimate branch of a developing foreign state. Advising requires relationship building and candid discourse to influence development of a professional security force. Advisors conduct partnership shaping functions, shape discussions with their counterparts, and create opportunities for the partner units.

5-17. The DRT may be under the operational control (OPCON) of an advisor team. The troop's primary mission is to provide security. However, it can also be assigned to accomplish some of the advisor team's missions, to include conducting individual and collective training of host nation forces.

INFORMATION ENGAGEMENT

5-18. Information engagement is the integrated employment of public affairs to inform U.S. and friendly audiences; military information support operations (MISO), combat camera, U.S. government strategic communications and defense support to public diplomacy, and other means necessary to influence foreign audiences; and leader Soldier engagements to support both efforts. (See FM 3-0.)

5-19. In stability operations the DRT Soldiers operate among the people of the host country. The troops are under the view of the media; therefore, IE is inseparable from the successful initiative of the stability mission. Dismounted reconnaissance troop leadership and Soldiers, through IE, can seize, retain, and exploit the initiative, drawing on cultural awareness and media engagements to achieve positive results. For the DRT, leader engagement may be the most critical component of IE. Leader engagement meetings may include:

- Key local communicators.
- Civilian leaders.
- Others whose perceptions, decisions, and actions affect mission accomplishment.

5-20. All engagement meetings should be planned and conducted with detailed preparation to ensure the outcomes of building local support for military operations, providing opportunity for persuasion, and reducing friction and mistrust are met. For the DRT, the keys to leader engagements include:

- Identifying key leaders, which includes:
  - Identifying persons of influence.
  - Determining the potential for long-term influence.
  - Evaluating the key leader network.
- Preparing intelligence of the AO, which includes:
  - Confirming/denying key leader's capability in relation to desired effects (Is this the right person to engage?).
  - Determining ethnicity; tribal background and perspective, if applicable; and religious background.
  - Defining resources.
  - Identifying social network.
  - Discerning key leader's agenda, motivation, and interest.
  - Determining information operations vulnerabilities assessment (hot button issues).
  - Developing contingencies and counters to unfavorable responses.
  - Reviewing post-engagement reports.
  - Using forward-thinking options to build on prior engagements and gather critical information from key leaders for increased operational benefits.
  - Leveraging other collection assets.
- Identifying desired effects, which includes:
  - Identifying what is to be achieved.
  - Identifying supporting objectives.
  - Identifying primary conditions required to achieve the desired effect(s).
  - Predetermining what to offer in order to get the desired outcome.
  - Identifying the probability of a favorable response to the request/desired effect.
  - Developing the best alternative to a negotiated agreement.
  - Considering utilizing other enablers.
- Preparing for the meeting, which includes:
  - Consulting with interpreters and cultural advisors.
  - Identifying roles.
  - Determining who leads.
  - Practicing.
  - Learning gift-exchange.
  - Being prepared to confront corruption.
  - Showing respect.
  - Learning a few key words of the local dialect.
  - Understanding the key leaders will have their own agenda.
- Executing the meeting, which includes:
  - Following local meeting etiquette.
  - Being patient.
  - Knowing when to speak.

- Looking at the host and not the interpreter.
- Focusing on the objective.
- Promising only what can be delivered.
- Installing local ownership.
- Concluding the meeting by clarifying agreements.
- Preparing debrief/reports, which includes.
  - Conducting after action review.
  - Submitting report per SOP.
  - Entering report into a troop/squadron continuity file.

AREA SECURITY MISSIONS

5-21. The troop may be tasked to conduct an area security mission as part of stability operations. Most area security missions are focused on securing the local population. The focus may be on the population centers in the DRT AOs and establishing a secure environment for the population. The same urban centers will also be the focus of the enemy to counter the Army and host nation presence and to influence the local population.

5-22. The following are area security-related tasks that the DRT conducts during stability operations:

- Liaison/negotiation.
- Joint military and/or civilian commission meetings.
- Compliance inspections.
- Support presence operations.
- Tactical questioning.
- Local security.
- Fixed site security.
- High-value target security.

5-23. The DRT commander considers the following when establishing local area security in a stability operation:

- Establishing and defending combat outposts and overt observation points.
- Rotating one platoon that conducts security operations while the other platoon provides combat outpost security, convoy escort, and QRF. The platoons rotate on a random schedule.
- Using the mortar section to support the QRF or attaching it to a platoon unless mortar firing missions are to be expected.
- Requesting tactical vehicle augmentation.
- Requesting Army aviation support to deliver patrols to outer areas of the AO where they can patrol back to the combat outpost.
- Establishing checkpoints and roadblocks.
- Conducting patrols. Patrols can accomplish the following:
  - Gathering information on the threat, on the terrain, or on the populace.
  - Regaining contact with the threat or with adjacent friendly forces.
  - Engaging the threat in combat to destroy them or inflict losses.
  - Reassuring or gaining the trust of a local population.
  - Preventing public disorder.
  - Deterring and disrupting insurgent or criminal activity.
  - Providing unit security.
  - Protecting key infrastructure or bases.
  - Conducting searches.
  - Conducting cordon and searches.
  - Countering IEDs.

- ■ Conducting compliance monitoring.
- ■ Conduct crowd control.
- Negotiating and conducting leader engagements.
- Establishing a reserve or QRF. For this mission the DRT should be augmented with tactical vehicles or helicopter support.

COMPANY INTELLIGENCE SUPPORT TEAMS

5-24. Company intelligence support teams (COIST) are formed at the company, troop, or battery level. They are generally formed during stability and counterinsurgency operations to perform intelligence tasks as directed by the commander, usually during stability operations. The COIST accomplishes many intelligence tasks to support the DRT commander. These tasks include:

- Answering the squadron commander's information requirements.
- Conducting IPB.
- Tracking SIGACTs.
- Assisting with site exploitation and database information.
- Supporting HUMINT-related operations such as key leader engagements and detainee operations.
- Assisting with biometric tools, using automated information collection and analysis tools.
- Supporting troop targeting with detailed intelligence products.

5-25. The COIST should develop a mission intelligence briefing plan. The plan should sensitize Soldiers to specific information and reporting requirements, information gaps, current events in the area of responsibility, and unique mission requirements. The COIST can use the same form for both prebriefing and debriefing the patrol. The information the patrol is looking for can be put on the sheet prior to leaving on the mission and the remainder of the data placed on the sheet during or after the mission is complete.

OTHER STABILITY MISSIONS

5-26. The DRT conducts economy of force within its capabilities. Its size and combat power limits its effectiveness against a strong and well-organized enemy. Its light foot prints and ability to traverse almost any terrain gives the DRT an advantage in broken and restricted terrain. The following are other missions that the DRT conducts during stability operations (see FM 3-21.10 and FM 3-20.971 for additional information on other DRT stability missions):

- An attack (may require augmentation based on METT-TC).
- A squadron movement to contact (normally a search and attack or cordon and search may require augmentation).
- Defending an AO.
- Defending a perimeter.

Chapter 6

Other Tactical Operations

Reconnaissance units are often required to conduct other tactical operations that facilitate or support the accomplishment of their primary reconnaissance or security mission. Other tactical operations are tasks that must be accomplished for a unit to carry out or continue its main operation and to help achieve or sustain the tactical advantage. Since reconnaissance operations by a DRT are often conducted with stealth while avoiding direct fire contact, they normally do not perform many of the enabling operations conducted by other maneuver units. Other tactical operations most often conducted by the DRT include those that require direct contact with other friendly units during a tactical transition such as a linkup, a passage of lines, an infiltration, or an exfiltration.

SECTION I – TEXT REFERENCES

6-1. Table 6-1 consolidates the references to additional information.

Table 6-1. Guide for subjects referenced in text

Subject	References
The Infantry Rifle Company	FM 3-21.10
The Infantry Platoon and Squad	FM 3-21.8
Special Forces Air Operations	FM 3-05.210
Long-Range Surveillance Unit Operations	FM 3-55.93
Reconnaissance and Scout Platoon	FM 3-20.98
Reconnaissance and Cavalry Squadron	FM 3-20.96
Engineer Reconnaissance	FM 3-34.170
Air Assault Operations	FM 90-4
Survival, Evasion, and Recovery	FM 3-50.3
Army Personnel Recovery	FM 3-50.1

SECTION II – GROUND MOVEMENT

6-2. The purpose of ground movement is to position units on the battlefield to prepare them for combat operations. Combat operations for the DRT focus on ensuring continuous reconnaissance. The DRT uses a variety of movement methods during their operations. Movements during DRT missions are most often used to conduct reconnaissance without becoming directly engaged with the enemy. For protection, however, the DRT normally conducts movements within the range of indirect fires. Movements to, through, or out of an area may be accomplished through a variety of means to include operations by ground, air, or water. Movements are used to position DRT units for reconnaissance missions and other operations. Movements are conducted in conjunction with infiltration and exfiltration operations as discussed in Section V of this chapter as well as missions where infiltration and exfiltration is not required.

6-3. Ground operations involve movements by foot or other ground-assisted transportation means. Dismounted reconnaissance troop units most often move on foot using common dismounted Infantry tactical movement formations and techniques as discussed in FM 3-21.10 and FM 3-21.8.

FORMATIONS AND TECHNIQUES

6-4. Tactical movement includes:
- Formations, including:
  - Column.
  - Line.
  - Vee.
  - Wedge.
  - File.
  - Echelon right/left.
- Techniques, including:
  - Traveling.
  - Traveling overwatch.
  - Bounding overwatch.

6-5. The troop commander is involved in planning, supervising, and refining both the execution of movements during the move and the follow-on operations after the destination is reached.

TACTICAL FOOT MARCH

6-6. The DRT also conducts a tactical foot march. A tactical foot march is a movement used to relocate units within an AO to prepare for other combat operations. Whenever possible, the troop marches in multiple columns over multiple routes to reduce closing time. A large column may be composed of a number of subdivisions, each under the control of a subordinate leader. March columns are composed of four elements:
- Reconnaissance party.
- Quartering party.
- Main body.
- Trail party.

RECONNAISSANCE PARTY

6-7. The reconnaissance party consists of at least one scout section per assigned route and, if available, supporting aerial assets. The reconnaissance party moves out as early as possible to reconnoiter the assigned route(s). Depending on the expected threat, the reconnaissance party is supported with engineers or other combat assets. The reconnaissance party's critical tasks are to:
- Determine trafficability.
- Identify choke points.
- Identify and mark bypasses; clear obstacles within capabilities.
- Systematically report progress.
- Establish traffic control points, as required.

QUARTERING PARTY

6-8. The troop employs a quartering party—actually a composite of the quartering parties from the scout platoons—if it plans to occupy an assembly area upon arrival at the march destination. The DRT 1SG normally controls troop quartering party activities. The quartering party normally follows the reconnaissance party and usually moves by infiltration.

MAIN BODY

6-9. The main body is composed of the bulk of the troop organized into serials and march units. The DRT moves as platoon, section, and team-size units. Units move and halt under the control of a single commander using voice, visual signals, or digital communications. March units move as task organized for the follow-on mission whenever possible.

TRAIL PARTY

6-10. The trail party is the last march unit in the troop serial. The DRT likely contains all unit vehicles and sustainment elements of the troop under control of the troop XO.

PLANNING CONSIDERATIONS

6-11. The following factors of foot march planning are considered:
- Time available.
- Distance of the move.
- Current threat and friendly situation.
- Follow-on mission.
- Availability and condition of routes.
- Task organization.
- Numbers of personnel to move.
- Mobility assets available.
- Fire support planning.
- Aviation support (SUAS, rotary, fixed wing).

6-12. Discipline is necessary to execute a foot march with precision. The troop TACSOP should consider the following:
- March unit organization and order.
- March rate factors.
- March unit intervals.
- Intervals between personnel.
- Actions on contact.
- Actions at halts.
- Security.
- Any contingency plans necessary.
- Communications.
- GCMs.

SECTION III – AERIAL MOVEMENTS

6-13. The DRT may use fixed-wing or helicopter assets to conduct troop air movements. Assault and ground support helicopter units routinely support the DRT by inserting the reconnaissance element via fast-rope, single-point, or landing in an LZ. These missions may require special patrol infiltration/exfiltration system (SPIES) or fast rope insertion/extraction system (FRIES) equipment, rappelling ropes, hoists, auxiliary fuel tanks, and additional training or rehearsals. The inserting or extracting aviation element during an infiltration operation commonly consists of UH-60s and AH-64s (or other armed escort). In accordance with unit TACSOP, UH-60s conduct multiple false insertions before and after actual insertion. Providing security, AH-64s may conduct feints or demonstrations to help cover the operation.

PLANNING CONSIDERATIONS

6-14. The squadron and the IBCT plan all air movement for the DRT. Planning may include requirements for the air infiltration and exfiltration and include:

- Coordinating with the supporting aviation unit(s) of the IBCT.
- Planning and rehearsing with the supporting aviation unit prior to the mission, if possible. If armed escort accompanies the operation, the PL as well as the assault or ground support aviation unit should ensure the attack reconnaissance aircrews are included in the planning and rehearsal.
- Gathering as much information as possible, such as enemy situation, in preparation for the mission.
- Ensuring joint suppression of enemy air defense coordination as appropriate.
- Determining planned insertion and extraction points.
- Determining emergency extraction rally points.
- Planning for actions at danger areas.
- Planning aerial resupply.
- Planning aerial MEDEVAC.
- Determining lost communications extraction points.

6-15. The DRT commander should plan and rehearse LZs and pick-up zones (PZs), emergency extraction rally points, and required communications to verify the preplanned pick-up time or coordinate an emergency pick-up time window. Planning must also include details for extraction when communication between the squadron and the DRT is lost. The lost communications extraction point involves infiltration teams moving to the emergency extraction point as preplanned or as per unit TACSOP. (See FM 90-4.)

SPECIAL PATROL INSERTION/EXTRACTION SYSTEM OPERATIONS

6-16. Units use SPIES for inserting and extracting reconnaissance personnel where a helicopter landing is impractical. The system provides a means of transporting up to 14 Soldiers over short distances. Since the SPIES exposes team members the entire time, the use of SPIES for infiltration carries increased risk. Due to the nature of SPIES operations, a thorough briefing is required for all participants before the operation. Careful coordination is crucial when additional assets (attack reconnaissance helicopters, aerial observers, or artillery support) participate with the extraction helicopter.

6-17. The commander ensures that Scouts are trained and rehearsals are completed prior to conducting SPIES. (For detailed information on SPIES, refer to FM 3-05.210 and FM 3-55.93.)

FAST ROPE INSERTION/EXTRACTION SYSTEM OPERATIONS

6-18. Fast rope insertion/extraction system operations RIES provide the capability to insert troops and equipment into areas not suitable for helicopter landing. The FRIES operation is used for fast rope insertion or extraction of Scouts without the aircraft contacting the ground or an obstacle. It is the fastest method of deploying troops from a helicopter that is unable to land. The UH-60 has provisions for two fast ropes, one on either side of the cargo door area. The CH-47 has provisions for up to three fast ropes—one out the forward right door and two out the ramp.

6-19. The commander ensures Scouts are trained, thoroughly briefed, and have completed rehearsals prior to conducting FRIES operations. (For detailed information on FRIES, refer to FM 3-05.210 and FM 3-55.93.)

HELICOPTER CAST AND RECOVERY OPERATIONS

6-20. A helicopter cast and recovery (helocast)) operation involves inserting/extracting Scouts or equipment from a helicopter over water. Helocasting is a very effective means of inserting or extracting reconnaissance elements. Units plan and conduct a helocast operation much the same as an air movement operation, except the LZ is in the water. (Refer to FM 3-55.93 for detailed information on helocast operations.)

PICK-UP ZONE/LANDING ZONE OPERATIONS

6-21. The troop may be required to establish its own PZ to conduct air operations for insertion or extraction of Scouts. They may also be required to establish a PZ or LZ for sustainment operations such as to resupply MEDEVAC or CASEVAC as discussed in Chapter 8 of this ATTP. (For specific conditions, markings, responsibilities, actions, and loading/unloading of personnel and equipment in the PZ/LZ, see FM 3-20.98.)

SECTION IV – WATERBORNE MOVEMENTS

6-22. Dismounted reconnaissance troop units may choose or be required to use waterways or cross water obstacles during the course of their mission. Using the water to their advantage can improve the speed, stealth, and flexibility of an insertion or extraction. Waterborne operations include using surface craft, swimming on the surface, helocasting, or a combination of these. Whichever they choose, they should execute the mission during limited visibility for maximum stealth.

PLANNING CONSIDERATIONS

6-23. While planning waterborne operations, leaders must consider the following factors:
- Enemy situation.
- Civilian situation.
- Shipping.
- Beach landing site, which must allow the team to infiltrate and support movement to the inland objective.
- Environmental factors such as winds, waves, tides, fog, thunderstorms, and lightning.
- Equipment.
- Time schedule. Leaders use reverse planning to schedule operational events.
- Drop site. The team debarks a larger vessel at a planned drop site then begins infiltration.
- Launch point. A point where swimmers enter the water and begin infiltration.
- Method of loading. Supervisors inspect to ensure loads and lashings, especially waterproofing, adhere to unit TACSOP.

6-24. Dismounted reconnaissance troop units must plan waterborne operations to the same detail as other operations with emphasis on additional water safety considerations. Common DRT missions involving waterborne operations include using inflatable landing crafts and helocast operations. (For more detail on these waterborne operations see FM 3-55.93.)

INFLATABLE LANDING CRAFT

6-25. Inflatable landing crafts, often called "rubber boats," are organic equipment to the DRT for small boat operations use. The landing craft currently issued as organic equipment to the DRT are actually not rubber but made from a neoprene-coated, tough, scratch-resistant cloth. Each boat can transport a scout section. Section members are assigned duties and responsibilities such as coxswain and paddler. They may also be an assistant coxswain, timekeeper, observer, or navigator.

HELOCASTING OPERATIONS

6-26. Helocasting can be an effective means of inserting and extracting DRT platoon elements and equipment. The speed, range, and lift capability of rotary-wing aircraft make them excellent waterborne delivery and recovery vehicles. Helocast preparations include the following:
- The leader uses the standard planning figures for loading troops when planning for the number of personnel for each type of aircraft. He can adjust these figures based on aircraft configuration, type of equipment, and casting or recovery procedures. He coordinates these items in advance with the aircrew.

- Rehearsals include all jumpers, the crew, the accompanying equipment, and support personnel. During live casting rehearsals, the leader emphasizes the commands, positions, and timing of body exit and water entry.
- All equipment attaches to the jumper with ¼-inch, 80-pound test cotton webbing. In or on this webbing, he normally carries a mask, fins, web belt with knife, flare(s), and life vest.

6-27. When using rubber boats in conjunction with helocasting, the team must tie down and secure all equipment inside the boat, waterproof all equipment in the boat in case of submersion, and tape or pad all sharp edges or items.

SECTION V – INFILTRATION

6-28. Infiltration is a form of maneuver that the DRT uses to penetrate the threat security zone or main battle area to accomplish its mission. Infiltration often entails using stealthy forms of movement including movement by aerial and waterborne platforms. Small unmanned aircraft system assets may also be employed using infiltration to gain information if this is within system capabilities. Units planning this type of infiltration must acknowledge the risk of the SUAS being engaged and becoming unrecoverable.

PURPOSE

6-29. The primary focus of infiltration is to move to a designated point without being detected or engaged by the threat. During infiltration, the DRT elements use pre-designated lanes to reach their objective. The infiltrating elements employ cover, concealment, and stealth to move through identified or templated gaps in the threat.

6-30. Dismounted reconnaissance troop elements infiltrate using a variety of movement methods. Infiltration may be conducted as an entire element at once or through movement into the area, by echelon, at different times.

6-31. Purposes for infiltration include the following:
- Reconnoiter a specified area and establish OPs.
- Emplace remote sensors.
- Establish communications relay capability for a specific period in support of other reconnaissance operations.
- Determine threat strengths and weaknesses.
- Locate unobserved routes through threat positions.
- Determine the location of high-payoff threat assets.
- Emplace small unit kill teams for interdiction missions.
- Recover SUASs to protect technologies from the enemy.
- Provide surveillance for follow-on echelons moving into the AO.

PLANNING

6-32. Infiltration imposes a number of distinct, and often difficult, operational considerations on the DRT, which include methods of infiltration, extended operations time, reaction force requirements, CASEVAC resources, and escorted or covert exfiltration methods.

6-33. The amount of intelligence information available to the commander during the planning process determines the risk involved in conducting the infiltration. Leaders conduct a thorough mission analysis, focusing on enemy activities in the areas of movement, historical locations of attacks, and likely areas of future ones to prevent accidental contact. While planning the operation, the commander must conduct IPB to include selecting appropriate routes and movement techniques based on the mission, the terrain and weather, the likelihood of threat contact, the expected or necessary speed of movement, and the depth to which elements must penetrate. The commander's infiltration plan must provide elements with enough time for preparation and initial movement. The initial plan should also cover a CASEVAC, evasion, extraction, and reinforcement plan, as well as any special equipment requirements.

6-34. Coordination with friendly elements through which the unit will pass when executing infiltration tactics must be accomplished. This includes integration of communications, fires, and sustainment activities. In addition, the squadron must coordinate the activities of adjacent friendly units to ensure that they do not compromise the troop and its elements as they conduct the infiltration. Coordination should include SUAS support, aerial or satellite imagery, and HUMINT briefings when possible.

6-35. The size of the infiltrating elements depends on several factors:

- The mission.
- Time available.
- Cover and concealment.
- The target acquisition capabilities of both friendly and threat forces.
- Available communications assets.
- Navigation capabilities and limitations.

6-36. If the troop is tasked to gather information over a wide area, platoons may employ several sections or small teams to cover the complete AO. In most situations, smaller elements are more suitable to take advantage of available cover and concealment. Another consideration is that some elements may not use infiltration. If moving into an AO in echelon, the initial echelons may infiltrate to a specific location and provide surveillance for follow-on echelons that are moving with a more conventional movement technique. A reconnaissance patrol is typically composed of four scouts. It becomes more difficult for patrols to hide as patrol size increases.

EXECUTION

6-37. The troop commander assigns the platoons an infiltration lane or zone, requiring the PL to gather the necessary information and intelligence to prepare for the mission. The PL decides whether to move the entire platoon along a single lane or to assign separate lanes for each section or vehicle.

6-38. Each alternative presents distinct advantages and disadvantages. Moving the entire platoon on a single lane makes navigation and movement easier to control, but can also increase the chance of the platoon being detected by threat forces. Moving on multiple lanes may require development of additional control measures, make C2 more difficult, and can create navigation problems. On the other hand, it can reduce the chances of detection by the threat. (For more specific information on platoon infiltration lanes, see FM 3-20.98.)

COMMUNICATIONS

6-39. In general, infiltrating elements should maintain radio listening silence except to send critical information that the commander has directed to be reported immediately or to report contact with threat forces. Message formats and communications windows should be established IAW squadron and troop TACSOP. When operating out of range of normal radio communications, an infiltrating element that must transmit required information should move to high ground or set up a long-range expedient antenna. Units may utilize HF and or TACSAT for communications during long-range operations, if equipped.

FIRE SUPPORT

6-40. Infiltration plans should always include employment of indirect fires, although these are used only in limited circumstances. Planning includes restricted fire areas, NFAs, and phase lines coordinated through the troop FIST and the squadron FS element. The most common use is when the infiltrating unit makes threat contact. The DRT commander or PL may employ indirect fires in other areas to divert attention away from the infiltration lanes. Indirect fires can also be useful in degrading the threat's acquisition and observation capabilities by forcing them to seek cover. The use of obscurant munitions (such as smoke) can have positive and negative effects. Scouts can employ smoke to screen their movements through terrain; however, this draws the attention of observers. Obscuration may also be used to break contact from the enemy during an infiltration. In some cases, the smoke screen may hinder the unit's ability to see enemy movements.

ACTIONS ON CONTACT

6-41. Actions on contact are discussed in detail in Chapter 3 of this ATTP. Each infiltrating element, however, must develop and rehearse a plan that clearly defines his actions when faced with one or more of the eight forms of contact. If detected, an infiltrating element will most often return fire, break contact, and report. Fighting through the threat force is the least preferred COA. Direct fire engagements are normally limited to whatever actions are required to break contact. To prevent compromise of their established locations and to retain the ability to report information, elements already established in the AO may choose not to provide direct FS for follow-on echelons in contact.

6-42. During an infiltration using multiple lanes, the detection of one element may alert the threat and compromise other units in the infiltration zone. The OPORD must clearly state the criteria under which elements will either continue the mission or return to friendly lines if they are detected by the threat. If an element makes visual contact but is not detected, he should continue the mission once certain he has not been observed.

SECTION VI – EXFILTRATION

PURPOSE

6-43. Exfiltration is the removal of personnel or units from areas under enemy control. The DRT and its elements may have to conduct exfiltration in certain tactical situations. Reconnaissance units that infiltrate an AO often have to conduct exfiltration once they gather the required information to remain undetected by enemy forces.

PLANNING

6-44. In all situations, exfiltration must be planned as carefully as infiltration. Planning includes identifying CCPs and emergency resupply points along exfiltration routes to provide supporting elements with a more secure, stealthy route into the AO to conduct these support operations. An effective exfiltration plan is essential in terms of mission accomplishment and morale. In most cases, planning for an exfiltration operation begins at the same time as planning for the infiltration (or other tactical operation) that precedes it. The commander must anticipate contingency measures that may be required if his elements must conduct an unplanned exfiltration during a reconnaissance operation. His exfiltration plan should factor in additional time that the platoon may need to react to unforeseen circumstances, such as inadvertent contact with threat forces or unexpected restricted terrain.

6-45. Leaders plan to integrate both indirect and direct FS for protection during the exfiltration. SUAS assets can assist by locating overwatch positions from which FS assets can provide fires. Whether the unit plans to exfiltrate on foot or by another transport method (ground vehicles, aircraft, or watercraft), detailed planning is required to establish criteria for a passage of lines to minimize the chances of fratricide. The exfiltrating force must also be prepared to plan for contingencies once the operation is under way, particularly if threat contact occurs.

6-46. Exfiltration in an urban environment requires movement in and around multistory buildings that can both conceal movement and provide advantageous threat locations with superior fields of view for engaging scouts.

EXECUTION

6-47. The DRT may have to conduct emergency exfiltration if it is detected or engaged by a threat force. This type of operation requires activation of an escape and evasion plan or deployment of a reaction or support force to assist with the extraction of friendly elements. Employment of the reaction force and supporting fires must be carefully coordinated and rehearsed before the insertion and infiltration (or other tactical mission, if applicable) is initiated. In all situations, the heavier the support, the louder the sound signature will become. All DRT leaders should be involved in the coordination and rehearsal of these assets since they will be most likely to assist in the exfiltration and extraction of their scouts. Dismounted reconnaissance troop units may use successful infiltration routes as their exfiltration routes as well. However, repeated movement in one area increases the likelihood of being detected and ambushed. If possible, exfiltration should be conducted during periods of limited visibility to conceal movement of friendly forces.

EXTRACTION METHODS

6-48. Extraction may be conducted by air, water, or land. Plans for extraction must be developed before the operation, covering procedural contingencies such as the evacuation of sick and wounded personnel and disruption of communications. These plans should address various contingencies for movement such as evasion. Hazards in the area of movement must be avoided to improve the scouts' chances of escape.

6-49. Extraction by air or water means is favored when the resources are available and their use will not compromise the mission. These methods are used when long distances must be covered, when time of return is essential, when the extraction zone lacks adequate cover and concealment, when the threat does not have air or naval superiority, or when complex terrain or heavily populated hostile areas obstruct ground extraction.

6-50. Reconnaissance forces normally conduct extraction via land routes when friendly lines are close or no other extraction method is feasible. Ground extraction is preferred when areas along the route are largely uninhabited, when threat forces are widely dispersed or under such pressure that they cannot conduct counterreconnaissance and security operations. In addition, ground extraction is preferred when terrain is sufficiently restricted to degrade threat efforts to use mobile forces against the exfiltrating/extracting reconnaissance unit.

EXTRACTION POINTS

6-51. Extraction points for DRT units should be carefully planned based on factors of METT-TC and far enough away from OPs to ensure that the threat does not hear vehicle or helicopter noises. The exfiltrating force should use mountains, dense foliage, and other terrain features to screen these noises.

6-52. Under normal conditions in flat, open terrain on a clear night, rotary-wing aircraft lose most of their audio signature at a distance of approximately five kilometers. In mountainous terrain, aircraft conducting the extraction can be seen or detected much easier when enemy observers are in place on the hilltops that offer superior observation.

6-53. For motorized ground extractions, rolling terrain can assist in hiding vehicle sounds as long as they maintain low-engine revolutions per minute (RPM).

6-54. In urban areas, motorized extractions may be down narrow roads and alleys to mask movement. Extraction points may be easily hidden among the materials and debris found in the urban area. While the actual point may be in buildings or in open areas such as an intersection, units may use surface or below surface hide locations to avoid detection. This may include inside and outside of buildings. Scouts must avoid detection because they are not prepared to fight decisive engagements.

SECTION VII – LINKUP

6-55. A linkup is a meeting of friendly ground forces. A DRT conducts a linkup in the following situations:
- The troop conducts linkup to conduct RHO or BHO.
- The troop reaches an objective that has been previously seized.
- An encircled element breaks out to rejoin friendly forces.
- Converging forces meet.

6-56. Linkup can be a platoon or section leader meeting another platoon or section leader from a unit on the other side of a lateral boundary or as complex as the troop joining support units for support and supplies. (See 3-20.96 for additional information.)

FORMS

6-57. There are two forms of linkup operations: moving and stationary forces or two moving forces.

LINKUP OF A MOVING FORCE WITH A STATIONARY FORCE

6-58. To ensure forces achieve linkup without committing fratricide, linkup points are selected at locations where the advance of the moving force intersects elements of the stationary force. These points will be recognizable to both forces and depend on the terrain and number of routes used by the moving force. Personnel in moving and stationary forces will be familiar with near/far recognition signals, TACSOP, and combat identification procedures. Both units will have a linkup point and other requirements stated in their OPORD and annotated on their graphics. This information can also be posted in leaders' digital systems. The stationary force supports the linkup by breaching or removing selected obstacles, furnishing guides, and designating assembly areas.

LINKUP OF TWO MOVING UNITS

6-59. Linkup between two moving units is conducted to complete the encirclement of a threat force. Primary and alternate linkup points for two moving forces are established on boundaries where the two forces are expected to converge. Both units will have the linkup point and other requirements stated in their OPORD and annotated on their graphics. This information can also be posted in the leaders' digital systems. As linkup units move closer, they must use fire control measures to prevent fratricide and interdict the threat to prevent their escape.

PLANNING

6-60. The headquarters directing the linkup establishes the command relationship between the DRT and the other force, specifies responsibilities of each force, and directs the linkup. If this headquarters cannot adequately control the operation, responsibility is delegated to one of the forces involved. Often the moving force is placed under control of the stationary force, or the force out of contact is placed under OPCON of the force in contact.

6-61. If the threat is between the forces conducting a linkup, coordination is then accomplished by radio or through digital systems if available. During the operation, the two forces attempt to maintain continuous radio contact with each other. Before initiating a linkup operation, the headquarters elements of the stationary force and the linkup force must share SA data, including the following:

- Digital graphic overlays with linkup graphic controls measures, obstacles, and FSCM.
- Manual/digital identification procedures.
- Manual/digital recognition signals.
- Threat and friendly situation plans.
- Communications plans.
- Contingency plans.

6-62. The communications plan includes radio frequencies, digital communications, SOI, and COMSEC variables for communication between the two forces. The plan establishes recognition signals (day, night, limited visibility) to prevent fratricide. The plan also includes the call signs and frequencies of all units in the AO that may not have knowledge of the ongoing operation.

6-63. Linkup operations may require one unit to resupply another. If sustainment requirements exceed the haul capability of the unit performing the resupply, the troop commander may have to request additional vehicles or resupply by air.

6-64. Evacuation of equipment and enemy prisoners of war (EPWs) or detainees can create problems for reconnaissance units. Typically, the 1SG will move forward to a CCP to take on wounded and EPWs, recover inoperable equipment, and transfer supplies. When ground routes are not secure, helicopters may be used for evacuation of the wounded, while damaged equipment may be moved forward with the linkup forces until a suitable opportunity for evacuation is available.

6-65. Additional planning considerations for linkup operations include:

- Distance to the linkup.
- Time the objective area is to be held.
- Planned operations or movement out of the objective area.
- Resupply of the linkup force.
- Movement of FS and sustainment assets involved in the linkup.
- Whether follow-on forces will secure LOC.

PREPARATION

6-66. Due to the time-sensitive nature of the operation, the troop commander, at a minimum, issues his order and attempts to rehearse the critical events of the operation with his subordinate leaders. Areas of particular emphasis include movement along the route, reaction to contact, contingency planning up to the linkup point, and actions to ensure that linkup coordination is executed without confusion.

6-67. The troop commander ensures linkup units (moving and/or stationary) have the higher unit's FS plan, current enemy situation, and digital updates if appropriate. If any control measures are changed during the operation, he announces updates to both elements.

EXECUTION

6-68. The initial conduct of the linkup is similar to a zone reconnaissance (Chapter 3 of this ATTP), depending on the threat situation. Reports of threat forces should be monitored throughout the mission to allow the leaders to react to changes in the threat situation. As the units begin to maneuver, they attempt to establish and maintain contact with each other.

6-69. At the SP, leaders establish long-range communications, stating that movement has started, and then establish short-range communications prior to the near recognition point. As the two forces draw closer, the tempo of the operation slows to help prevent fratricide. Each force uses coordinated signals to identify itself as it approaches the linkup point. The forces should be able to monitor each other's location via digital systems and take the appropriate actions to control the physical linkup. Fire support coordination measures are changed based on the progress of the forces and the threat situation. The linkup point can be moved IAW the stated timeline, if necessary.

SECTION VIII – PASSAGE OF LINES

6-70. A passage of lines is the controlled movement of one unit through the positions of a stationary unit, conducted so that neither unit interferes with the other's scheme of maneuver. A passage of lines often becomes necessary because the combat situation does not permit one unit to bypass another unit's position (See FM 3-20.96 for additional information).

6-71. The DRT may conduct either a rearward or forward passage of lines. When a unit moves toward the threat through a stationary unit, it is considered a forward passage. In a rearward passage, the unit moves away from the threat through friendly units.

6-72. A passage of lines may be conducted for the following purposes:

- Continue an attack or counterattack.
- Envelop a threat force.
- Pursue a fleeing threat.
- Withdraw security forces or main battle area forces.
- Facilitate route, zone, or area reconnaissance.
- Execute a defense or a delay.
- Execute a screen or guard operation.

6-73. The DRT may perform some of these operations independently (screen and reconnaissance); otherwise, it usually will take part in a passage of lines as part of a BHO.

> *Note.* A BHO is an operation generally associated with a passage of lines in which a stationary unit and a passing unit transfer responsibility for fighting a threat force from one unit to another. Its purpose is to sustain continuity of the combined arms fight and to prevent the threat from moving unopposed on the battlefield as one force picks up the fight from another. It also preserves the fighting capabilities of both friendly units.

CRITICAL TASKS

6-74. There are three key elements in passage of lines: the stationary unit, the passing unit, and the common commander.

6-75. The DRT, acting independently or as part of a larger element, may be either the stationary or the passing unit. The troop normally assists in some portion of the passage of lines and may be required to coordinate the passage. In many cases, the troop is required to conduct a passage separate from the squadron.

6-76. The commander exercising command authority over both the stationary unit, and the passing unit designates the battle handover line (BHL); this is a phase line forward of the stationary unit that is recognizable on the ground. He normally does this in coordination with the stationary unit commander, who recommends the position of the BHL. The line is drawn where elements of the passing unit can be effectively protected by direct fires of the forward combat elements of the stationary unit until the passage of lines is complete. The area between the BHL and the stationary force is the responsibility of the stationary unit commander. The common commander provides GCMs to the troop, depicting the BHL and contact points, on an overlay issued to subordinate units with the OPORD or FRAGO.

6-77. Battle handover begins on the common commander's order. Defensive handover is complete when the passing unit is clear and the stationary unit is ready to engage the threat. Offensive handover is complete when the passing unit has deployed and crossed the BHL. The common commander prescribes the specific criteria that mark completion of handover and ensures that both subordinate commanders understand these criteria.

PASSING UNIT CRITICAL TASKS

6-78. The passing unit must accomplish several critical tasks during passage of lines in BHO, including the following:
- Immediately establish communications, entering the command, intelligence, and FS nets of the stationary unit.
- Collocate a unit or vehicle with the TAC CP or main CP of the stationary unit as soon as possible to enhance communications and unity of effort.
- In a rearward passage, continuously report to the stationary unit the location, size, and composition of all threat forces, as well as the threat's current activity. If the threat is attacking, the passing unit reports the direction of movement, movement formation, and estimated rate of advance of threat elements. If the threat is defending, passing unit reports include threat locations, orientation, composition, EAs, reserves (if known), obstacle systems, and flanks.
- Continuously report to the stationary unit the location, size, and activity of all parent unit elements, including augmentation, sustainment, and C2 assets.
- Based on the current dispositions of the parent unit, coordinate with the stationary unit to determine contact points at which subordinate elements (such as reconnaissance sections) will meet to coordinate handover and passage of lines with representatives of the stationary unit. Once contact points are determined, the passing unit leader sends a FRAGO to all elements specifying where they will coordinate the passage with the stationary unit. In addition, the passing unit confirms recognition signals used during passage.
- Ensure that each subordinate element acknowledges where it must coordinate the passage and that it dispatches representatives to the assigned contact points to coordinate passage for the element. At the contact points, the representatives confirm recognition signals and exchange required information with their counterparts from the stationary unit.

- In a rearward passage, maintain visual contact with all threat units and conduct movement back to the BHL, avoiding decisive engagement.
- During the passage, display correct recognition signals and use the correct challenge and password as specified in the SOI.
- Maintain proper weapons orientation.

STATIONARY UNIT CRITICAL TASKS

6-79. The stationary unit must accomplish a variety of critical tasks when ordered to conduct passage of lines during BHO. These tasks include the following:

- Establishing communications with the passing unit, coordinating necessary contact points, and directing the passing unit to the contact points based on current dispositions of the designated units.
- Ensuring that contact points are manned and secured and that passing elements have established personal communications with their representatives.
- Ensuring that representatives at the contact points assign each passing element a passage point into the AO and a route that extends from the passage points to the rear boundary or assembly area (in a rearward passage) or to the attack position (in a forward passage).
- Ensuring that representatives at the contact points exchange required information, including FBCB2, with the passing unit as outlined in their unit TACSOP.
- Positioning elements along the BHL where they have the best possible observation of threat avenues of approach, adjusting as necessary during limited visibility.
- If obstacles are emplaced between the forward edge of the battle area (FEBA) and the BHL, ensuring that routes through the obstacle system are clearly marked and physically controlled by guides or that escorts are provided to the passing unit.
- Ensuring that all routes of withdrawal obligated to the passing unit are unobstructed and facilitate rapid movement to the rearward passage.
- Ensuring that obligated routes of advance, attack positions, and routes to the BHL are clear and facilitate rapid movement (forward passage).

PREPARATION

6-80. Units are particularly vulnerable during a passage of lines. Effective preparation is critical because subordinate elements may be concentrated, stationary unit fires may be masked temporarily, and the passing unit may not be disposed properly to react to threat action. The commander may task subordinate units with a number of missions, including detailed reconnaissance and coordination, to assist him in preparing for the passage.

GRAPHIC CONTROL MEASURES

6-81. Graphic control measures for BHO and passage of lines are illustrated in Figure 6-1 (forward passage) and Figure 6-2 (rearward passage). Graphics control measures include the following:

- **Battle handover line.** The BHL is established by the common commander in consultation with both commanders. The stationary commander has the major responsibility for determining the location of the BHL because his force must be able to overwatch the line with direct fires.
- **Contact points.** These are established on identifiable terrain and are normally in the vicinity of the passage lanes. For rearward passage of lines, the contact points are established forward at the BHL. For forward passage, the contact points are established in the stationary unit's AO rearward of the passage lanes.
- **Passage points.** The passage point is the location on the passage lane at which the moving unit passes responsibility for the operation to the stationary unit. It is usually placed where the passage lane begins.
- **Passage lanes.** The stationary unit establishes passage lanes to move the passing unit quickly through defending unit positions. This could include passing through gaps in friendly obstacles

and moving near or through friendly EAs and BPs. Lanes are restrictive; however, they should ideally be wide enough to allow the passing unit to move in a tactical formation. The passage lane begins at the passage point and ends at the rear of the stationary unit BPs. The passage is considered complete when the moving unit exits the lane.

- **Routes.** Routes are used to move the passing unit through the stationary unit. The number of routes designated will vary based on METT-TC, but as a general rule, multiple lanes/routes should be planned to facilitate rapid passage of moving units and to avoid unnecessary massing of units. The stationary unit may escort or guide the passing unit along the lane/route.

- **Assembly area.** An assembly area in the AO of the stationary unit allows the passing unit to conduct hasty reorganization and emergency sustainment actions. This assembly area is temporary in nature.

- **Infiltration points.** Leaders should plan infiltration points and lanes for personnel unable to complete the passage with their unit. Passing unit liaison officers (LNO) may remain located with stationary unit CPs to serve as a point of contact for infiltrating personnel/equipment. Personnel who infiltrate must have some way of contacting the stationary unit before crossing into friendly territory. (See Section V and VI of this chapter, covering infiltration and exfiltration.)

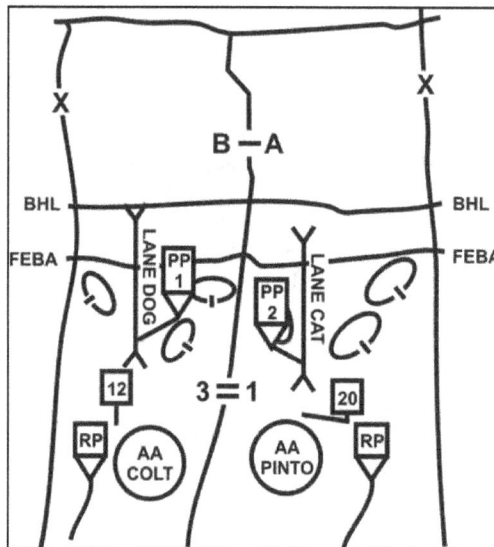

Figure 6-1. Forward passage line

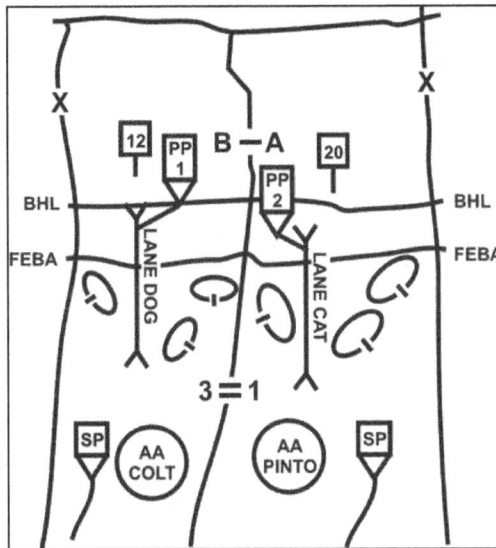

Figure 6-2. Rearward passage line

TROOP CONSIDERATIONS

6-82. At troop level, the passage of lines is usually performed as part of the squadron or IBCT. The passage may be forward, such as to pass through a defending unit to conduct a zone reconnaissance, or rearward, such as when a screening force unit withdraws through units in the main battle area.

6-83. The troop is particularly vulnerable during a passage of lines. The unit may be concentrated and the fires of the stationary unit may be temporarily masked. Furthermore, the possibility of fratricide increases considerably. Thorough reconnaissance and detailed coordination are critical to ensuring the operation is successful.

6-84. The troop commander has numerous critical tasks to ensure a successful passage of lines. During reconnaissance, he confirms the following:

- The disposition of the stationary force through which the troop will pass.
- The location of contact points where both units are required to make physical contact at a predetermined time.
- The location of passage points on the BHL through which friendly forces will pass.
- The location of passage lanes that provide a clear route through friendly positions to facilitate a smooth and continuous passage. Areas selected for passage should be unoccupied or on the flanks of units in position. If possible, multiple routes are used to reduce vulnerability during the operation.
- The location of a screen line (for forward passage) or assembly area (for rearward passage).
- The initial location for enabling and sustainment elements.

6-85. Based on the reconnaissance, the DRT commander coordinates and plans for the following:

- **Fires.** The stationary force supports the passing unit with direct and indirect fires up to the BHL. In a forward passage, the stationary force supports the passing unit's move through the passage lane until it crosses the BHL. In a rearward passage, the stationary unit supports the passing unit's move back across the BHL and through the passage lane.
- **Time factors.** The DRT commander determines and/or coordinates the time of transfer of responsibility for control of the AO and handover of the enemy.
- **Troop density.** The passing troop commander plans for multiple routes of passage to ensure rapid movement and to avoid congestion.

- **Traffic control.** Guides from the stationary unit pick up passing elements at each contact point and guide them through the position. The passing unit commander provides the stationary unit with the type, number, and order of vehicles passing through each contact point.
- **Communications.** The OPORD must identify, synchronize, and integrate communications architecture, digital systems, COMSEC instructions, recognition signals, and communications procedures and requirements. Effective communications planning and coordination ensure that units share data and pertinent combat information, maintain an up-to-date combat outpost, and avoid or prevent fratricide.
- **Engineer support.** A passage of lines may require either the reduction of some obstacles or the opening and closing of lanes through friendly obstacles. The passing and stationary units' staff engineers coordinate via digital means or face-to-face meetings. As a minimum, this coordination addresses the following:
  - Location and status of friendly and enemy tactical obstacles.
  - Routes and locations of lanes and bypasses through friendly and enemy obstacles.
  - Responsibility to close lanes through obstacles.
  - Transfer of obstacle and passage lane responsibilities.
  - Location of lane-marking materials.
  - Placement of far and near recognition markers.
  - Employment of deception and obscurants to confuse or deceive the enemy as to actual unit locations and passage points.
- **Sustainment.** The sustainment plan is integral to a successful passage of lines. Sustainment assets are positioned to support the passage. Maintenance collection points and emergency refueling points are positioned where they can best keep lanes open and vehicles moving. In addition, because a number of ground ambulances from the supporting medical company will be using the same road networks, coordination and synchronization are essential. The sustainment elements of the stationary force provide area support to the passing force. This preserves continued mobility for the passing force.
- **Liaison officers.** The troop commander designates a representative to perform the critical duties of an LNO. The commander normally performs liaison duties in coordinating a forward passage of lines, while the XO coordinates a rearward passage. If the commander or XO is unavailable, a PL performs liaison duties. Liaison officers are normally located at critical points during the passage.

CHEMICAL, BIOLOGICAL, RADIOLOGICAL, AND NUCLEAR CONSIDERATIONS

6-86. Because of potential congestion of units at passage points and along routes, stationary and passing units must take protective measures against CBRN attack. Techniques to reduce vulnerability include the following:

- To minimize exposure time, passing units move as rapidly as possible through passage points and along passage routes to their RPs.
- Passing and stationary units conduct CBRN monitoring.
- Passing and stationary units put on chemical-protective clothing as prescribed by the commander.
- If required, the stationary unit requests assistance through channels for decontamination of the passing unit. Units normally conduct operational decontamination and then move to a rear assembly area for thorough decontamination. The DRT does not have the internal assets for thorough decontamination of personnel or equipment; it requires assistance from a chemical company.

FRATRICIDE AVOIDANCE

6-87. Since passage of lines during BHO is often conducted in contact with the threat, extreme care must be taken to avoid fratricide. All units involved must know the correct recognition signals as well as the exact number of vehicles and time of passage. There will be times when some elements fail to receive necessary information or when stragglers are unaware of the current operation. Planning and coordination must cover the following considerations:

- Fratricide assessment.
- Vehicle marking systems.
- Obstacle marking system.
- Navigational aids such as GPS.
- Threat situation and composition.
- Obscuration (limited visibility).
- IFF techniques for ground forces.
- Effective TACSOP.
- Direct fire plans for both units.
- Indirect fire considerations, including specific procedures for requesting and clearing indirect fires.
- Communications procedures and potential problems.

6-88. For more detailed information concerning fratricide and risk reduction measures, refer to Appendix A, FM 3-21.10.

SURVIVAL, EVASION, AND RECOVERY

6-89. Survival and evasion are processes whereby Soldiers isolated in hostile or unfriendly territory avoid capture and return to areas under friendly control. Personnel recovery is the return of such evaders to friendly control, with or without aid, as the result of plans, operations, and individual actions by recovery planners, conventional or unconventional forces, and sometimes the evaders themselves. Evasion is considered the highest form of resistance. Both evasion and recovery are integral to military operations.

6-90. Personnel assigned to reconnaissance units are considered high-risk-of-capture and subject to isolation in hostile territory. Therefore, they should prepare for the possibility of being in an evasion situation. Successful evasion is dependent on detailed planning, as well as peacetime training and proficiency in survival and evasion and recovery tactics, techniques and procedures. The DRT commander must ensure his units are trained on evasion techniques. He must also be prepared to initiate personnel recovery operations if necessary. (See FM 3-50.3 and FM 3-50.1 for detailed information on survival, evasion, and personnel recovery.)

This page intentionally left blank.

Chapter 7

Augmenting Combat Power

Critical combat power augmentation provided by other units help support the maneuver of the DRT during reconnaissance missions. Combat power augmentation is employed by the commander to enhance the effectiveness of DRT operations. The troop commander and his subordinate leaders must understand the capabilities and limitations of these elements to effectively integrate them into troop operations. These units assist the troop commander in accomplishing his mission while ultimately achieving the squadron commander's intent for reconnaissance and security operations. Maneuver enhancement units should complement, not detract, from the troop mission and as such should be well synchronized with all troop operations. The integration of these combat power augmenting units begins during DRT planning and continues through rehearsals and execution.

SECTION I – TEXT REFERENCES

7-1. Table 7-1 consolidates the references to additional information.

Table 7-1. Guide for subjects referenced in text

Subject	References
Multi-service Tactics, Techniques, and Procedures for Joint Application of Firepower	FM 3-09.32
The Infantry Rifle Company	FM 3-21.10
Combined-Arms Breaching Operations	FM 3-34.2
Engineer Operations–Brigade Combat Team and Below	FM 3-34.22
Human Intelligence Collector Operations	FM 2-22.3
Sniper Training and Operations	FM 3-22.10

SECTION II – FIRES

7-2. Fires include the collective and coordinated use of indirect fire weapons and armed aircraft in support of the operation plan (OPLAN). Assets include mortars, field artillery (FA) cannons, rockets, missiles, fixed and rotary-wing aviation fires. Desired effects from these assets can be achieved through a combination of both lethal and nonlethal means. For the DRT, the employment of fires, if needed, is used to assist in breaking contact rather than in an offensive action directed toward attacking a threat force. The commander's reconnaissance guidance, however, may direct the troop to call fires on targets contained in the HPTL as directed by the commander. Regardless of their mission, they normally operate within the range of the IBCT's indirect fire assets.

7-3. Fire personnel who may assist the troop during the mission include a FIST and/or a combat observation and lasing team (COLT).

FIRE SUPPORT TEAM

7-4.   A FIST is an FA team organic to each maneuver battalion and the squadron to plan and coordinate all available company/troop supporting fires, including mortars, FA, naval surface FS, and CAS. The squadron commander can direct that FISTs be task-organized within the squadron and employed according to the observation plan. Fire support teams employed at the DRT level can provide the troop with FS coordination, targeting, and assessment capabilities. Each FIST vehicle possesses a target acquisition/communications suite with a laser capability to accurately locate targets or designate them for laser-guided munitions.

DISMOUNTED RECONNAISSANCE TROOP FIRE SUPPORT OFFICER

7-5.   The FSO is the troop's principle FS advisor and works directly with the commander during combat operations. This allows greater flexibility in conducting or adjusting the FS plan. At times, the troop FSO is positioned away from the commander to provide overwatch and better control supporting fires. While the DRT commander is responsible for integrating FS and maneuver, the FSO must fully understand tactics and the scheme of maneuver. Based on the commander's guidance, the FSO synchronizes FS within the maneuver plan for the DRT commander's approval. The troop FSO and the other FIST HQ personnel are trained FOs.

7-6.   The DRT FSO's responsibilities are to:

- Plan, coordinate, and execute FS.
- Assist the DRT commander in developing the troop OPORD/OPLAN to ensure the inclusion of any squadron-assigned FS tasks and the full integration of fires.
- Prepare, brief, and disseminate the FS plan to key personnel as part of the troop OPORD/OPLAN.
- Recommend and refine targets to support the maneuver plan. Integrate platoon targets into the DRT target overlay and target worksheet, and send the resulting products to the squadron fires cell.
- Advise the DRT commander on FS matters, to include capabilities, limitations, and employment of all FS assets available to support the unit mission.
- Recommend FSCMs and methods of target engagement.
- Alert the DRT commander if a request for fires against a target has been denied.
- Advise the DRT commander on the threat's indirect fire capabilities.
- Monitor the location and capabilities of friendly FS units and assist the DRT commander in the clearance of indirect fires.
- Determine the specific FS tasks and instructions required to execute the troop FS plan and ensure that FS tasks are adequately addressed during rehearsals. Coordinate with PLs to ensure they understand any FS responsibilities given to their platoon.
- Keep key personnel informed of pertinent information (by SPOTREP and SITREP).
- Maintain the friendly and enemy situations to include SITTEMP, target overlay, FSCMs, GCMs, and locations of troops.
- Train the FIST in applicable FS matters.
- Request, adjust, and direct all types of FS, including CAS and naval gun fire in the absence of qualified personnel.
- Assist the DRT commander to coordinate the employment of CCA, joint air attack teams, and SUASs.
- Advise the DRT commander on the positioning and use of unit mortars.
- Develop an observation plan, with day and night visibility contingencies, that supports the DRT and squadron missions. The plan would:
  - Allocate FOs and other observers to maintain surveillance of TAI and, if possible, NAI.

■ Plan, direct, and manage the employment of FIST observer platforms and laser equipment where they will best support the troop commander's concept of operation.

■ If augmented by a COLT for the DRT's use, integrate and employ the team in planned operations.

FORWARD OBSERVER

7-7. Platoon FOs are part of the squadron's FISTs and are normally allocated to a DRT and sent to a platoon. The FOs are the primary FS observers in the troop. They are normally collocated with the PLs. Forward observers provide target refinement; execute planned fires, and request fires for their supported platoons. The FO may control CAS as a non-joint terminal attack controller (JTAC)-qualified individual in emergencies when no U.S. Air Force Forward Air Controller (Airborne), Tactical Air Control Party, or JTAC is available. With additional training and certification, the FO can qualify as a joint fires observer (JFO).

7-8. Forward observer duties include:

● Refining or submitting key targets for inclusion in the DRT FS plan.

● Calling for and adjusting indirect fires.

● Preparing maps, overlays, terrain sketches, and target lists.

● Maintaining the grid coordinates of his location.

● Establishing and maintaining communications with the DRT FIST HQ.

● Informing the FIST HQ of the platoon's situation, location, and FS requirements. Standard operating procedure should specify when the FO provides update information; for example, every time an FO moves more than 300 meters or on a time-specific trigger (every 20 to 30 minutes during movement).

● Advising the PL of the capabilities and limitations of indirect FS.

● Updating the PL on FS assets and current and planned FSCMs.

● Reporting battlefield intelligence.

● Selecting OPs and movement routes to observe his target area.

● Operating and maintaining FO-related devices.

● Conducting CAS in the absence of a FAC (A), JTAC, or JFO and requesting and providing information to Army aviation during CCA. (See FM 3-09.32.)

● Requesting NGF when NGF spotters are not present.

JOINT FIRES OBSERVER

7-9. A JFO is a trained and certified service member who can request, adjust, and control surface-to-surface fires, provide targeting information in support of Type 2 and 3 CAS terminal attack controls, and perform autonomous terminal guidance operations (see FM 3-09.32). The JFO is not an additional Soldier in his Army FS organization, but rather an individual who has received the necessary training and certification to receive the JFO's additional skill identifier. Joint terminal attack controllers cannot be in a position to see every target on the battlefield. Trained JFOs, in conjunction with JTACs, will assist maneuver commanders with the timely planning, synchronization, and responsive execution of all joint fires. Autonomous terminal guidance operations independent of CAS requires the JFO to have direct or indirect communications with the individual commanding the delivery system plus C2 connectivity with the JFO's maneuver commander, or appropriate weapons release authority. Joint Fires observers provide the capability to exploit opportunities that exist in the AO to efficiently support air delivered fires and facilitate targeting for the JTAC. The goal is to have a JFO-trained and certified service member with each Armor company and each Infantry platoon.

COMMUNICATIONS

7-10. The FIST operates on multiple radio nets. The use of each radio net varies according to the mission, experience level of the FIST, and degree of control desired. Types of nets include:

- Fires battalion assigned fire direction net (as necessary).
- Troop command net (when the FSO is not physically located with the troop commander).
- Troop fires net.
- Through the pocket-sized forward entry device. The pocket-size forward entry device is a small hand-held digital call for fire device used by the FOs to call for fire. The device is integrated with the Advanced Field Artillery Tactical Data System.
- Squadron fires net (for example, when the FSO is physically located with the commander and calls for FS from assets other than FA observers).
- Additional nets as necessary.

PLANNING AND COORDINATION

7-11. To provide the DRT commander with the necessary support, the FIST conducts planning specific to the type of operation that the troop is conducting. Fire support planning and coordination begin on receipt of a mission and continue throughout planning and execution. (For additional details of this process, including the roles of the commander and FSO, refer to the discussion of fires planning and coordination later in this chapter.)

COMBAT OBSERVATION AND LASING TEAM

7-12. A COLT is a FIST controlled at the brigade level that is capable of target acquisition day and night and has both laser range finding and laser designating capabilities.

7-13. The DRT may request indirect fire through the COLT, which has a secondary mission of processing these requests. The COLT may monitor the reconnaissance platoon net and handle the fire request and subsequent adjustments in the same manner as a FIST. The COLT can enter the information gained through its primary mission, laser target location, or laser target designation for guided munitions and CAS, directly into the fire control system. When pushed forward with the DRT, the COLT may collocate with one of the platoon OPs for local security and protection. Leaders often link a COLT's observation of a TAI with a scout team's coverage of an NAI. This technique allows the scout team to act as a trigger, with the COLT executing and adjusting fires.

INDIRECT FIRE ASSETS AND CAPABILITIES

7-14. Indirect fire systems available to the DRT include organic mortars and the brigade fires battalion. Other systems that may be available include mortar systems found in the mounted troops, rifle battalions, and cannon or rocket/missile systems from a fires brigade.

MORTAR EMPLOYMENT

7-15. The troop mortar section provides organic indirect FS that is extremely responsive to the troop's tactical needs. The section can place a heavy volume of accurate, sustained indirect fires that can disrupt threat fires and movement, allowing the troop to maneuver to positions of advantage. Mortars are effective in covering obstacles or dead space, engaging dismounted threats, marking targets for air attack, or providing screening smoke. They are ideal weapons for attacking targets on reverse slopes, in narrow ravines, in built-up areas, and in other areas that are difficult to strike with low-angle fires. The DRT has a section of two 60-mm mortars and a fire direction center.

7-16. The troop commander uses available indirect fires from organic mortars to:
- Cover scouts during the conduct of their mission.
- Suppress the enemy while scouts are maneuvering to develop the situation or disengage.
- Screen enemy observation of scouts.
- Cover a likely enemy avenue of approach.
- Support the scouts on a screen line.

CONSIDERATIONS

7-17. The commander considers the following while planning for the employment of the mortars:

- METT-TC analysis.
- ROE.
- Scheme of maneuver.
- Ammunition constraints by type and quantity.
  - The mortar section is dismounted and must carry their mortars either conventional (with bipod and base plate) or hand-held mode (with small base plate without bipod).
  - DRT platoon scouts carry a designated amount of mortar rounds for the mortar section when conducting a tactical move. The rounds are dropped off at the mortar firing position. If the mortars displace, the unfired rounds are moved also.
  - Colocating the mortar section with the DRT CP would allow for additional security and the possible use of CP vehicles to support the displacement of the mortar section and ammunition.
- Priority of fire to a designated platoon.
- Anticipated changes in mortar employment.
- Communications constraints.
- Designation of positions (mortar firing points).
- Movement guidance including triggers.
- Coordination requirements.
- Clearance of fires.
  - If firing from the hand-held mode, fires are normally cleared at the troop level.
  - Normally, due to the maximum ordinate of fire, the conventional mode is more restrictive.
- Resupply.
- Capabilities.
  - A close working relationship with reconnaissance platoons.
  - Fast response time.
  - Effectiveness against low-density targets.
- Limitations.
  - Range is 3,500 meters conventional mode and 1,350 meters hand held mode.
  - Limited types of ammunition.
  - Vulnerability to threat counterfire radars because of the high angle of fire.
  - Limited basic loads of ammunition.

TYPES OF MORTAR SUPPORT

7-18. Troop mortars are organic to the DRT and are most often used for immediate suppression and disengaging of fires. Without revealing their locations, all scouts engage targets through the fires network with a variety of indirect means, depending on the requirement.

7-19. Mortar firing positions are often planned to allow the mortars to fire two-thirds maximum range forward of the reconnaissance troop or to cover likely enemy avenues of approach. Troop mortars are always placed in positions that effectively support the indirect fire plan. The range limits of the DRT mortars may not allow for full mortar coverage of the troop based on the mission.

7-20. The DRT uses its organic mortars for three main types of support: suppression, obscuring and screening smoke, and illumination.

Suppression

7-21. Unless a direct hit is achieved, high explosive (HE) rounds will not destroy armored vehicles; however, their use can greatly disrupt threat movement. High explosive rounds can force mounted threat units to button up or move to less advantageous positions. High explosive is highly effective against slowing and disrupting dismounted threats. High explosive is also valuable in urban environments.

Smoke

7-22. White phosphorus (WP) rounds are used for incendiary effects against equipment, obscuration, marking of targets, and screening. In obscuration, smoke is placed on or just in front of threat positions to obscure their vision. Smoke can be employed to support infiltration and exfiltration. Screening is achieved by placing smoke between the threat and the troop's positions to conceal movement. Mortar-delivered smoke can be used to mark threat positions, which can help to enhance friendly maneuver and orient direct fires or CAS. Smoke can also be effectively employed in urban environments where structures minimize the impact of winds that normally disperse smoke effects. Smoke rounds may, however, start fires that cause collateral damage. In any situation, however, scouts must be careful not to allow friendly smoke to work against them by marking their own positions.

Illumination

7-23. White light illumination rounds are used to light a point or area target during periods of limited visibility. This can increase the effectiveness of image intensification devices and sensors. It also assists the troop in gathering information, adjusting mortars or artillery, or engaging threat targets with direct fire. Ground-burst illumination can also be used to mark threat positions and to provide a thermal target reference point (TRP) for control of direct and indirect fires. As with smoke, however, care must be taken not to illuminate friendly positions. In addition, because U.S. NVDs are superior to those of most potential adversaries, white light illumination can be unnecessary or even counterproductive. Whenever they employ illumination, scouts must pay close attention to wind direction and speed to ensure proper placement of the rounds. Infrared illumination rounds may be employed, which will allow for the use of NVDs and other infrared devices.

EMPLOYMENT TECHNIQUES

7-24. The troop mortar section is employed as a separate element during operations. It moves independently of the platoons and provides its own security. The commander normally designates positions for the section sergeant and provides guidance for indirect fires forward of the platoons. The commander can also delegate this responsibility to the FSO, which allows the FSO and section sergeant to work together to develop a firm FS plan. If METT-TC permits the collocation of the mortar section with the DRT CP, this would provide additional security, closer coordination with the FSO, and the possible use of the FSO vehicle for displacement of the mortar section.

Communications

7-25. The mortars can operate on two nets: the troop command net and the troop fires net. If the FSO is responsible for moving the section, both nets may be on the troop fires net. In this case, the FSO provides the mortars with updates on the situation. Because, however, many SPOTREPs over the troop command net can become fire missions, the mortars can eavesdrop and provide more responsive fires if they stay abreast of the situation themselves. If the commander gives the mortar section sergeant authority to move the section and select firing positions, the section sergeant operates on the troop command net to maintain SA and effectively integrate fires.

Reconnaissance and Security Operations

7-26. During reconnaissance and security missions, the troop often operates within a large AO that cannot be completely covered by the mortar section. In that situation, the commander decides whether to position the mortars to cover the most critical area or to move them to a position where they can cover a portion of multiple areas and adjust as necessary. Knowing what other fires assets are available helps the commander make that decision.

7-27. During reconnaissance operations, the movement of the mortars is based on the progress of the troop. While the section is on the move, it is prepared to provide immediate fires using direct lay, direct alignment, or hip shoot techniques. The movement of the section is planned to be in position to support the troop at critical times, such as when the troop is crossing danger areas or clearing complex terrain. As stated earlier, the repositioning of mortar rounds should be a planning consideration.

7-28. Considerations for using mortars in security operations are similar to those for reconnaissance operations. To reduce potential sustainment problems during security operations, the commander and section sergeant plan for prestocking of ammunition at subsequent firing positions if METT-TC factors permit.

Mortars in Urban Operations

7-29. Mortars are well suited for operations in urban areas because of their high rate of fire, short minimum range, and the steep angle of fall of mortar ammunition, which minimizes dead space behind buildings. For mortar fire, dead space on the gun-target line beyond a building is about one-half the height of the building.

7-30. The DRT 60-mm mortar round cannot penetrate most rooftops, even with a delay setting. Small explosive rounds, however, are effective in suppressing snipers on rooftops and preventing roofs from being used by enemy observers. The 60-mm WP round is not normally a good screening round because of its small area of coverage. In UO, however, several factors make it more effective, including the tendency for smoke to linger and the smaller areas to be screened. Fragments from 60-mm HE rounds landing as close as 10 feet cannot penetrate a single sandbag layer or a single-layer brick wall. The effect of a 60-mm mortar HE round that achieves a direct hit on a bunker or fighting position is equivalent to 1 or 2 pounds of TNT. Normally, this blast will not collapse a properly constructed bunker, but it can cause structural damage. The 60-mm mortar will not normally crater a hard-surfaced road.

Other Indirect Fire Assets

7-31. The IBCT has an organic 105-mm fires battalion for providing indirect fires to the brigade; however, indirect fire assets from other units may be available to assist the troop if needed. Indirect fire assets offer a destructive, accurate, and flexible combat multiplier immediately available to units on the battlefield. Table 7-2 lists the capabilities of common indirect fire systems.

Table 7-2. Indirect fire capabilities

Capabilities of the Indirect Fire System						
CALIBER	60-mm	81-mm	120-mm	105-mm	155-mm	155-mm
MODEL	M224	M252	M285	M119	M198/M777-series	M109A6
MAX RANGE (HE)(m)	3,490	5,608	7,200	14,000 w/ charge 8	30,000	18,600 w/M232A1
PLANNING RANGE (m)	(2/3 max)	(2/3 max)	(2/3 max)	11,500 2/3 max range of the largest powder and projectile lots of the appropriate type of shells at the firing unit	2/3 max range of the largest power and projectile lots of the appropriate type shell available at the firing unit	2/3 max range of the largest powder and projectile lots of the appropriate type of shells at the firing unit
PROJECTILE	HE, WP, illum, IR illum	HE, WP, illum, RP, IR illum	HE, SMK, illum, IR illum	HE M760 illum, HEP-T, APICM, RAP	HE, WP, illum, smk, RAP, FASCAM, CPHD, Excalibur, APICM, DPICM	HE, WP, illum, smk, RAP, FASCAM, CPHD, Excal bur, APICM, DPICM
MAX RATE OF FIRE	30 RPM for 4 min	30 RPM for 2 min	16 RPM for 1 min	8 RPM for 3 min	4 RPM (M198) for 3 min / 5 RPM (M777-series) for 2 min	4 RPM for 3 min
SUSTAINED RATE OF FIRE (rd/min)	20	15	4	3 for 30 minutes	2 as determined by thermal warning device	1
MINIMUM RANGE (m)	70	83	200	Direct fire	Direct fire	Direct fire
FUZES	PD, VT, time, dly, MO	PD, VT, time, dly, MO	PD, VT, time, dly, MO	PD, VT, MTSQ, CP, MT, dly	PD, VT, CP, MT, MTSQ, dly	PD, VT, CP, MT, MTSQ, dly

LEGEND

AP	armor piercing		MO	multioption (VT, PD, dly)
APICM	antipersonnel improved conventional munitions		MT	mechanical time
chem	chemical		MTSQ	mechanical time super quick
CP	concrete piercing		nuc	nuclear
CPHD	copperhead		PD	point detonating
dly	delay		RAP	rocket assisted projectile
DPICM	dual purpose improved conventional munitions		RD	round
FASCAM	family of scatterable mines		RP	red phosphorus
HE	high explosive		RPM	rounds per minute
HEP-T	high explosive plastic-tracer		smk	smoke
illum	illumination		time	adjustable time delay
IR	infrared		VT	variable time
min	minute		WP	white phosphorus

EMPLOYING FIRES

7-32. Except as specifically directed, the DRT rarely engages the enemy with direct fire. When lethal fires are needed, the DRT most often employs indirect fire, CAS, or CCA assets. The reconnaissance troop may direct fires on specific targets to disengage from the enemy or to attack targets provided in the commander's HPTL.

PLANNING CONSIDERATIONS

7-33. As mentioned earlier, the DRT main mission is reconnaissance as opposed to direct contact engagements with the enemy. Most often indirect fires are used as a means of disengaging from the enemy. Depending on the commander's guidance, they may also employ indirect fires against HPTs as they present themselves during troop operations. In either case, the troop must effectively employ indirect fires when needed. One of the commander's greatest challenges is effectively synchronizing and concentrating all available assets at the critical time and place.

7-34. The planning process begins with receipt of the mission. The commander, XO, and FSO interact throughout planning and execution to ensure that necessary support is continually provided. While developing plans for employment of forces, the commander and the FSO plan for the best use of fires by determining:

- Fires and nonlethal assets that will be tasked to support the troop and subordinate elements.
- Targets to be attacked (to include the commanders HPTL).
- Indirect fires and nonlethal assets to be employed (ammunition and delivery).
- Desired target effects.
- Engagement priorities.

7-35. The commander clearly states his intent for fires and ensures that the fires plan is developed accordingly to support each phase of the operation. The following list covers areas that the commander coordinates with the FSO:

- **Scheme of maneuver.** This includes the AO, timing of advance, rate of movement, passage of lines, and Army aviation in the AO.
- **Priority of fires.** This identifies which platoon has priority of fires.
- **Priority targets.** These are identified, along with how long they will be in effect.
- **HPTL.** These are targets whose loss to the enemy will significantly contribute to the success of the friendly COA.
- **CAS.** The commander and FSO, in coordination with the squadron TACP, determine what CAS assets are available, when they are available, and how they will be used (including target selection and desired effects).
- **FS coordination center.** These control measures—existing or proposed, permissive or restrictive—are established.
- **Ammunition restrictions.** These place limitations on the use of smoke, improved conventional munitions, or other ammunition (including established controlled supply rates).

7-36. The FS plan outlines how both lethal and nonlethal fires will be used. The plan is developed by the troop FSO and is constantly refined as the operation continues. It ranks targets in priority order, matches them with the available indirect fires systems, eliminates duplication with squadron targets, and allows fires to be executed quickly and without specific direction from the commander. A FS plan includes:

- The general concept of how indirect fires will support the operation.
- A target list that includes locations where fires will be used.
- Priority of fires.
- HPT and priority targets.
- Allocation of priority targets and FPF, if available.
- Execution matrix.
- Required airspace coordination areas (ACA).
- FSCMs.
- ROE.
- Clearance of fires.

7-37. The FSO disseminates the FS plan within the troop OPORD or by other means, such as a digital message. It contains all the elements listed above and is modified as platoon indirect fire plans are received. Updated fire plans are then returned to the PLs.

COORDINATION CONSIDERATIONS

7-38. The troop FSO has the following responsibilities in coordinating fires:

- Ensure the squadron FSO, the troop mortar section, and any other supporting elements have the correct FS plan.
- Conduct fires rehearsals prior to every operation, when feasible.
- Keep the squadron FSO informed of the tactical situation.
- Select the appropriate fires method to engage targets.
- Ensure the troop commander is kept informed regarding the status of all fires assets.
- Modify the FS plan as necessary and ensure changes are disseminated.
- Coordinate requests for additional fires, if needed.
- Monitor execution of the FS plan throughout the operation.

7-39. The troop FSO ensures that the FS plan remains supportable. Because the FSO must immediately inform the commander if the plan becomes unworkable or if circumstances dictate changes to the plan, the FSO has to stay abreast of the tactical situation and coordinate, refine, and anticipate all FS requirements.

FIRES IN CLOSE SUPPORT

7-40. For the DRT, close supporting fires are most commonly used to aid in disengaging from the enemy. Close supporting fires may be used in either offensive or defensive situations depending on the nature of the operation.

EFFECTS

7-41. The DRT mission often does not require the use of indirect fires. Usually, reconnaissance is the purpose of their operation as opposed to engaging in direct conflict with the enemy. The use of close supporting fires may be used for disengagements, however. The purpose is often to slow the enemy by degrading their effectiveness. Indirect fires may cause the enemy to seek cover or fight with their vehicles buttoned up. This gives the reconnaissance unit more freedom of maneuver to disengage. Suppression of the enemy and obscuration of friendly movements is usually the desired effect for DRT units.

ACCURACY

7-42. Many variables affect the accuracy of the indirect fire weapon systems. The FSO has the technical knowledge to assist the troop commander. Artillery and mortars are area weapons systems, which mean that every round fired from the same tube impacts in an area around the target or aiming point. This dispersion is greater in length than in width. The weather conditions (wind, temperature, and humidity), the condition of the weapon, and the proficiency of the crew also affect the accuracy.

PROTECTION

7-43. If the unit is in well-prepared stationary positions with overhead cover, an FPF can be adjusted very close, just beyond bursting range. If required, the troop commander can even call for artillery fires right on his position using proximity or time fuzes for airbursts. The commander considers the terrain, the breach site, and the enemy positions to determine how close to adjust supporting indirect fires.

INTEGRATION OF SUPPRESSIVE FIRES

7-44. When integrating indirect suppressive fires to support disengagements or other operations, the following points should be considered:

- Danger increases with the size of weapons. Mortars and artillery should be used on enemy positions further away from friendly units. Sixty-mm mortars, grenade launchers, and direct fire weapons should be used for close suppression.
- If the rounds are coming over the head of friendly elements, the margin of safety is reduced.

- Troop mortars firing direct lay or direct alignment achieve quicker and greater success. They are able to observe the rounds' impact and adjust accordingly.
- Ideally, the firing units register prior to firing close support missions. If not, the first rounds fired might be off target by a considerable distance. Once the firing units are adjusted on a target, then any shifts from that target are much more reliable.
- Risk estimate distances should always be considered when firing close to friendly units. (For further information on risk estimate distances, see FM 3-21.10.)

AVIATION

7-45. Aviation fires may come from joint service fixed-wing aircraft or Army aviation rotary-wing aircraft. The troop commander should be aware of the assets available to support his mission and plan the use of aviation fires. Aviation fires should be based on mission need, to include preplanned targets if required, and immediate missions for unscheduled attacks. (For more information on aviation support, see FM 3-21.10.)

CLOSE AIR SUPPORT

7-46. The DRT may employ CAS from fixed-wing aircraft to augment other supporting fires or to attack targets in the HPTL. The speed, range, and maneuverability of aircraft allow them to attack targets that other supporting arms may not be able to effectively engage because of limiting factors such as target type, range, terrain, or the ground scheme of maneuver. Ground commanders are the ultimate authority for all supporting fires in their respective AOs. The ground commander at the lowest level is responsible for employment of CAS assets unless responsibility is specifically retained by a higher level commander in the ground force chain of command. (See FM 3-09.32 for additional information on the role of JTAC personnel and JFOs.)

TYPES OF CLOSE AIR SUPPORT MISSIONS

7-47. Close air support missions may be either preplanned or immediate.

Preplanned Close Air Support

7-48. Preplanned CAS missions are requested 72 hours in advance of the operation. They may or may not include detailed target information due to the lead time for the mission. These requests, however, must include potential targets, desired effects, proposed times, and a general priority. Preplanned CAS is categorized as follows.

Scheduled Mission

7-49. This entails CAS strikes on a planned target at a planned time or time on target (TOT).

Alert Mission

7-50. Alert (or on-call) CAS entails strikes on a planned target or target area executed upon request. Usually, this mission is launched (or scrambled) from a ground alert status, but may be flown from an airborne on-call alert status. Alert CAS allows the ground commander to designate a general target area within which targets are to be attacked. The ground commander designates a conditional period within which he will later determine specific times for attacking targets.

Immediate Close Air Support

7-51. Requests for immediate CAS are used for requirements that were identified too late to meet the air tracking order cutoff time. If there are no immediate CAS sorties available and HPTs have been identified, then other aircraft may be diverted to engage these targets or provide CAS for DRT missions.

CLOSE AIR SUPPORT PLANNING CONSIDERATIONS

7-52. Close air support mission success is directly related to thorough mission planning based on these considerations:

- **Weather.** Weather is one of the most important considerations when visually employing weapons. It can hinder target identification and degrade weapon accuracy. Does the weather favor the use of aircraft? What is the cloud ceiling? What is the forecast for the immediate future?
- **Target acquisition.** Targets that are well camouflaged, small and stationary, or masked by natural and man-made terrain are difficult to identify from fast-moving aircraft. Marking rounds can enhance target identification and help ensure first-pass success.
- **Target identification.** This is critical if CAS aircraft are to avoid fratricide. It is accomplished by providing a precise description of the target in relation to terrain features easily visible from the air. Smoke and laser devices can also be used for marking purposes. The remotely operated video enhanced receiver by JTACs greatly enhances the ground commander's SA and simplifies the targeting process.
- **Identification of friendly forces.** This is a key consideration in using CAS or rotary-wing aircraft. The primary cause of fratricide is misidentification of friendly troops as threat forces. Safe means of friendly position identification include mirror flash, marker panels, and direction and distance from prominent land features or target marks.
- **General ordnance characteristics.** These identify types of targets to be engaged and the desired weapon effects.
- **Final attack heading.** The final attack heading depends on considerations of troop safety, aircraft survivability, and optimum weapon effects. Missiles or bombs are effective from any angle. Cannons, however, are more effective against the flanks and rear of armored vehicles.
- **SEAD.** Suppression of enemy air defense is required based on the capabilities of the aircraft and presence of threat air defense systems in the target area.
- **CAS/artillery integration.** Army artillery and combat air power are complementary. Because artillery support is more continuous and faster to respond than CAS, close air support missions must be integrated with artillery so that limited firing restrictions are imposed. The airspace coordination ACA is the FSCM used to accomplish this integration.

AIRSPACE COORDINATION AREA

7-53. An ACA is a means of providing airspace for the relatively safe travel of aircraft and for facilitating the simultaneous attack of targets near each other by multiple FS assets. Airspace coordination areas are classified as either formal or informal. This classification is based on the amount of time available and the level of control desired.

Formal Airspace Coordination Area

7-54. This is a three-dimensional block of airspace that provides lateral and altitude separation between aircraft and other fires. It is designed to be in effect for longer periods of time. The formal ACA is established at IBCT or higher headquarters.

Informal Airspace Coordination Area

7-55. The informal ACA is used more frequently than the formal type and is the preferred method. An informal ACA can be established at the squadron or higher level by using one of four standard separation plans: lateral, altitude, timed, or lateral and altitude. It is in effect for very short periods of time—only long enough to get aircraft into and out of the target area.

NIGHT CLOSE AIR SUPPORT OPERATIONS

7-56. As with weather considerations, the use of GPS and laser-guided munitions has enhanced the ability of CAS assets to provide support at night. The two most important requirements of a night CAS operation remain the same:

- Identification of the target.
- Positive marking/identification of friendly unit locations.

7-57. Flares released from forward air controllers-airborne, other CAS aircraft, or "flare ships" can effectively illuminate target areas. However, artillery- and mortar-fired illumination is preferred because these assets provide a longer sustained rate of fire.

7-58. The commander also relies on his own assets to accomplish marking and illumination requirements. Marking of friendly unit locations improves safety and provides target area references. Tracers and infrared beacons can serve both purposes. Forty-millimeter illumination grenades and flares are effective, but may be useful to the threat as well. Flares used during limited visibility conditions (such as fog or smoke) can make it more difficult for aircraft to find targets. When used under a low cloud ceiling, flares can also highlight the aircraft against the clouds. Strobe lights, used with blue or infrared filters, can be made directional by the use of any opaque tube. In overcast conditions, they can be especially useful. Aside from the obvious security considerations, almost any light that can be filtered or covered and uncovered can be used for signaling aircraft.

CLOSE AIR SUPPORT REQUEST

7-59. The CAS request provides the crew of CAS aircraft with the SA and information necessary to successfully engage their target(s). The terminal controller, normally a JTAC or joint operations center, will transmit via radio (such as VHF, UHF, or FM) to the attack aircraft, providing the aircrew with enough time to write down the information and set up their navigational equipment. The controller does not transmit the line numbers. Units of measurement are standard unless otherwise specified. Table 7-3 provides the CAS request format. Lines 4 and 6 and any restrictions are mandatory read-back items (indicated by **boldface type** in Table 7-3). The controller may request read-back of additional items as required.

Table 7-3. Close air support nine-line request format

CAS Briefing (Nine-Line)
Do not transmit line numbers. Units of measure are standard unless briefed. Lines 4, 6, and restrictions are mandatory readback (*). JTAC may request additional readback. JTAC may request additional readback. JTAC: *this is* (Aircraft call sign; JTAC)
"Type_____ (1, 2, or 3) Control" 1. IP/BP: " "
2. Heading: " " *(Deg Magnetic; IP/BP to target)* Offset: " " *(Left/right, when required)*
3. Distance: " " *(IP to target in nautical miles, BP to target in meters)*
4.* Target Elevation: " " *(in feet/MSL)*
5. Target Description: " "
6.* Target Location: " " *(Latitude and longitude, grid coordinates to include map datum such as WGS-84, offsets, or visual description)*
7. Type Mark: " " Code: " " *(WP, Laser, IR, Beacon) (Actual Code)*
8. Location of Friendlies: " " *(From target, cardinal directions and distance in meters)* Position marked by: " "
9. Egress: " " Remarks (as appropriate): " " *(Restrictions*, **o**rdnance delivery, threats, FAH, hazards, ACAs, weather**,** target info, SEAD, LTL ,GTL {degrees magnetic north}, night vision, danger close [plus commander's initials]).* Time on Target (TOT): " " or Time to Target (TTT): " __ " *"Standby plus, Hack."* *(minutes) (seconds)*
Note. When identifying position coordinates for joint ops, include map data. Grid coordinates must include 100,000-meter grid identification.

CLOSE COMBAT ATTACK

7-60. Close combat attack is defined as a hasty or deliberate attack in support of units engaged in close combat. During CCA, armed helicopters engage enemy units with direct fire that impact near friendly forces. Targets may range from a few hundred meters to a few thousand meters. Close combat attack is coordinated and directed by a team, platoon, or by company-level ground-unit Soldiers using standardized CCA procedures in unit TACSOP's. The DRT may require the use of Army aviation for CCA operations. The integration and synchronization of CCA operations is key to ensuring the successful completion of the commander's intent for the use of the aircraft.

PLANNING CONSIDERATIONS

7-61. Digital transmission of information, such as coordinates, is faster and more accurate, if available. Voice communications are necessary to verify information and to clarify needs and intentions. The minimum information required by the Army aviation team to ensure accurate and timely support is listed below:

- Situation including friendly forces' location and composition, enemy situation highlighting known ADA threat in the AC, mission request, and tentative EA coordinates.
- Brigade- and squadron-level graphics update via MCS, AMPS or via radio communications, updating critical items—such as LOA, fire-control measures, and maneuver graphics—to better integrate into the friendly scheme of maneuver.
- FS coordination information: location of direct support artillery and organic mortars, and call signs and frequencies.
- Ingress/egress routes in the AO. This includes passage points into sector or zone and air route to the holding area or LZ.
- Call signs and frequencies of the squadron in contact, down to the troop in contact; air-ground coordination must be done on command frequencies to provide SA for all elements involved.
- GPS and SINCGARS time coordination; care must be taken to ensure that all units are operating on the same time.

MARKING

7-62. Ground units must ensure that aircraft have positive identification of the locations of friendly units and targets. There are various ways to mark a location or target. (Table 7-4 lists various marking methods.) The effectiveness of vision systems on helicopters compares to those found on ground vehicles. During the day, the vision systems of the AH-64 and the OH-58D allow accurate identification of targets. During periods of reduced visibility, resolution is greatly degraded, requiring additional methods of verification. This situation requires extra efforts from both the ground unit and aviation element. Some U.S. weapons can kill targets beyond the ranges that thermal, optical, and radar acquisition devices allow positive identification. Both aviation and ground forces might become overloaded with tasks in the heat of battle. Simple, positive identification procedures must be established and known to all.

Marking U.S. Troops

7-63. A method of target identification is direction and distance from friendly forces. Friendly forces can mark their own positions with infrared strobes, infrared tape, NVG lights, smoke, signal panels, body position, meals ready to eat (MRE) heaters, chemical lights, and mirrors. Marking friendly positions is the least desirable method of target location information. It should be used with extreme caution. Marking friendly positions can take more time than directly marking a target, but it can reveal friendly positions to the enemy.

Marking Enemy Positions

7-64. Target marking aids aircrews in locating the target that the unit in contact desires them to attack. Ground commanders should provide the target mark whenever possible. To be effective, the mark must be timely, accurate, and easily identifiable. Target marks might be confused with other fires on the battlefield, suppression rounds, detonations, and marks on other targets. Although a mark is not mandatory, it improves aircrew accuracy, enhances SA, and reduces the risk of fratricide.

Table 7-4. Techniques for marking of target or location

METHOD	DAY	NIGHT	NVG	NVS	FRIENDLY MARKS	TARGET MARKS	REMARKS
Smoke	Go	No Go	Marginal	No Go	Good	Good	Easy ID. May compromise friendly position, obscure target, or warn of FS employment. Placement may be difficult because of terrain, trees, or structures.
Smoke (infrared)	Go	Go	Go	No Go	Good	Good	Easy ID. May compromise friendly position, obscure target, or warn of FS employment. Placement may be difficult because of terrain, trees, or structures. Night marking is greatly enhanced by the use of infrared reflective smoke.
Illumination, Ground Burst	Go	Go	Go	No Go	N/A	Good	Easy ID. May wash out NVDs.
Signal Mirror	Go	No Go	No Go	No Go	Good	N/A	Avoids compromise of friendly location. Depends on weather and available light. May be lost in reflections from other reflective surfaces such as windshields, windows, or water.
Spot Light	No Go	Go	Go	No Go	Good	Marginal	Highly visibility to all. Compromises friendly position and warns of FS employment. Effectiveness depends on the degree of ambient lighting.
Infrared Spot Light	No Go	No Go	Go	No Go	Good	Marginal	Visible to all NVGs. Effectiveness depends on the degree of ambient lighting.
Infrared Laser Pointer (below .4 watts)	No Go	No Go	Go	No Go	Good	Marginal	Effectiveness depends on the degree of ambient lighting.
Infrared Laser Pointer (above .4 watts)	No Go	No Go	Go	No Go	Good	Good	Less affected by ambient light and weather conditions. Highly effective under all but the most highly lit or worst weather conditions. IZLID-2 is the current example.
Visual Laser	No Go	Go	Go	No Go	Good	Marginal	Highly visibility to all. High risk of compromise. Effective, depending upon degree of ambient light.
Laser Designator	Go	Go	No Go	Go	N/A	Good	Highly effective with precision-guided munitions. Very restrictive laser-acquisition cone and requires LOS to target. May require precoordination of laser codes. Requires PGM or LST equipped.
Tracers	Go	Go	Go	No Go	No Go	Marginal	May compromise position. May be difficult to distinguish mark from other gunfire. During daytime use, may be more effective to kick up dust surrounding target.
VS-17 Panel	Go	No Go	No Go	No Go	Good	N/A	Easy to see when visibility is good. Must be shielded from the enemy.
Infrared Paper	No Go	No Go	No Go	Go	Good	N/A	Must be shielded from the enemy. Affected by ambient temperature.

Table 7-4. Techniques for marking of target or location (continued)

METHOD	DAY	NIGHT	NVG	NVS	FRIENDLY MARKS	TARGET MARKS	REMARKS
AN/PAQ-4C Infrared Aiming Light	No Go	No Go	Go	No Go	N/A	Good	Effective to about 600 meters.
AN/PEQ-2A Infrared Aiming Light, Pointer, Illuminator	No Go	No Go	Go	No Go	N/A	Good	Effective to about 1300 meters. Can illuminate the target.
Chem Light	No Go	Go	Go	No Go	Good	N/A	Must be shielded from enemy observation. Affected by ambient light. Spin to give unique signature.
Infrared Chem Light	No Go	No Go	Go	No Go	Good	N/A	Must be shielded from enemy observation. Affected by ambient light. Spin to give unique signature
Strobe	No Go	Go	Go	No Go	Excellent	N/A	Visble to all. Affected by ambient light.
Infrared Strobe	No Go	No Go	Go	No Go	Excellent	N/A	Effectiveness depends on ambient light. Coded strobes aid acquisition. Visble to all with NVGs.
Flare	Go	Go	Go	Marginal	Excellent	N/A	Visble to all. Easily seen by aircrew.
Infrared Flare	No Go	No Go	Go	No Go	Excellent	N/A	Easily seen by aircrews with NVGs.
Glint/Infrared Panel	No Go	No Go	No Go	Go	Good	N/A	Not readily detected by enemy. Effective except in high ambient light.
Combat ID Panel	Go	No Go	No Go	No Go	Good	N/A	Provides temperature contrast on vehicles or buildings.
Chemical Heat Sources, MRE Heater	No Go	No Go	No Go	Go	Poor	N/A	Can be lost in thermal clutter. Difficult to acquire. Best to contrast a cold background.
Briefing Pointer	No Go	Go	Go	No Go	Fair	Poor	Short range.
Electronic Beacon	N/A	N/A	N/A	N/A	Excellent	Good	Ideal friendly marking for AC-130 and some USAF CAS. Not compatible with Navy/Marines. Can be used as a TRP. Coordination with aircrew essential.
Hydra 70 Illumination	Go	Go	Go	Go	N/A	Good	Assists with direct fire and adjustment of indirect fire.

CLOSE COMBAT ATTACK REQUESTS

7-65. A request for CCA may be sent when targets of opportunity require engagement from Army aviation elements. Time is the primary constraining factor for coordinating aviation fires. Requests for CCA should follow the briefing format shown in Table 7-5. The CCA briefing is the joint standard five-line format with minor modifications for Army helicopters and is also used for request for support from Specter gunships. This briefing provides clear and concise information in a logical sequence enabling aircrews to employ their weapons systems. It also provides appropriate control to reduce risk of fratricide. Transmission of the brief constitutes clearance to fire except in a danger close situation. When applicable, danger close missions must be declared in line 5.

Table 7-5. Close combat attack briefing

CLOSE COMBAT ATTACK BRIEFING (Ground to Air)
1. Observer-WARNO: "(Aircraft call sign) THIS IS (Observer call sign). FIRE MISSION. OVER."
2. Friendly Location/Mark: "MY POSITION (TRP, GRID). MARKED BY (STROBE, BEACON, IR STROBE or others)."
3. Target Location: "(Magnetic Bearing and Range (meters), TRP, Grid.)"
4. Target Description/Mark: "(Target Description) MARKED BY (IR, pointer, Tracer, or others). Over."
5. Remarks: "(Threats, Danger Close Clearance[1], Restrictions, At My Command[2], or others.)"
As Required:
1. Clearance: Transmission of the fire mission is clearance to fire, unless danger close. Danger close ranges are IAW FM 3-09.32. For closer fire, the observer/commander must accept responsibility for increased risk. State, "CLEARED DANGER CLOSE" on line 5. This clearance may be preplanned.
2. At my command. For positive control of the gunship, state "AT MY COMMAND" on line 5. The gunship will call "READY TO FIRE" when ready.

SNIPER EMPLOYMENT

7-66. Sniper teams play a critical role in tactical operations. Well-trained snipers provide commanders accurate and precisely targeted long-range small-arms fire. Accurate and unexpected sniper fires can affect the threat's morale, ability to move, and mission accomplishment. Snipers are also well trained and equipped to observe, collect, and provide critical, detailed information. It is in this role that they are often employed for reconnaissance units.

TROOP SNIPER OPERATIONS

7-67. The DRT commander or sniper squad leader controls the sniper teams from a central location. Once deployed, sniper teams may operate independently in support of the troop mission. To successfully contribute to mission accomplishment, they must clearly understand the commander's intent, concept of the operation, and purpose for their assigned tasks. The commander and his supporting sniper elements must retain flexibility. Snipers are effective only in areas with good fields of fire and observation. They should have the freedom of action to choose their own positions once on the ground. (See FM 3-22.10.)

7-68. The sniper squad leader assigns tasks based on the commander's intent and the concept of operations. The common sniper tasks are discussed below. While the DRT sniper squad is capable of accomplishing each task, their main role in DRT operations remains that of surveillance, information gathering, and reporting of information. Below are common tasks snipers are able to perform. Tasks prevalent during UO are marked with an asterisk.

- Conduct surveillance operations.*
- Provide overwatch for OPs and fire positions.
- Cover obstacles while friendly forces cross them.
- Observe and control indirect fire onto threat positions.
- Conduct countersniper operations.*
- Target key threat leaders.*
- Target threat C2 nodes.
- Target vehicle operators.*
- Target threat crew-served weapons and crews.*
- Target threat sappers.*
- Cover demolition guards and supply columns.

- Place accurate fire into bunkers and embrasures.
- Disable or destroy key threat equipment and material.
- Ambush or harass withdrawing threat elements.
- Deny threat access to certain areas (such as obstacles) or avenues of approach (such as defiles).

PLANNING

7-69. The planning process for employment of snipers is the same as that for employment of other forces. The variables of METT-TC are used for mission analysis of sniper employment.

Mission

7-70. The mission assigned to a DRT sniper team for a particular operation consists of the task(s) the commander wants the sniper team to accomplish and the reason (purpose) for it. The DRT commander decides how he wants his sniper team to affect the AO. He then assigns missions to achieve this effect using these guidelines:

- The commander assigns target priorities so snipers can avoid involvement in sustained engagements. Because sniper teams often conduct independent missions and may have to make quick decisions, the team leader has to understand the commander's intent and have a high level of flexibility in how to accomplish his mission.
- The commander describes the effect or result he expects and allows the sniper team to select key targets.
- The commander also designates the sniper to act as an observer of a target or an area rather than task conventional forces to do so. The sniper's ability to remain undetected for long periods may make this a more practical mission than dedicating other forces to do so.
- The commander assigns specific types of targets to achieve a desired effect or endstate.
- The commander assigns specific point targets such as bunkers, checkpoints, or crew-served weapons positions.

Enemy

7-71. The DRT commander considers the following in analyzing the threat situation:

- What are the attributes of the AO?
- How is the threat organized?
- What are the threat's characteristics, including capabilities, limitations, and dispositions?

7-72. The answers to questions like these help the DRT commander to determine the threat's susceptibility and then to predict the reaction to effective sniper operations. Obviously, a well-rested, well-led, well-supplied, and aggressive threat with armored protection poses a greater challenge to snipers than one that is poorly led, poorly supplied, lax, and unprotected. Additionally, the commander needs to know if threat snipers are present and effective, since they can pose a significant danger to his operations and his snipers.

Terrain And Weather

7-73. The DRT commander evaluates and considers the terrain to and within the sniper's AO; the time and effort snipers will need to get into position; and the effects of weather on the sniper and his visibility. Snipers prefer positions at least 300 meters from their target area. Operating at this distance allows them to avoid effective fire from enemy rifles, while retaining much of the effective range (800 to 1,000 meters) of the sniper rifle. Snipers need AOs with good observation, fields of fire, and firing positions. Bad weather can conceal their approach to and exit from the target area.

Troops And Support Available

7-74. The DRT commander decides how many sniper teams to use depending on their availability, the duration of the operation, expected opposition, the availability of other units to support the insertion and extraction phases, and the number and difficulty of tasks and targets assigned. He also considers assigning a dedicated element to conduct emergency extraction based on availability of assets. The commander also considers the snipers' level of training and physical conditioning to determine the effects of these human factors on sniper operations. Furthermore, the commander considers the time required to properly prepare and rest teams, recognizing that using multiple teams simultaneously can limit their availability at a later time.

Time Available

7-75. The DRT commander considers how much time the snipers have to achieve the result he expects. He must allocate time for snipers to plan, coordinate, prepare, rehearse, move, and establish positions. He understands how the snipers' risk increases with inadequate time to plan or to perform other tasks such as moving to the AO. The length of time a sniper team can remain in a position without loss of effectiveness due to eye fatigue, muscle strain, or cramps depends mostly on the type of position the team occupies. Generally, snipers can remain in an expedient position for six hours before they must be relieved. They can remain in belly positions or semi-permanent hides for up to 48 hours before they must be relieved. The average mission takes about 24 hours. Movement factors for snipers operating with a security element are the same as for any Infantry force. When snipers move alone in the AO, they move slowly; their movement can be measured in feet and inches. The sniper team is the best resource in determining how much time is required for their movement.

Civil Considerations

7-76. The DRT sniper can be employed to gather information or to dominate an AO by delivering selective, precision fire against specific targets IAW the applicable ROE. A sniper team's ROE may differ from those applied to the rest of the troop. The sniper team must have clearance to reduce high-risk targets, at the team's discretion, to save lives. Some of the specialized tasks that commanders can assign to snipers include the following:

- As authorized by local orders or instructions, engage individual targets involved in such activities as hijacking, kidnapping, weapons emplacement, or IED/EFP emplacement.
- Engage threat snipers as opportunity targets or as part of a deliberate clearance operation.
- Covertly occupy concealed positions to observe selected areas.
- Record and report all suspicious activity in the area of observation.
- Help coordinate the activities of other elements by taking advantage of hidden observation positions.
- Protect other elements of the controlling forces, including auxiliaries such as firemen and repair crews.

PREPARATION

7-77. Mission preparation comprises several steps: learning the mission, understanding the DRT commander's intent, and determining the resources that will be required from receipt of the order through debriefing. Troop-leading procedures assist the commander and sniper squad/section leader in preparing the mission (as well as in planning and execution). This discussion covers several TLP considerations.

Mission Alert

7-78. The DRT sniper team receives the mission in oral or written form. The team analyzes it to ensure that all Soldiers understand it and then begins making plans.

Warning Order

7-79. Normally, the entire sniper team receives the mission brief. If only the sniper team leader receives the brief, however, he issues a WARNO as soon as possible afterward.

Tentative Plan

7-80. The DRT sniper team leader makes a tentative plan for accomplishing the mission. If the mission is complex and time is short, he may be able to make only a quick mental estimate. If he has time, he makes a more thorough estimate. The sniper team members learn as much as they can about the threat and mission requirements and apply what they learn to the terrain in the assigned area.

Coordination

7-81. Coordination checklists included in the troop TACSOP are vital tools for sniper planning. The troop commander and the team coordinate with all elements involved in the operation. All parties use checklists to ensure that they cover all the required areas. Sniper coordination requirements include the following:

- Intelligence.
- Operations.
- Fire support.
- Insertion/extraction.
- Adjacent units.
- Routes.
- Rehearsal area.
- Army aviation support.
- Vehicle movement.
- OPORD.

7-82. The sniper team leader completes his plan based on his map/imagery reconnaissance and on any changes in the threat situation. He may or may not change the tentative plan, but he can add critical details. He focuses mainly on actions in the objective area and carefully assigns specific tasks to his snipers for all phases of the operation. He issues the OPORD in the standard five-paragraph format. He includes terrain models, sketches, and chalkboards to highlight important details such as routes, planned rally points, and actions at known danger areas.

Backbrief

7-83. The sniper team rehearses the backbrief before presenting it to the commander.

Equipment Check

7-84. The sniper team ensures that all equipment is operational. The team leader ensures that weapons are clean, functional, and test-fired to confirm zeroing. The team makes a communications check with all elements participating in the operation.

Final Inspection

7-85. Snipers make any last-minute changes and correct any deficiencies found during equipment checks. The commander and sniper squad/section leader conduct the final inspection and review the mission with team members.

Rehearsals

7-86. Rehearsals ensure team proficiency. During rehearsals, the sniper squad/section leader reviews and refines his plan based on revised threat assessments or any additional guidance from the DRT commander.

EXECUTION

7-87. A sniper mission has three general phases: insertion, execution, and extraction.

Insertion Phase

7-88. Insertion is the first critical phase of any sniper operation. The team may have to pass through terrain where the enemy might use sophisticated detection devices. The method of insertion selected depends on METT-TC. The team can be part of a mounted or dismounted patrol, moving away as it approaches the insertion point.

Execution Phase

7-89. The execution phase includes the sniper team's movement from the insertion site to the target area, execution of the mission, and movement to the extraction site.

Movement to the Target Area

7-90. After leaving the insertion site, the sniper team transmits an initial entry report as required by unit TACSOP. This report ensures that radio equipment operates properly. It also informs the commander and CP of the team's status.

Occupation of Position

7-91. During mission planning, the team selects a tentative final firing position (FFP), objective rally point (ORP), and route based on map and aerial photograph reconnaissance. The snipers move close to the tentative FFP and establish the ORP. Then, they move forward to search for a specific FFP site, ensuring that it is suitable and that they can observe the target area at ground level. They reconnoiter the FFP during limited visibility. After they locate an FFP, they return to the ORP, secure all mission-essential equipment, move to the FFP and occupy it, and begin to construct the hide position.

Primary Positions

7-92. Snipers position themselves where they can observe or control one or more avenues of approach into the defensive position. Sniper employment can increase all-around security and allow the commander to concentrate his assets against the most likely threat COA. Snipers can support the troop by providing extra optics for target acquisition and precise long-range fires to complement the fires of other weapon systems. This arrangement takes advantage of the effectiveness of all of the unit's weapons. In an economy of force role, snipers can cover dismounted enemy avenues of approach into troop positions.

Alternate and Supplementary Positions

7-93. Snipers establish alternate and supplementary positions for all-around security. Multiple sniper teams, if used, can be positioned for surveillance and mutual FS. If possible, they establish positions in depth for continuous support during the operation. (For more information on establishing alternate and supplemental positions, see FM 3-22.10.)

Reports

7-94. The sniper team follows the troop communications TACSOP. Team members maintain communications throughout the mission using directional antennas, masking, and burst transmissions.

Extraction Phase

7-95. The sniper team exfiltrates as soon as it accomplishes the mission. The extraction site is coordinated with supporting forces before the mission. The situation, however, will dictate whether the sniper team conducts extraction at the planned site, exfiltrates, or has to escape and evade.

SECURITY ELEMENT

7-96. During insertion and extraction, sniper teams move with a security element (section or platoon) whenever possible. Initially, sniper teams can also move with a motorized element, which allows them to enter an area more quickly and safely than if they operated alone. The security element also protects the snipers during the operation. When moving with a security element, snipers use the following guidelines:

- Snipers should appear to be an integral part of the security element. Based on METT-TC, they conceal their sniper-unique equipment—such as optics, radios, and ghillie suits—from view whenever possible.
- Snipers wear the same uniforms as the members of the security element. Snipers and element members maintain proper intervals and positions in the element formation.

URBAN OPERATIONS

7-97. The DRT sniper's value to a unit conducting UO depends on several factors, including the type of operation, level of conflict, and ROE. Where ROE allow destruction, snipers may not be needed since other weapon systems have greater destructive effect. But where ROE prohibit collateral damage, snipers can be the commander's most valuable tool. During stability operations in urban terrain, the sniper can provide greatly enhanced observation of an area or population and can apply precise firepower within the limits of the ROE more easily than more powerful weapon systems.

SECTION III – ARMY AVIATION

7-98. Army aviation assets can enhance troop operations through additional support in reconnaissance, security, and movement of personnel and equipment. Aviation assets are often used en route to and from the objective and can assist in operations at the objective site.

ORGANIZATION

7-99. Organization of aviation units in support of the troop will be designed, tailored, and configured for specific operational support based on mission guidance and the specific AO in which the units operate. The organization could be any combination of attack reconnaissance, assault, lift, and maintenance units.

CAPABILITIES

7-100. Aviation units support operations by:

- Conducting day, night, and limited visibility combat, enabling, and sustainment operations.
- Weighting the combat power of the supported unit by rapidly maneuvering forces to achieve mass at critical times and places.
- Shaping the AO by providing near-real-time combat information on threat locations and dispositions throughout the AO.
- Influencing the tempo of friendly and threat operations.
- Conducting joint air attack team operations.
- Conducting SEAD.

LIMITATIONS

7-101. Aviation units are subject to the following limitations:

- The effects of weather and obscuration on observation, acquisition, and engagement ranges of combat systems, as well as on the employment of all aviation forces.
- Limited capability to secure aviation assembly areas.
- Limited employment times based on distance and fuel consumption.

PRINCIPLES OF AVIATION EMPLOYMENT

7-102. The principles and guidelines for employment of aviation assets are to:

- Fight as an integral part of the combined arms team.
- Exploit the capabilities of other branches and services.

- Capitalize on intelligence-gathering capabilities.
- Suppress threat weapons and acquisition means.
- Exploit firepower, mobility, and surprise.
- Mass forces.
- Use terrain for survivability.
- Displace forward elements frequently.
- Maintain flexibility.
- Exercise staying power.

PLANNING CONSIDERATIONS

7-103. The squadron staff plans aviation missions. Planning considerations for operations that include aviation assets are similar to those of any other tactical operation. The two primary factors are the higher commander's intent and METT-TC factors. At the same time, others factors, such as sustainment and risk analysis, must be integrated from the start. Two specific areas in the planning process are of critical importance to the troop: requesting procedures for aviation support and integrating aviation and ground forces.

7-104. The troop requests aviation support through the squadron, which requests through the IBCT aviation element.

7-105. The squadron staff plans the integration of aviation and ground forces. The planning for such operations capitalizes on the strengths of each combat system. In whichever role the aviation assets are used, the plan is all-encompassing and ensures coordination of effort. All planning begins with the ground tactical plan. Army aviation assets are integrated into the plan, coordinated, and controlled by the reconnaissance squadron staff under the squadron commander's guidance. Planning considerations include:

- Ground tactical plan.
- Landing plan factors, including:
  - Location and size of LZs.
  - Troop is most vulnerable during landing.
  - Multiple insertions require multiple LZs.
  - Troop elements must land with tactical integrity.
  - Soldiers are easily disoriented if not briefed when landing direction changes.
  - There may not be any other friendly units in the area; the troop must be prepared for enemy in any direction.
  - Landing plan should be flexible with several options available.
  - Fire support must be planned, (artillery, naval gunfire, CAS, and attack helicopters).
  - Organic 60-mm mortars may be brought into the LZ early if the LZ is beyond supporting fires.
  - Resupply and MEDEVAC is done by air.

7-106. Marking of friendly positions and targets is an indispensable aspect of planning and must be considered thoroughly regardless of the time available to the ground and air commanders. The proximity of friendly forces to targets makes positive identification and accurate marking of friendly units and targets a critical factor in avoiding fratricide while maximizing responsive aerial fires. Aircrews must be able to easily observe and identify ground signals and marking methods. The signals and marking methods—or combination of these means—must be based on items commonly carried by ground maneuver units, must be acquirable by the night vision or thermal imaging systems on the aircraft, and must be recognizable by the aircrews.

AVIATION MISSIONS

7-107. Aviation missions generally fall within three categories: attack/reconnaissance, utility, or enabling.

ATTACK/RECONNAISSANCE MISSIONS

7-108. Aviation attack and reconnaissance missions include the following:
- Reconnaissance.
- Area.
- Route.
- Zone.
- Surveillance.
- Security.
- Screen, guard, and cover (if applicable).
- Aerial security.
- Convoy security.
- Area security.
- Movement to contact.
- Attack.
- Close combat attack.
- Interdiction attack.

UTILITY/CARGO MISSIONS

7-109. Aviation utility/cargo missions include the following:
- Air assault.
- Air movement.
- Aerial resupply.
- Aerial CASEVAC.
- Aerial MEDEVAC.
- Personnel recovery.
- C2 support.

ENABLING MISSIONS

7-110. Aviation enabling missions include the following:
- Air traffic services.
- Forward arming and refueling point operations.
- Aviation maintenance.
- Downed aircraft recovery.

ATTACK RECONNAISSANCE SUPPORT

7-111. Attack reconnaissance assets can be placed under OPCON of the squadron; therefore, the squadron, troops, and platoons must establish close working relationships with attack reconnaissance units whenever possible. Through mobility and speed, attack reconnaissance assets give the ground commander added flexibility, increasing the speed with which reconnaissance is conducted.

EMPLOYMENT CONSIDERATIONS

7-112. The primary mission of attack reconnaissance in support of the troop is conducting reconnaissance. Table 7-6 summarizes the capabilities and limitations of attack reconnaissance assets.

Table 7-6. Attack reconnaissance aviation capabilities and limitations

CAPABILITIES	LIMITATIONS
Terrain-independent maneuver. Addition of speed, agility, and depth to operations. Increased tempo of operations. Digital connectivity. Enhanced optics in an elevated observation platform. Video reconnaissance. Long-range direct fire. Precision guided munitions. Enhanced fires. Enhanced night survivability.	Degraded limited visibility capabilities. Lack of detailed reconnaissance. Limited station times. Crew endurance. Aircraft maintenance requirements. Inability to retain terrain. Increased Class III/V requirements. Forward arming and refueling point survivability. Weather conditions. Assembly area survivability. Reaction time from decreased readiness condition. Survivability in close operations.

AIR-GROUND INTEGRATION IN RECONNAISSANCE TROOP OPERATIONS

7-113. The DRT commander and subordinate leaders may employ attack reconnaissance assets as a maneuver force. To achieve effective air-ground integration, they must consider basic fundamentals that enhance overall effectiveness and ensure attack reconnaissance assets are synchronized with troop operations. These fundamentals include the following:

- Understanding capabilities and limitations of attack reconnaissance assets.
- Adhering to TACSOP.
- Employing effective C2.
- Maximizing available assets.
- Synchronizing efforts of air and ground forces.

Standing Operating Procedures

7-114. Although it is difficult to establish habitual working relationships with aviation elements that are not organic to the squadron, TACSOP should, where possible, be established to provide a common basis for more efficient air-ground integration. Applicable TACSOP considerations include, but are not limited to, the following:

- Common terminology.
- Conditions for air-ground team (AGT) employment.
- Specialized task organizations.
- Roles and responsibilities for planning and preparation.
- Air-ground coordination checklists.
- BHO checklists.
- Air passage of lines procedures.
- Recognition signals.
- Fratricide prevention procedures.
- Clearance of fires procedures.
- Liaison requirements.
- Reporting procedures.
- Communications architecture.
- Movement techniques.
- Actions on contact drills.
- Battle drills.

Command and Control

7-115. There are two methods for controlling air and ground operations. These are squadron control and AGT control. In both methods, control rests with the commander who owns the terrain upon which the operation is executed.

Squadron Control

7-116. With the squadron control method, the attack reconnaissance commanders operate on the squadron command net and can coordinate detailed actions with the troops on the attack reconnaissance or ground troop command nets. The squadron commander ensures the focus of the attack reconnaissance units remains synchronized. He clarifies coordination and issues orders to units as necessary. At the same time, this method never precludes cross-talk between troops and attack reconnaissance units.

7-117. Advantages of squadron control include:
- Enhanced SA at the squadron level.
- Additional flexibility for the squadron as the situation develops.
- Enhanced squadron awareness of attack reconnaissance unit's sustainment status.
- Reduced C2 requirements for the ground troop commander.
- Streamlined reporting and fires requests.
- Reduced planning, liaison, and rehearsal requirements at troop level.
- Increased tempo of squadron-level operations.
- Ease in establishing and executing the squadron-level Army airspace C2 plan.

7-118. Disadvantages of squadron control include:
- Degraded SA below the troop/attack reconnaissance unit level.
- More difficult air-ground synchronization at the troop/attack reconnaissance unit level.
- Greater potential for fratricide.
- More difficult clearance of direct and mortar fires.
- More difficult air passage of lines.
- Increased difficulty in RHO and target handover.
- Increased traffic on the squadron command net.

Air-Ground Team Control

7-119. The second method of C2, the formation of AGTs, is a temporary relationship to deal with a specific situation. Operational control is the command relationship used. Air-ground teams are best employed when decentralized troop operations are required. Operations that can be enhanced by the formation of AGTs include route reconnaissance, area/zone reconnaissance, reconnaissance in force, screens, and area security. Control can be exercised by either the ground troop commander or the attack reconnaissance unit commander.

7-120. Control by the ground troop is appropriate when ground reconnaissance owns the AO. Control by the attack reconnaissance unit is appropriate when that unit owns the AO.

7-121. The advantages of forming AGTs are METT-TC dependent. They can include:
- Enhanced SA below the troop/attack reconnaissance unit level.
- The squadron commander's ability to weight the main effort.
- Enhanced reconnaissance and security operations.
- Decentralized operations.
- Streamlined clearance of direct and mortar fires in the close fight.
- The troop's enhanced ability to observe mortar fires.
- Reduced traffic on the squadron command net.
- The attack reconnaissance unit's ability to provide enhanced C2 and observation for the DRT over extended distances.

- Enhanced response for downed aircraft in the close fight.
- Greater security for the attack reconnaissance unit in daytime reconnaissance and security missions.

7-122. Disadvantages of AGTs, also METT-TC dependent, can include:
- Reduced SA of attack reconnaissance assets at squadron level.
- Limited ability of the squadron commander to reorient/retask the attack reconnaissance unit.
- Increased time required to clear fires.
- Limited knowledge of the attack reconnaissance unit's sustainment requirements.
- More difficult squadron-level Army airspace command and control.
- Increased C2 and liaison requirements at troop level.

ATTACK RECONNAISSANCE HELICOPTERS IN STABILITY OPERATIONS

7-123. The attack reconnaissance helicopter unit's mobility, advanced surveillance and targeting capabilities, and lethality provide the troop commander with a flexible platform for power projection and information acquisition in stability operations. Troops operating in stability operations can expect to be dispersed throughout expansive AOs where it is difficult to maintain a constant ground force presence and effective surveillance. Attached or OPCON attack reconnaissance assets allow the troop to increase its presence in these types of operations.

ASSAULT (UTILITY) AND CARGO (LIFT) HELICOPTER SUPPORT

7-124. The Army utility helicopter, the UH-60 Blackhawk, is a general-purpose aircraft with limited carrying capability. It is used for such missions as transport of troops and cargo or MEDEVAC of casualties. The Blackhawk can carry 8,000 pounds of cargo internally, externally, or as a combination of both.

7-125. The Army cargo helicopter, the CH-47D Chinook, has the capacity for carrying loads of greater weight and size than those carried by the utility helicopter. The cargo helicopter can lift heavy, oversized loads, such as artillery and ammunition. With a maximum external load of 26,000 pounds, the Chinook can also recover downed aircraft or vehicles.

CAPABILITIES

7-126. During operations, the utility and cargo helicopter unit significantly influences the troop commander's mission by:
- Conducting day, night, and limited visibility operations across the AO.
- Influencing the tempo of friendly operations.
- Rapidly moving tactical units over great distances from contiguous and non-contiguous areas of operation.
- Bypassing threat positions and obstacles to achieve surprise.
- Enhancing the command, control, and communications process.
- Moving large amounts of supplies and equipment to sustain combat operations.
- Moving critical repair parts quickly to increase the combat power of the force.
- Emplacing Volcano minefields to disrupt, delay, turn, or block threat forces.
- Conducting operations beyond the FLOT.
- Providing personnel recovery coverage in the AO.
- Conducting MEDEVAC/CASEVAC and personnel replacement operations.
- Providing refueling capabilities using wet/fat hawk/fat cow/jump forward arming and refueling points (FARPs).

LIMITATIONS

7-127. Utility and cargo helicopter units are subject to the following operational limitations:

- Extreme environmental effects (temperature, altitude) may reduce the capabilities of the aircraft to perform full range of missions.
- The unit has limited capability to secure unit assembly areas with organic assets.
- Missions require adequate planning and coordination time to fully capitalize on utility and cargo helicopter assets.
- The unit may be subjected to inadequate sustainment because of extended range of operations and limited organic sustainment assets.
- Terrain may limit the availability of adequate PZs and LZs.
- Helicopters require large amounts of fuel (Class III) and repair parts (Class IX).
- Some units can provide only a limited number of aircraft to support a combat force.
- Battlefield obscuration (smoke, dust) degrades utility and cargo helicopter operations.
- Helicopters require extensive maintenance support for extended operations.

AERIAL RESUPPLY

7-128. Aerial resupply operations provide the troop commander with a flexible, responsive means to resupply his force. Although limited by weather and threat air defense systems, aerial resupply enables the commander to bypass congested supply routes, destroyed bridges, and most terrain obstacles to deliver supplies where they are most needed.

7-129. Close coordination must occur between all participants in the aerial resupply operation. They review the entire mission and resolve all limitations and problem areas. If a particular problem cannot be resolved, another mode of transport should be considered.

7-130. The squadron plans for aerial resupply. Planning factors include:

- Type/amount of cargo to be carried.
- Helicopter assets available.
- Sling/cargo net/cargo container requirements.
- Ground crew training requirements.
- Selection of the PZ/LZ.
- Integration into the tactical plan.
- Priorities of cargo/unit resupply.

SECTION IV – ENGINEERS

7-131. Combat engineers increase the effectiveness of troop operations by accomplishing mobility and countermobility tasks. They are integrated with the commander's maneuver and indirect fires assets to enhance opportunities for the commander to accomplish combined arms missions. Additionally, they may perform reconnaissance and Infantry combat missions when required. General (construction) engineers may employ their technical capabilities to support the troop for specialized missions when close combat is less likely since they are not equipped for combat tasks. Engineer reconnaissance support capabilities include both a tactical and technical focus for combined arms reconnaissance operations. Organic engineer assets in the IBCT are limited. The engineer company is equipped with enough squads to support one squad per rifle company. As such, the DRT will rarely have engineers available to specifically support their reconnaissance efforts. If assets are available, their employment is primarily through application of specialty skills that are not available within the troop.

MISSIONS

7-132. The tactical missions of combat engineers correspond to those of IBCT Infantry units. Combat engineer units can operate in restrictive terrain such as forests, jungles, mountains, and urban areas.

Because of their austere nature, IBCT engineers have limited tactical mobility. To compensate for this, IBCT engineers train to operate in a decentralized manner. Like their supported maneuver force, they are very well suited to operate under conditions of limited visibility.

CAPABILITIES

7-133. The IBCT combat engineer company was designed with a focus on mobility support. For the DRT, this may include, among other missions, route reconnaissance or clearance and obstacle reduction support. They may also identify potential enemy counterattack routes and support to establishment of countermobility measures such as scatterable mines to protect the force. Infantry Brigade Combat Team engineers train in Infantry skills and are able to move undetected when close to the enemy. (For a complete listing of weapons and engineer assets, see FM 3-21.10 and FM 3-34.)

MOBILITY

7-134. Mobility operations create and preserve freedom of movement for friendly forces. Engineers reduce the effects of existing or reinforcing obstacles, providing gap crossings, and constructing and maintaining combat roads and trails. These activities support forces by performing mobility tasks that aid in movement and maneuver of friendly forces. (For more information on combined arms mobility operations, see FM 3-34.2.) Engineers support forces mobility through:

- Bridging.
- Constructing new routes.
- Repairing or upgrading existing routes.
- Constructing, repairing, or upgrading airfields and heliports.
- Preparing or repairing LZs, FARPs, and landing strips.

7-135. While the DRT may not often require engineer assets to assist with the same mobility needs as many vehicular based units, they often use engineer specialty capabilities. These assets and capabilities include:

- Using robots in mine or explosive detection.
- Assisting with the classification of bridges.
- Assessing route or roadway trafficability.
- Assessing and/or clearing obstacles.
- Using military working dogs for mine and explosive detection.

COUNTERMOBILITY

7-136. Countermobility operations attack the threat's ability to maneuver through construction of reinforcing obstacles that are integrated with fires and existing obstacles. These operations inhibit the maneuver of an enemy force, increase time for target acquisition, and increase weapon effectiveness. Commanders integrate obstacle planning into the MDMP, integrate obstacles into the concept of operations (primarily through proper siting), and maintain integration through obstacle turnover, protection, and tracking.

7-137. The following considerations govern obstacle employment:

- Observing restrictions imposed by the squadron.
- Integrating obstacle employment into the scheme of maneuver.
- Covering obstacles with direct and indirect fires.
- Integrating reinforcing obstacles with existing obstacles.
- Employing obstacles in depth.
- Employing surprise.
- Preventing stealth breaching or infiltration.
- Conducting final siting of obstacles on the ground (accomplished by the responsible maneuver commander and the emplacing engineer).

7-138. Dismounted reconnaissance troop units do not have a major role in countermobility operations and rarely use engineers in this capacity.

SURVIVABILITY

7-139. Survivability operations provide cover and concealment and reduce the effects of enemy weapons on personnel, equipment, and supplies while simultaneously deceiving the enemy about the force's intentions. These operations include the employment of camouflage, concealment, and deception. They also include the construction and/or hardening of facilities, C2 nodes, and critical infrastructure to protect personnel and critical equipment and supplies. The most extensive aspect of the survivability effort involves defensive operations, creating vehicle fighting positions, and digging individual and crew-served weapon positions.

7-140. Although DRT units use cover and concealment when performing operations such as reconnaissance, engineer assets are normally not required for establishment of DRT short- or long-duration (less than 24 hours) surveillance positions unless the DRT positions become extended-duration OPs (beyond 24 hours).

ORGANIZATION

7-141. The combat engineer company of IBCT is tailored to fight as part of the combined arms team within the IBCT. It focuses on mobility but also provides limited countermobility and survivability engineer support. One engineer company is organic to the IBCT. Depending on the mission and other METT-TC conditions, the DRT may have or need support from engineer assets. These assets may be a supporting engineer element such as a sapper squad. The engineer company can be augmented according to the mission with units that have brigades at echelons above the IBCT. Augmentation provides additional engineer capability and functions.

ENGINEER COMPANY

7-142. The IBCT engineer company is assigned and executes engineer missions that are identified by the IBCT commander. Their employment depends on the IBCT commander's analysis of METT-TC. The engineer company commander may receive augmentation from other engineer units. He directs his unit in the execution of mission support to the IBCT. The engineer company is self-sufficient for mobility purposes.

ENGINEER PLATOON

7-143. Based on the IBCT commander's analysis of METT-TC, an engineer platoon (sappers) might be task organized to the reconnaissance squadron. The engineer platoon can be employed to accomplish almost any engineer mission. However, the engineer platoon lacks organic sustainment assets and has minimal C2 depth and combat systems. Thus, it will most likely require augmentation or external support to conduct continuous operations over a sustained period of time (more than 48 hrs). The engineer platoon might also require some augmentation to conduct combined arms tasks such as breaching operations. The engineer platoon may receive augmentation from its engineer company or other units as required.

SAPPER SQUAD

7-144. As mentioned earlier, there are six combat engineer squads, or sapper squads, per IBCT. The IBCT commander may choose to employ the company as a single unit or attach engineer assets to the battalions. Often, one sapper squad is associated with each of the six rifle companies. A sapper squad consists of eight combat engineers. It might be task organized to a reconnaissance troop. It executes engineer tasks to support the troop mission. Task organization is based on the squadron commander's analyses of METT-TC. The squad is the smallest engineer element that can be employed with its own organic C2 assets and as such can accomplish tasks such as reconnaissance, manual breaching, demolitions, or route clearance as part of a platoon or DRT mission. The sapper engineer may receive augmentation of engineer equipment such as a small emplacement excavator or other specialized engineer equipment based on METT-TC.

ENGINEER RECONNAISSANCE TEAM

7-145.   In the IBCT, ERTs are ad hoc reconnaissance units organized specifically for a reconnaissance mission. Engineer reconnaissance teams may collect information about the terrain, enemy engineer activity, obstacles, and weather effects within an AO. Engineer reconnaissance team operations share many of the characteristics that define reconnaissance operations. Reconnaissance support is normally guided by the same objective, receives the same commander's guidance, and is conducted at the same tempo as the overall reconnaissance operation. Engineer reconnaissance team operations take the basic form of a route, area, or zone reconnaissance and use techniques compatible with those of the supported force. (Refer to FM 3-34.170 for additional discussion of engineer reconnaissance support capabilities.)

7-146.   Engineer reconnaissance teams may operate independently or may assist the troop in conducting zone, area, and route reconnaissance to answer the applicable CCIR, with a specified additional focus on required technical information. Most often, the smallest ERT task organized to support the troop will be an engineer squad. In addition to reconnaissance support in M/CM/S operations, engineer reconnaissance support may be critical in UO, search operations, tunnel and subsurface operations, and other operations in complex terrain. Engineer capabilities also are critical in supporting environmental and infrastructure classification in support of reconnaissance operations. Both environmental assessment and infrastructure assessment are generally intended to support the performance of a more detailed survey when the situation permits.

SUPPORT TO RECONNAISSANCE AND SECURITY OPERATIONS

7-147.   During reconnaissance operations with the DRT, priority of effort for engineer units working with the troop is mobility. Priority of mobility effort is the designated route the troop or follow-on forces travel. The following considerations guide the employment of engineers in support of reconnaissance or offensive security missions:

- Normally move well forward, either with or immediately behind the troop.
- Supplement route reconnaissance by assessing specific roadway features that are damaged or require more technical engineer analysis.
- Create bypasses around obstacles.
- Reduce obstacles beyond troop capability. Those that significantly affect the mission of follow-on forces deserve attention. Others are marked and reported.
- Emplace tactical bridging.
- Improve ford sites.
- Improve embankments at vehicle swim sites.
- Emplace protective minefields on exposed flanks.
- Construct combat trails.

OTHER SUPPORT CONSIDERATIONS

7-148.   The DRT receives engineer support from the combat engineer company organic to the IBCT or from combat or general engineer units augmenting the IBCT. Elements of the organic engineer company are typically task organized in a command relationship at either the squadron or troop level. This is especially true for ERTs supporting a combined arms reconnaissance mission. The troop receives an ERT in situations requiring highly detailed or technical engineer information as a focus for the reconnaissance operation.

SUPPORT RELATIONSHIPS

7-149.   The engineer unit is placed in a supporting relationship with the troop for an operation in which this arrangement best accomplishes the mission. Troop assets provide security to engineers as they work on their tasks and are prepared to provide sustainment as well. These actions ensure the engineer effort is focused. The engineer platoon or squad leader best manages the collective effort of the entire platoon/squad and supporting equipment, using assets as needed to accomplish the commander's intent. An ERT also augments the troop to perform specific focused reconnaissance. (For additional guidance on engineer missions and employment, see FM 3-34.)

OBSTACLE INTELLIGENCE

7-150. In any operation where enemy obstacles interfere with friendly maneuver, obstacle intelligence (OBSTINTEL) is one of the information requirements and could become a PIR. Obstacle classification is one of the high-frequency tasks conducted by ERTs. The task is to conduct classification focused on answering OBSTINTEL information requirements, including obstacle location, length, width, and depth; obstacle composition (such as wire or mines by type); soil conditions; locations of lanes and bypasses; and the location of enemy direct fire systems. An ERT moves with scouts and conducts dismounted reconnaissance of templated or confirmed obstacles. The purpose of the reconnaissance is not only to locate the obstacle, but also to determine how best to overcome the effects of the obstacle, whether by reduction or bypass. The following tasks may be associated with the reconnaissance:

- Locating and marking a bypass.
- If the obstacle is to be bypassed, employing ERT to provide guides as well as mark the bypass.
- Locating and marking the best location to reduce.
- Estimating the reduction assets necessary to reduce the obstacle.

Note: OBSTINTEL is an engineer term for gathering information on obstacles.

CLEARING OPERATIONS

7-151. Clearing operations are designed to clear or neutralize explosive hazards and other obstacles from a route or area. As with most mobility operations, clearing operations are often conducted by a combined arms force built around an engineer-based clearing force. Clearing operations include route clearance and area clearance. The engineer focus in clearing operations is again on OBSTINTEL. In support of clearing operations, the OBSTINTEL must be comprehensive and detailed to enable the neutralization of all obstacles along or in the route or area. The task is to conduct detailed reconnaissance of obstacles focused on answering OBSINTEL information requirement: obstacle location, length, width, and depth; obstacle composition (such as wire or mines by type); and soil conditions. The location of lanes and bypasses as well as information on enemy positions is also collected, but the focus is on detailed OBSTINTEL.

SECTION V – INTELLIGENCE

7-152. Intelligence drives the conduct of operations; therefore, the IBCT S2 is responsible for ensuring that the intelligence warfighting function operates smoothly and efficiently so that the commander receives timely, relevant, accurate, predictive, and tailored information in a timely manner. The commander requires intelligence about the enemy and the environment prior to engaging in operations to effectively execute battles, engagements, and other missions within full-spectrum operations. Intelligence assists the commander in visualizing the environment, organizing the forces, and controlling operations to achieve the desired objectives or endstate. Intelligence supports protection by alerting the commander to threats and assisting in preserving and protecting the force.

HUMAN INTELLIGENCE

7-153. Human intelligence is the collection of information by a trained HUMINT collector from people and their associated documents and from media sources to identify elements, intentions, composition, strength, dispositions, tactics, equipment, personnel, and capabilities. It uses human sources as a tool and a variety of collection methods, both passive and active, to gather information to satisfy the commander's information requirement and cue other intelligence disciplines. Human intelligence tasks include, but are not limited to, the following:

- Sourcing operations using tactical and other developed sources.
- Acting as liaison with host nation officials and multinational counterparts.
- Collecting information from the civilian populace, including transients.

- Identifying individuals as potential information sources.
- Debriefing U.S. and multinational forces and civilian personnel.
- Interrogating detainees.
- Supporting the translation and exploitation of threat documents, media, and other materials.

7-154. The DRT has no organic HUMINT capability. If needed, these missions will be supported by nonorganic assets from the IBCT, or external assets to the brigade, that the mission/situation requires. The IBCT military intelligence company (MICO) contains three HUMINT collection teams (HCTs).

HUMAN INTELLIGENCE COLLECTION TEAM

7-155. Human intelligence collection teams are elements comprised of HUMINT collectors who collect information from human sources. Human intelligence collection teams usually deploy in teams of approximately four HUMINT personnel—three collectors and one technician.

7-156. The HCT can be augmented based on factors of METT-TC. Military interpreters or civilian contractors with appropriate security clearances are added when necessary. Technical intelligence personnel or other specific subject matter experts can also augment the team to meet technical collection requirements. (See FM 2-22.3.)

Human Intelligence Sources

7-157. Human intelligence collectors use human sources and a variety of collection methods to gather information to satisfy the commander's information requirement and to cue other intelligence disciplines. Human intelligence collection teams conduct operations throughout the AO. They play a crucial role in supporting operating forces by conducting debriefings, screenings, military source operations, liaison, interrogations, and support to document and media exploitation. Human intelligence focuses on the threat and assists the troop commander in understanding the threat's capabilities, characteristics, vulnerabilities, intentions, and decision-making process.

Capabilities

7-158. The HCT is integrated into the squadron/troop reconnaissance and security plan. The HUMINT operational management team chief advises the troop commander on the specific capabilities and requirements of the team to maximize mission success.

7-159. Team members conduct mission analysis and planning specific to the troop AO. Backwards planning and source profiling are used extensively to choose HUMINT targets. To verify adequate area coverage, the HCT uses analytical tools that help illustrate the HUMINT situation, identify gaps, and refocus the collection effort.

7-160. The HCT is also in constant contact with the troop commander, squadron S2, and other assets (scouts, MISO, civil affairs (CA), and MPs) to coordinate operations.

7-161. The HCT collectors provide the squadron with an organic, trained HUMINT collection capability. The HUMINT collectors:

- Advise on HUMINT collection operations.
- Provide initial assessment and quality control of HUMINT collection and source identification.

7-162. At the DRT level, the HCT's mission includes the following general tasks:

- Collecting information of value from detainees, refugees, civilians, and friendly forces in the AO.
- Collecting data allowing predictive analysis of events in the DRT's AOs.
- Identifying individuals for potential detailed exploitation by the counterintelligence (CI) teams in the brigade's MICO.

7-163. Specific missions for HCT collectors in a MICO include, but are not limited to, the following:

- Conducting interrogation of EPWs and detainees.
- Debriefing or interviewing civilians in the AO.

- Conducting HUMINT analysis.
- Supporting limited document and media exploitation.

7-164. HUMINT collection teams are not organized, equipped, or authorized at any level to perform tasks normally conducted by:
- Military police (to include riots and crowd control).
- Civil affairs.
- MISO.
- CI.

7-165. The troop plans security of the HCT to perform missions.

COUNTERINTELLIGENCE

7-166. Counterintelligence is focused on detecting, identifying, countering, exploiting, or neutralizing foreign intelligence and security and international terrorist organizations' threat intelligence collection activities against U.S. forces. Counterintelligence personnel conduct investigations, collections, operations, analysis, and production to deny, disrupt, or degrade the FIST threat and provide threat indications and warnings to U.S. forces. Counterintelligence personnel conduct screening operations to identify personnel who may be of CI interest or have CI-related information leads.

7-167. Counterintelligence investigations and operations cue other intelligence disciplines. Counterintelligence personnel work in conjunction with reconnaissance, CA, MISO, MPs, engineers, and medical personnel to create threat assessment and vulnerability assessments. These assessments provide commanders with a comprehensive assessment, comparing pertinent threat capabilities to existing conditions.

7-168. Counterintelligence teams are also assigned specific missions from a higher headquarters and operate independently within the troop AO. When a team operates independently, the troop commander is notified by the squadron and is prepared to provide support, if necessary.

COUNTERINTELLIGENCE SOURCES

7-169. Counterintelligence sources include:
- **Casual.** These are one-time sources or casual contacts that provide atmospheric data, protection, threat indications, and warnings. The CI special agent has minimal control over the operation beyond planning and coordinating meetings and debriefing the source on CI areas of interest.
- **Developmental.** These sources are routinely contacted and provide more detailed information than a casual source. Developmental sources are never tasked to obtain information on behalf of U.S. forces; they include contacts who have demonstrated positive views or sentiments towards U.S. forces.
- **Controlled.** These sources have an established reporting history, are deemed credible, and have been vetted by CI elements. Controlled sources meet and cooperate with the CI special agent to provide information.

OTHER INTELLIGENCE ASSETS

7-170. Other intelligence assets available to the troop include those found in the MICO and its own organic SUAS.

MILITARY INTELLIGENCE COMPANY

7-171. The MICO mission is to conduct intelligence analysis, synchronization, and HUMINT collection that support the IBCT and its subordinate commands across the full spectrum of conflict. The MICO provides analysis and intelligence synchronization support to the IBCT S2. The MICO supports the IBCT and its subordinate commands through collection, analysis, and dissemination of intelligence information. It supports the IBCT S2 in synchronizing and maintaining a timely and accurate picture of the enemy situation. This threat portion of the combat outpost aids in predicting future enemy COAs and in answering the IBCT commander's intelligence requirements. The MICO also assists the IBCT S3 with intelligence, surveillance, reconnaissance synchronization, and integration tasks. It coordinates and executes tactical HUMINT operations as directed by the IBCT S3 and S2X. The primary purpose of the MICO in the IBCT is to assist the S2 in maintaining a timely and accurate picture of the enemy situation. Their input to the combat outpost will aid in predicting future enemy COAs and in answering the IBCT commander's intelligence requirements.

Small Unmanned Aircraft System Platoon

7-172. The SUAS platoon conducts missions in response to requirements from the IBCT S2 and receives technical steerage from the MICO. The SUAS is the primary aerial asset to provide visualization of the battlefield to the IBCT commander. The SUAS platoon exercises extensive flexibility and agility in mission planning and execution.

SMALL UNMANNED AIRCRAFT SYSTEMS

7-173. Small unmanned aircraft systems may be used to support the DRT in planning and conducting their missions. The reconnaissance squadron has no organic SUAS; however, a common brigade asset available to the squadron or troop is the Shadow. Small unmanned aircraft systems are vulnerable to weather-related issues such as high winds and cloud cover. A higher level SUAS, such as the Shadow, may impose a security risk if downed in threat areas due to the sensitive items it contains.

SUAS Support in Reconnaissance Operations

7-174. When SUASs complement the troop during reconnaissance operations, they normally operate 1 to 10 kilometers forward of the troop, dependent on the METT-TC variables. The SUAS conducts detailed reconnaissance of areas that are particularly dangerous to ground reconnaissance elements, such as open areas and defiles. They are also effectively employed in support of operations in urban terrain. They conduct route reconnaissance forward of the troop or are employed in conjunction with the troop when it is necessary to reconnoiter multiple routes simultaneously. The SUAS also conducts screening in support of the troop during area or zone reconnaissance missions. Upon contact, it provides early warning for the troop and maintains contact until the troop conducts RHO from the SUAS to a ground element.

SUAS Support in Security Operations

7-175. In security operations, SUASs complement the troop by assisting in identification of threat reconnaissance and main body elements and by providing early warning forward of the troop. In addition to acquiring threat elements, they play a critical role in providing security through the depth of the screen by observing dead space between ground OPs. They support the troop during area security missions by screening or conducting reconnaissance. They provide early warning when the troop is conducting convoy security missions or securing a critical point. Small unmanned aircraft systems identify threat ambush positions forward of the convoy or locate a bypass to allow the convoy to move around an obstacle.

Shadow

7-176. The Shadow is a brigade-level SUAS employed for intelligence, reconnaissance, target acquisition, and BDA, and operates in or near the DRT AOs. The Shadow wingspan is about 12.5 feet with a length of just over 11 feet. It is powered by a 38-horsepower rotary engine. It uses EO and infrared cameras and communications equipment for C2. It provides the brigade with four hours of coverage at 50 kilometers from the launch site. It has a maximum range of up to 125 kilometers, and identifies targets from a range of 3 to 5 kilometers. It uses a hydraulic launcher for takeoff. Landing requires the use of a portable tracking system, an airborne transponder, and an arresting cable. The Shadow is capable of automatic target tracking, and its imagery can be shared with other intelligence assets via data links.

DIGITAL/ELECTRONIC SYSTEMS

7-177. The troop has many other organic digital and electronic systems to aid in gathering and transmitting information to be used for intelligence processing. Currently these systems include equipment such as:

- Radios.
- FBCB2.
- GPS systems.
- Command launch unit.
- Digital cameras.

SECTION VI – CHEMICAL, BIOLOGICAL, RADIOLOGICAL, AND NUCLEAR

7-178. Chemical, biological, radiological, and nuclear assets are limited within the DRT and external support is required from external assets for most circumstances involving CBRN incidents.

SQUADRON AND TROOP ASSETS

7-179. The only CBRN elements organic to the squadron are the squadron CBRN officer and NCO. The squadron CBRN officer uses decision-support tools embedded in the joint warning and reporting network. He does this to plan CBRN defense, provide battle tracking during squadron operations, and gain and maintain CBRN SA. The CBRN battle staff assists the squadron commander, and the troop CBRN NCO assists the troop commander, in CBRN defense through the integration of contamination avoidance, protection, and decontamination.

DECONTAMINATION SUPPORT

7-180. When thorough decontamination is required, the troop receives support from a CBRN company decontamination platoon, which is part of a maneuver enhancement brigade. This normally occurs after contamination with a persistent agent or prolonged exposure to other agents. Thorough decontamination requires detailed planning and extensive manpower and equipment resources. It is conducted in a forward area to limit contamination spread, but in an area that is beyond the range of enemy direct fire systems.

7-181. The troop should be relieved by other units so that it can conduct thorough decontamination. Decontamination proceeds by either the troop alone or the entire squadron, which moves to the decontamination site. If the decontamination proceeds by troop and the squadron remains committed in a mission, the decontamination unit is placed under OPCON of the squadron. More often, the affected troop or the entire squadron moves to the established site and conducts thorough decontamination under squadron control. This method permits the most effective and expeditious use of decontamination assets.

SECTION VII – OTHER COMBAT AUGMENTATION

7-182. The troop does not possess the organic assets to complete many of the detailed requirements of some complex tasks, such as SE, for example. During mission analysis the commander should consider other enablers who can assist in the conduct of the mission. Depending on METT-TC, and the specific nature of the mission, unique enablers such as working dogs, interpreters, tactical MISO teams, explosive ordnance disposal (EOD) teams, or CA teams may be useful. If these assets are not immediately available, the troop commander and subordinate leaders must clearly identify their request for additional support to or through the squadron. Internally, they must identify subordinate elements available to the troop that can fulfill these roles while understanding their organic capabilities and limitations.

MILITARY WORKING DOGS

7-183. Military working dogs are trained for a variety of purposes. Military police units can provide working dog support for mine and explosives detection, and to locate personnel, contraband, weapons, ammunition, and other items. If available, Infantry units should employ working dogs to alert handlers to a variety of sources including personnel and material.

INTERPRETERS

7-184.   Interpreters are valuable assets during reconnaissance operations that require a close proximity to indigenous personnel. A troop may be operating near individuals who have had no previous contact with U.S. personnel and who are unsure of how to deal with U.S. Soldiers. Early in the planning process, the commander should request an interpreter who is either from the AO or familiar with the AO. Using interpreters, communications is improved between the local population and unit personnel. Interpreters also improve intelligence gathering and lead to acceptance of the unit within that AO. Interpreters are often used during searches, including operations at roadblocks/checkpoints.

TACTICAL MILITARY INFORMATION SUPPORT TEAMS

7-185.   Tactical MISO teams support the troop by coordinating broadcasts of information to influence the population on or near the objective with loudspeakers or other delivery means. Tactical MISO teams integrate with the IE process at the squadron level to meet the commander's objectives. The commander should consider withdrawing from the area when employing MISO capabilities since the presence of each unit has the potential to compromise the mission of the other.

7-186.   At the tactical level, MISO teams seek to influence targets directly through face-to-face encounters, dissemination of printed products, and use of loudspeakers. Tactical MISO teams can:

* Influence potential adversaries in the civil population not to interfere with friendly force efforts.
* Induce cooperation or reduce active opposition.
* Reduce collateral damage by giving instructions to noncombatants in the combat zone.

EXPLOSIVE ORDNANCE DISPOSAL

7-187.   The troop requires EOD support to destroy threat ammunition and equipment and to ensure that IEDs and UXO are rendered inoperable. Explosive ordnance disposal capabilities are not organic to the troop, and augmentation of EOD personnel may be needed to clear an identified explosive hazard or assist in the collection of explosive components. Requests for EOD support are processed through squadron operational channels to the IBCT, which in turn forwards the request to the supporting EOD headquarters. Once IEDs or UXOs are located and reported, the EOD headquarters determines which EOD assets can respond. If there is a constant presence of IED/UXO hazards, EOD teams can be attached to the troop.

CIVIL AFFAIRS TEAM

7-188.   Civil affairs teams collect information and conduct assessments to help friendly forces target their relief efforts or stabilize the civil environment. Civil affairs teams should be incorporated with the IE process to meet operational objectives. They assist in assessing the environment and evaluating the effect of search operations on the region. Civil affairs teams meet with local leaders to mitigate the impact of the search and outline the goals and objectives of the operation.

Chapter 8

Sustainment

Sustainment for the DRT is a potentially challenging operation due to the wide-ranging, low-profile, and sometimes decentralized nature of their mission. The DRT often operates well in front of maneuver forces while conducting reconnaissance and security missions. Sustainment or resupply operations for these units can be hindered by distance and the need to keep reconnaissance operations undetected by the threat. Since the duration of DRT missions are often limited, sustainment is accomplished through what the Soldier will carry with him. Missions of longer duration, which require resupply and other sustainment operations, demand further planning and coordination, and often include additional assets such as aerial support.

SECTION I – TEXT REFERENCES

8-1. Table 8-1 consolidates the references to additional information.

Table 8-1. Guide for subjects referenced in text

Subject	References
Infantry Platoon and Squad	FM 3-21.8
Infantry Rifle Company	FM 3-21.10
Air Assault Operations	FM 90-4
Survival	FM 3-05.70

SECTION II – OVERVIEW

8-2. Sustainment for the DRT and other reconnaissance units is characterized by the following basic fundamentals and imperatives.

FUNDAMENTALS

8-3. Tactical sustainment involves the following three interrelated functions:

- Sustainment (including supply, field services, transportation, and maintenance).
- Personnel services (including human resource, legal, and religious support, and financial management).
- Health service support.

8-4. The sustainment system faces significant challenges in supporting the troop's wide-ranging and decentralized missions in the fast-paced, noncontiguous AO. The sustainment structure throughout the IBCT or squadron is extremely austere, allowing for faster deployability and a reduction of the support footprint in the AO. Employment of the latest technological advances in sustainment increases the squadron's support-related SA, allowing for effective DRT support.

8-5. Sustainment is planned in advance and aggressively pushed forward to the troops without the delay imposed by reaction to requests. The FBCB2 provides sustainment functionality in the form of sustainment SITREPs, personnel SITREPs, digital call for support, task order messaging, SA, and task management capabilities. These functions enhance the synchronization of all sustainment support in the AO between the supported and the supporter.

IMPERATIVES

8-6.   Effective sustainment operations enable the DRT commander to accomplish the wide range of tasks the troop is assigned without the sustainment "tail" needlessly inhibiting the troop's operations. In conducting these operations, sustainment leaders are guided by the following five imperatives:

ANTICIPATION

8-7.   Personnel responsible for sustainment activities, including the XO, 1SG, PL, and PSG, anticipate the needs of the troop as operations occur and coordinate to push support forward. They update the commander on sustainment status and capabilities and inform the support echelons of requirements. These personnel, in conjunction with the squadron S4, plan when they will receive the WARNOs and FRAGOs. The S4 determines support requirements and coordinates changes to support relationships.

INTEGRATION

8-8.   The DRT commander, XO, 1SG, PL, and PSG integrate sustainment into the planning process. By discuss sustainment during rehearsals, they ensure the sustainment plan is integrated.

CONTINUITY

8-9.   Sustainment continues before, during, and after the troop mission. Continuous sustainment operations require careful personnel management. The DRT performs operator and organizational maintenance whenever the opportunity exists.

RESPONSIVENESS

8-10. Responsiveness is the ability to meet changing or unforeseen requirements on short notice. Sustainment must be as agile as maneuver to allow the commander to seize opportunities and exploit tactical advantage.

IMPROVISATION

8-11. Leaders often improvise to solve unanticipated problems. Normal operating procedures may be suspended and extraordinary measures taken to overcome them. Agility, initiative, and ingenuity are essential qualities for sustainment leaders.

SECTION III – ORGANIZATION

8-12. Dismounted reconnaissance troop sustainment units are organized similarly to those of other reconnaissance and maneuver units. The main supporting element for the DRT is the troop trains, which are supported by squadron trains operations.

TROOP TRAINS

8-13. The trains provide sustainment during operations. They can be collocated with the CP or may operate separately under the control of the 1SG. Generally, troop trains are located with at least one terrain feature between it and the enemy to be out of the enemy's direct fire range. The troop trains may also consolidate with the squadron trains if locations and distances allow for collocation. This method alleviates stress on the troop's limited sustainment assets.

8-14. Troop trains generally include command vehicles and MEDEVAC vehicles. Troop trains for the DRT also include a field maintenance team if the mission requires direct maintenance support.

SQUADRON TRAINS

8-15. Two types of squadron trains, combat trains, and field trains provide administrative and sustainment support. The squadron commander designates either the combat trains command post (CTCP) or the field trains command post (FTCP) as an alternate squadron main CP.

COMBAT TRAINS

8-16. The combat trains normally consist of the unit maintenance collection point (UMCP), emergency resupply trucks (for example, carrying Class III and V), and the SAS. Generally, the primary intent for location of the combat trains is to ensure they are outside of the enemy's mortar range. A UMCP may also be positioned where recovery vehicles have access or where major or difficult maintenance is performed. A suitable helicopter landing site for MEDEVAC should be nearby.

COMBAT TRAINS COMMAND POST

8-17. The CTCP plans and coordinates sustainment for tactical operations and is prepared to serve as an alternate for the squadron main CP. When established, the CTCP consists of elements from the squadron S1 and S4 sections. The S4 is the OIC of the CTCP and is assisted by the S1. The CTCP serves the following functions:

- Tracks the current operation.
- Controls sustainment of the current operation.
- Provides sustainment representation to the main CP for planning and integration.
- Forecasts and coordinates future requirements.
- Monitors MSRs and controls sustainment traffic.
- Coordinates the evacuation of casualties, equipment, and detainees.

FIELD TRAINS

8-18. The squadron field trains usually consist of the forward support company (FSC), troop supply sections, and elements of the squadron HHT, S1, and S4. Field trains personnel facilitate sustainment from the squadron to the troop by ensuring that LOGPACs are organized, configured, and dispatched. Generally, the primary intent for location of the field trains is to ensure they are outside of the enemy's artillery range.

FIELD TRAINS COMMAND POST

8-19. The FTCP is the primary direct coordination element between the squadron and the BSA/regimental support area. Generally, the HHT commander is the OIC of the FTCP. The FTCP serves the following functions:

- Tracks the current operation.
- Plans for sustainment of future operations.
- Provides sustainment representation to the main CP for planning and integration.
- Forecasts and coordinates future requirements.
- Coordinates the RTD of Soldiers and repaired equipment.

SECTION IV – LOGISTICS

8-20. The sustainment environment the DRT operates in is characterized by longer distances, greater dispersion, decentralized execution, and fluid situations. The commander, XO, and 1SG are careful not to use maneuver unit planning factors when assessing sustainment requirements for the troop.

SUSTAINING RECONNAISSANCE OPERATIONS

8-21. Maintaining the momentum of the operation is the overriding consideration in sustaining reconnaissance. The availability of adequate supplies and transportation to sustain the operation becomes more critical as the operation progresses. The XO and 1SG work closely with the S4 in the planning process to ensure that sustainment meets the demands of reconnaissance.

8-22. Considerations to support reconnaissance operations include the following:

- Using blivets for fuel, water, and caching for other classes of supply.
- Ensuring basic loads remain replenished.
- Planning for increased consumption of petroleum, oils, and lubricants.
- Recovering damaged vehicles to the UMCP or request assistance.
- Using push packages of preplanned and preconfigured essential sustainment items.
- Planning for increased vehicular maintenance.
- Keeping maintenance assets, if available, and other support teams well forward.
- Requesting additional sustainment assets from squadron to support attachments or extended operations.
- Planning aerial resupply.
- Planning and coordinating detainee operations.
- Planning for increased medical assets, including the following:
  - Using CCPs and ambulance exchange points.
  - Augmenting medical treatment elements.
  - Planning for longer transportation and turnaround times.
  - Planning for trains and convoy security.

SUSTAINING SECURITY OPERATIONS

8-23. As with reconnaissance, emphasis on any consideration varies with the mission assigned and shifts during mission execution. Considerations to support security operations include the following:

- Planning for increased use of Class IV and Class V.
- Requesting additional sustainment assets from squadron for attachments.
- Continuing routine resupply IAW the TACSOP.
- Resupplying during limited visibility to reduce the chance of threat contact.
- Preparing to conduct immediate resupply.
- Planning for destruction of supplies and equipment (except medical) that cannot be evacuated.
- Planning for alternate means of evacuation for casualties.
- Emphasizing recovery and evacuation of equipment over forward repair.
- Planning for trains and convoy security.

ATTACHMENTS

8-24. When a supporting element is attached to the DRT, the necessary sustainment augmentation is also attached. This augmentation is established by TACSOP and should be coordinated in advance. It normally consists of maintenance and recovery support and supply support for Classes III, V, and IX. Additional sustainment assets are attached to squadron sustainment elements or directly to the troop.

8-25. When receiving attachments, leaders receive basic information to anticipate support requirements. Planning considerations include the following:

- Number and type of vehicles, personnel, and weapon systems.
- Current status and/or strength.
- When the attachment is effective and for how long.
- What sustainment assets accompany the attachment.
- When and where linkup will occur, and who is responsible for linkup.

DETACHMENTS

8-26. If the situation requires, the squadron detaches reconnaissance troops for certain missions. The same considerations that apply to receiving attachments are used. Based on how long the troop is detached, it deploys with the appropriate level of support, including maintenance, Class III, V, and VIII resupply. This also applies when the DRT operates at a considerable distance from squadron sustainment assets. When the troop is detached to another unit, the squadron S4 sends the following information to the receiving unit's S4:

- Number and type of vehicles, personnel, and weapon systems.
- Current status or strength.
- When the attachment is effective and for how long.
- What sustainment assets accompany the troop.
- When and where linkup will occur, and who is responsible for linkup.

COMMUNICATIONS

8-27. The CTCP is the NCS for the squadron and troop administrative and logistics net. All sustainment leaders and sites operate on the A/L net to respond to requests and coordinate sustainment execution. The troop XO and 1SG use this net to submit sustainment reports and requests for support. The A/L net is used to control movement of sustainment assets during LOGPAC displacement and movement until the LOGPACs are turned over to 1SGs at logistics release points (LRP).

REPORTING

8-28. Accurate reporting of sustainment status is essential to keep the DRT combat ready. Tactical standing operating procedures establish report formats, reporting times, and FM voice brevity codes to keep sustainment nets manageable.

8-29. The DRT sends sustainment reports using two methods. Detailed information can be sent to both the supporting sustainment element and the higher TAC CP. Alternately, detailed FM voice reports are sent to the supporting sustainment element while a summarized status in each general category is given to the higher TAC CP using a brevity code. Routine reports are limited to a summary of those items changing during the reporting period. Immediate reports are submitted as necessary.

8-30. The commander knows the sustainment status of the DRT at all times. The CP tracks the status of subordinate elements by a code, allowing the commander to quickly assess the troop's combat capability using the percentage of combat power, fuel, ammunition, and personnel available. For example, the DRT assigns the following code words:

- GREEN for 90 to 100 percent.
- AMBER for 80 to 89 percent.
- RED for 60 to 79 percent.
- BLACK for less than 60 percent.

LOGISTICS PACKAGES

8-31. A LOGPAC is a grouping of multiple classes of supplies and supply vehicles under the control of a single convoy commander. This tactical grouping of sustainment elements is tailored to METT-TC, but adheres to fundamental tenets that are suitable for inclusion in TACSOP.

SUPPLY ROUTES

8-32. Main supply routes are designated within the AO where the bulk of sustainment traffic flows in support of operations. Alternate supply routes are planned when an MSR is interdicted by the threat or becomes too congested. Alternate supply routes meet the same criteria as the MSR. If CBRN contamination occurs, either the MSR or alternate supply route is designated as the "dirty MSR" to handle contaminated traffic. Security of supply routes in a noncontiguous AO dictates that the troop provide security for sustainment elements.

LOGPAC OPERATIONS

8-33. The DRT supply sergeant compiles and coordinates unique supply requests for the troop and routes them through the squadron S4. Based on the requests and the predetermined supply needs, he then organizes and assembles the LOGPAC in the squadron field trains. Supplies are usually configured to sustain the troop for a 24-hour period or until the next scheduled LOGPAC. Other items included in the LOGPAC are coordinated by the appropriate staff officer and delivered to the field trains. These items include replacement personnel and Soldiers returning from medical treatment facilities, vehicles returning to the troop area from maintenance, mail, and personnel actions.

8-34. The S4 ensures that LOGPACs contain requested or required supplies for the supported units. Additionally, the S4 determines which LRP best supports the operation and notifies all units. LOGPACs are normally organized every 24 to 72 hours for routine resupply. If necessary, the S4 organizes unscheduled LOGPACs to provide immediate or supplementary resupply.

Organization

8-35. The DRT supply sergeant organizes the troop LOGPAC in the field trains. The troop LOGPAC normally consists of the following:

- The troop supply truck, which brings replacements, incoming mail, and the troop water trailer.
- Class I rations.
- Bulk fuel and packaged petroleum, oil, and lubricant products (Class III).
- Class V, including demolitions and mines. The squadron TACSOP normally establishes a standard LOGPAC load of munitions. The S4 uses reports from the 1SG to adjust the standard load.
- Additional trucks as necessary to carry other classes of supply requested by the DRT.
- Class IX parts or other requested maintenance items.

Planning

8-36. The HHT 1SG ensures that the LOGPAC reaches the LRP. The LRP is the point along the supply route where the reconnaissance troop's 1SGs take control of the troop's LOGPAC. Likely areas for LRPs are near MSRs, at crossroads, or close to water (lakes, ponds, and reservoirs). In some situations, however, METT-TC requires placement of the LRP in a less conspicuous location. In all cases, LRP sites are secured.

Movement

8-37. Once the squadron LOGPAC is formed in the field trains, the HHT 1SG and/or supply sergeant moves it forward to the LRP. At the LRP, reconnaissance troop 1SGs, or their representatives, assume control of the troop LOGPACs. The S4 or CTCP representative should be present at the LRP to monitor the operation, coordinate with troop 1SGs, receive hard-copy sustainment reports, and deliver sustainment situation updates. The squadron identifies LOGPAC turnaround times in the TACSOP. Upon completion of resupply operations, the troops return the LOGPAC vehicles to the LRP. They are formed by the HHT 1SG for movement back to the field trains. The convoy commander also establishes security measures for the LOGPAC along the MSR. Movement of sustainment assets is primarily based on three methods:

- On order.
- Triggered by events (such as a troop going RED on Class V).
- Triggered by distance between sustainment assets and the supported elements.

8-38. Checkpoints or LRPs control the movement of assets and specifies which functions will occur at the checkpoint. Functions at checkpoints are activated or deactivated based on the three methods listed above, which are incorporated into the OPORD and/or TACSOP. (Figure 8-1 illustrates an example of sustainment graphics on a maneuver overlay [IBCT reconnaissance squadron]).

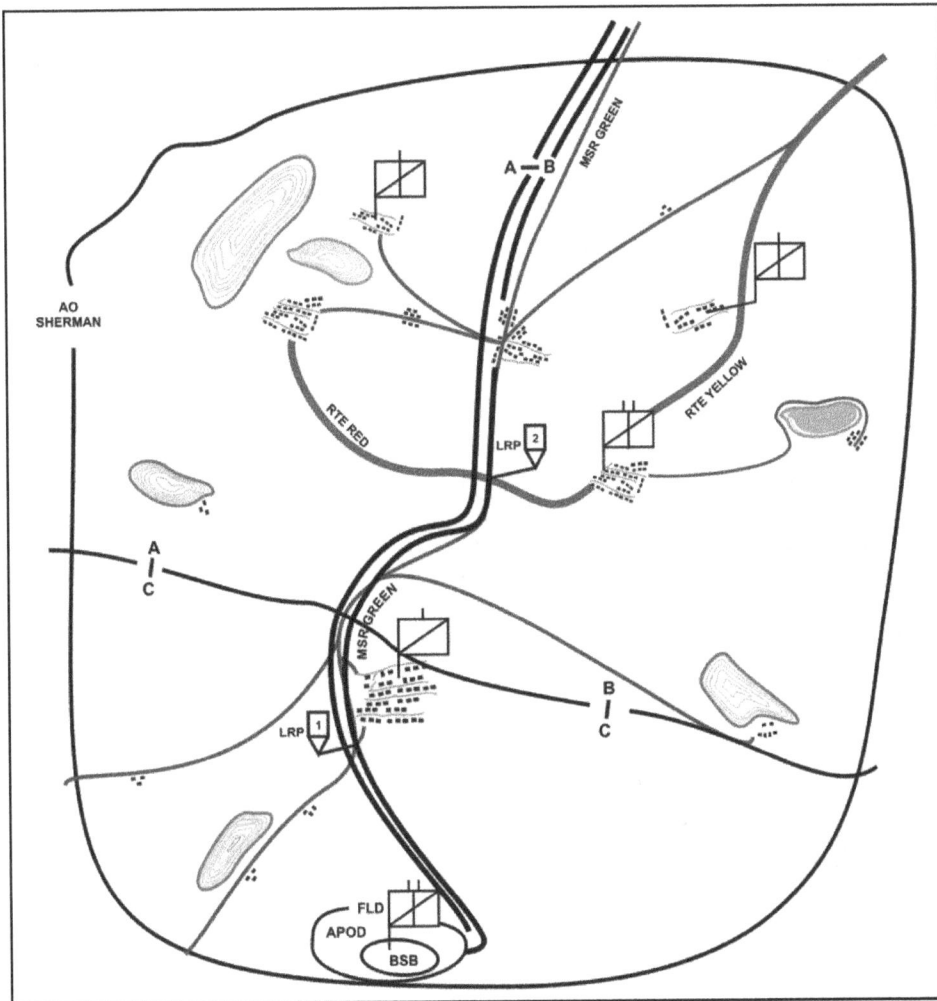

Figure 8-1. Example of sustainment graphics on maneuver overlay

Actions at the Logistic Release Point

8-39. When the LOGPAC arrives at the LRP, the DRT 1SG assumes control of the troop LOGPAC and continues tactical movement to the troop resupply point. The LOGPAC stops at the LRP only when the tactical situation dictates or when ordered by the commander. Security is maintained at all times.

Resupply Procedures

8-40. The DRT uses the service station, tailgate, or in-position resupply method as described under "Routine Resupply" in this section. The time required for resupply is an important planning factor. Resupply is conducted as quickly and efficiently as possible, both to ensure operational effectiveness and to allow the troop LOGPAC vehicles to return to the LRP on time. Service station resupply of the troop normally takes 60 to 90 minutes, but may take longer. Tailgate resupply usually requires significantly more time than service station resupply. At times, leaders use the in-position resupply method, although it takes more time to accomplish.

Return to the Logistic Release Point

8-41. Once resupply operations are complete, the LOGPAC vehicles are prepared for the return trip. Troop vehicles requiring evacuation for maintenance are lined up and prepared for towing. Human remains and personal effects are carried on cargo trucks, fuel trucks, or disabled vehicles. Enemy prisoners of war ride in the cargo trucks. They are guarded by the walking wounded or by other troop personnel. Supply requests and personnel action documents are consolidated for forwarding to the field trains, where the appropriate staff section processes them for the next LOGPAC. The supply sergeant leads the LOGPAC back to the LRP. The LOGPAC keeps moving through the LRP to avoid interdiction by enemy forces or artillery. Whenever possible, the reunited LOGPAC convoy returns to the BSA together. When METT-TC dictates, or when the LOGPAC arrives too late to rejoin the larger convoy, the vehicles return to the BSA on their own.

LOGPAC SURVIVABILITY

8-42. The very nature of an ambush—a surprise attack from a concealed position—places the ambushed unit at a disadvantage. Combat situations often prevent a convoy from taking all the measures necessary to avoid being ambushed; therefore, it takes all possible measures to reduce its vulnerability. These are generally passive measures, supplemented by active measures, taken to defeat or escape from an ambush. (For information on the types of ambushes, see FM 3-21.8.)

8-43. No single defensive measure, or combination of measures, prevents or effectively counters all ambushes or IED detonations. The effectiveness of counterambush measures is directly related to the state of Soldiers' training and the ability of their leaders.

Avoiding an Ambush

8-44. Leaders and Soldiers take the following actions to avoid an ambush:
- Select the best convoy route.
- Maintain vigilant observation of the route ahead of the convoy to detect anything suspicious.
- Conduct map (digital) reconnaissance.
- Conduct ground reconnaissance.
- Conduct aerial reconnaissance.
- Obtain current intelligence information.
- Use OPSEC to deny the threat foreknowledge of the convoy.
- Present a formidable target by:
  - Manning all crew-served weapons.
  - Maintaining 360-degree security.
  - Remaining vigilant and alert.
  - Maintaining a disciplined, aggressive posture.
- Never routinely schedule convoys by time or route.

Reducing the Effectiveness of an Ambush

8-45. Leaders and Soldiers take the following actions to reduce the effectiveness of an ambush:
- Harden vehicles.
- Cover loads.
- Space prime targets throughout the convoy.
- Wear protective equipment.
- Use assistant drivers.
- Carry troops and supplies.
- Use prearranged signals to warn the convoy of an ambush or IED.

- Coordinate for escort vehicles.
- Coordinate for reaction force support.
- Thoroughly brief all convoy personnel on immediate action drills.
- Rehearse immediate-action drills.
- Maintain the interval between vehicles.
- Move through the kill zone, if possible.
- Stop short of the ambush or IED.
- Do not block the road.
- Rapidly respond to orders.
- Aggressively return fire.
- Counterattack with escort vehicles.
- Call for fires support.
- Call in CAS.
- Call for the reaction force.

RESUPPLY OPERATIONS

8-46. Resupply of critical combat supplies is accomplished using standardized procedures to rearm, refuel, and refit the troop as fast as possible to sustain its continuity of effort. For the DRT, resupply operations are complicated by limited sustainment assets organic to the troop, locations of the platoons and other elements of the squadron in relation to friendly maneuver units, and the requirements to secure resupply assets that go to the troop's forward positions. Routine resupply (Classes I, III, V, and IX; mail; and other items required by the troop to effectively conduct the mission) occurs when the troop is out of contact range or when the troop commander decides the risk of not conducting resupply outweighs the risk of interrupting ongoing operations.

8-47. During mission preparation, the squadron staff conducts detailed planning and coordination for combat resupply of the troops forward of the FEBA. Resupply is often conducted prior to mission execution and sustains the units for the entire mission. The DRT often carries a three-day supply with plans to be extracted prior to the supply being used. If necessary, resupply is conducted forward of the FEBA in an assembly area. When resupply of the troop in an assembly area is not feasible, the troop XO and 1SG, along with the squadron staff, plan and coordinate for ground infiltration or aerial insertion of resupply at designated drop-off or cache points.

ROUTINE RESUPPLY

8-48. Routine resupply operations cover items in Classes I, III, V, and IX, as well as mail and any other items requested by the troop. Resupply operations normally occur once a day. Whenever possible, routine resupply should be conducted daily, ideally during periods of limited visibility.

Methods

8-49. As directed by the DRT commander or XO, the 1SG establishes the troop resupply point. He uses either a resupply point (service station method) or delivers resupply directly to the platoon (tailgate method). Occasionally the in-position resupply method is required. He briefs each LOGPAC driver on which method to use. When he has the resupply point ready, the 1SG informs the commander. The troop commander then directs each platoon or element to conduct resupply based on the tactical situation.

Service Station Resupply

8-50. The service station method allows platoons, squads, or Soldiers to move individually to a centrally located resupply point. This method requires the Soldiers to leave their fighting positions. Depending on the tactical situation, a section or platoon moves out of its position, conducts resupply operations, and moves back into position. The squads or platoons rotate individually to eat, pick up mail and sundries, and replenish water. This process continues until the entire platoon has received its supplies. This technique is normally used in assembly areas and when contact is unlikely. This technique also reduces vehicular movement such as the LOGPAC. Vehicles are stationary once they have established the resupply point.

Tailgate Resupply

8-51. When the platoons are dispersed or the tactical situation requires, the 1SG uses the tailgate method. The terrain must permit the movement of multiple vehicles to each platoon position. The 1SG brings LOGPACs to each platoon's area. Individual Soldiers or teams rotate back through the feeding area. While there, they pick up mail and sundries, and replenish other classes of supply. They centralize and guard any EPW. They take Soldiers killed in action and their personal effects to the holding area where the 1SG assumes responsibility for them. (See Figure 8-2.)

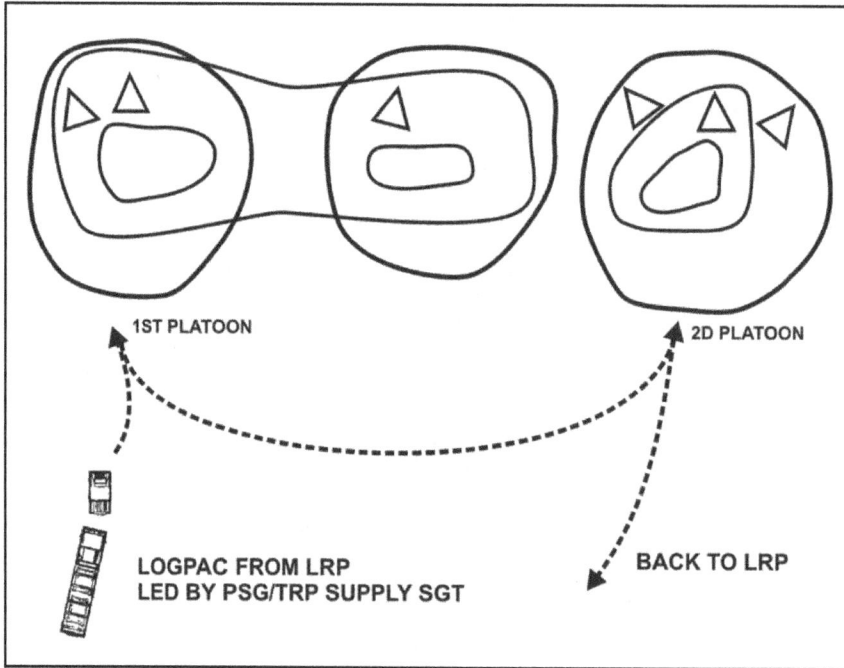

Figure 8-2. Example of tailgate resupply method

In-Position Resupply

8-52. Occasionally, during some reconnaissance and security operations, and with specific METT-TC conditions, the in-position resupply method is used to deliver supplies to the reconnaissance units. The in-position resupply method requires the DRT to bring forward supplies or equipment (or both) to individual unit positions. This method is used when resupply is better facilitated by keeping the units in position and resupply operations do not compromise mission operations. (See Figure 8-3.)

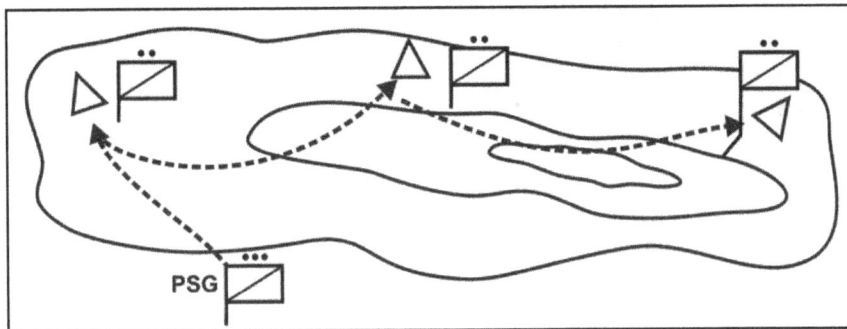

Figure 8-3. Example of in-position resupply method

EMERGENCY RESUPPLY

8-53. Occasionally (normally during combat operations), DRT units have such an urgent need for resupply that they cannot wait for a routine LOGPAC. Emergency resupply involves Classes III, V, and VIII, as well as CBRN equipment and, on rare occasions, Class I. Emergency resupply is conducted using either the service station or tailgate method, but more often the in-position method. The fastest appropriate means is normally used although procedures might have to be adjusted if using certain resupply techniques might compromise the mission. For DRT units operating at extended distances, emergency resupply by air should be considered.

8-54. Emergency resupply begins at section and platoon level by redistribution of supplies. The PSG reports his need for emergency resupply to the 1SG, who relays the request to the squadron S4. The unit's combat maintains a small load of Class III and V for these situations. The S4 coordinates a linkup between the combat trains and the troop 1SG. The 1SG meets the resupply trucks and moves back to the troop AO. The 1SG and troop XO choose a resupply point that is just behind the troop position and masked by terrain from threat direct fire and observation.

PRESTOCKAGE OPERATIONS

8-55. Prestock resupply, which includes pre-positioning and caching, is most often required when DRT elements support defensive operations and when DRT elements conduct missions of longer duration.

Pre-Positioned Supplies

8-56. Prestock operations must be carefully planned and executed at every level. All leaders know the exact locations of prestock sites, which they verify during reconnaissance or rehearsals. The troop takes steps to ensure survivability of the prestock supplies. These measures include digging in prestock positions and selecting covered and concealed positions. The DRT commander must also have a plan to remove or destroy pre-positioned supplies to prevent the enemy from taking them.

Caches

8-57. A cache is a pre-positioned and concealed supply point. It can be used in any operation. Caches are an excellent tool for reducing the Soldier's load and can be set up for a specific mission or as a contingency measure. Cache sites have the same characteristics as an ORP or patrol base, with the supplies concealed above or below ground. An above ground cache is easier to get to, but is more likely to be discovered by the enemy, civilians, or animals. A security risk always exists when returning to a cache. A cache site should be observed for signs of enemy presence and secured before being used; it may have been booby-trapped and might be under enemy observation.

8-58. In the offense, advance elements may set up a cache along the intended route of advance to the objective. Caches may also be set up in the AO to support continuous operations without allowing the enemy to locate the troop through air or ground resupply. Soldier's load considerations may limit the size of caches. Cache activities should not jeopardize the offensive mission. In some cases, special operations forces, multinational forces, or partisans may set up caches in an AO either for their own operations or to support a troop or squadron mission.

8-59. In the defense, a defending unit should set up caches throughout the AO during the preparation phase. A cache should also be in each alternate or subsequent position throughout the depth of the defense AO. During stay-behind operations, or in an area defense on a fluid battlefield where the enemy is all around, caches might be the only source of supply for extended periods.

Troop Prestock (Pre-Positioning and Cache)

8-60. The two methods of prestock resupply differ in the level of security provided for the supplies. With pre-positioning, supplies are generally left unattended, without security, although steps are taken to prevent detection of the location by threat elements.

8-61. Both pre-positioning and cache are used in a variety of reconnaissance and security operations. During reconnaissance, prestock positions are established by advance elements along the intended route of advance or near the objective. In security operations, reconnaissance elements set up prestock points throughout the AO. These points are in alternate or supplementary OPs, in addition to other locations throughout the depth of the AO. Scouts also use prestock to provide resupply for patrols.

8-62. Prestock operations are carefully planned and executed at every level. Prestock points are placed where they can be located by simple instructions that are clear to someone who has never visited the site. All leaders, including the lowest ranking member of the mission element, know the exact locations of prestock points. As noted, the troop sustainment team takes steps to ensure security and survivability of pre-positioned supplies by digging in prestock positions, selecting covered and concealed positions, and considering the effects of weather and terrain. A prestock plan must include plans for removal or destruction by the DRT element using the items.

SUPPLY CONSIDERATIONS

8-63. The techniques described in the preceding paragraphs are the normal methods for resupply within the troop. However, a basic understanding of nonstandard techniques, different modes of delivery, and specific supply issues are also required for the successful execution of the sustainment function.

Foraging and Scavenging

8-64. Foraging and scavenging are used infrequently and only under extreme conditions. Foraging is the gathering of supplies and equipment necessary to sustain basic needs, such as food, water, and shelter, in the AOs. Scavenging is the gathering of supplies or equipment (friendly or enemy) in the AOs to help the user accomplish his military mission. Leaders protect their Soldiers by determining whether the food or water is safe and whether the equipment is booby-trapped.

Aerial Resupply

8-65. Helicopters are a vital lifeline for reconnaissance units, especially when operating forward of friendly lines for extended periods. Aerial resupply operations reduce the risks associated with conducting ground resupply under such conditions; however, they require significant planning and entail consideration of a different set of risks. Because of these issues and limited ground transportation, troop personnel must know how to conduct aerial resupply (See FM 90-4). Dismounted reconnaissance troop units must have an understanding of PZs/LZs selection, sling loading, bundle drops, and allowable cargo loads to conduct an aerial resupply if needed.

8-66. Aerial assets are useful in resupplying DRT in OPs in restricted terrain. On the other hand, aerial resupply is sometimes not feasible, such as when helicopters are not available. In addition, the signature of resupply helicopters can compromise unit positions. Careful choice of resupply routes and LZs minimizes this risk.

8-67. In using aerial resupply, the DRT commander considers the threat's ability to locate his unit by observing the aircraft. Unless conducting the resupply in an area under friendly control and away from direct enemy observation (reverse slope of a defensive position with reconnaissance well forward), the commander locates the DZ or LZ away from the main unit in an area that can be defended for a short time. The delivered supplies are immediately transported away from the DZ or LZ.

Managing Consumption of Water

8-68. Ensuring that Soldiers receive and drink enough water is a vital sustainment and leadership function at all levels in the troop's chain of command. Even in cold areas, everyone needs to drink at least two quarts of water a day to maintain efficiency. Soldiers must drink water at an increased rate in a combat environment.

8-69. Water is delivered to the unit under troop or squadron control in 5-gallon cans, disposable bottles, trailers, or collapsible containers. When a centralized feeding area is established, a water point is set up in the mess area and each Soldier fills his canteen. When the troop distributes rations, it resupplies water either by collecting and filling empty canteens or distributing water cans to the platoons.

8-70. Water is habitually included in LOGPACs. The ability of the command to supply water is limited by the ability of the brigade support battalion's water section to purify, store, and distribute it. The sustainment system may not always be able to meet unit needs, particularly during decentralized operations. In most environments, water is available from natural sources. Soldiers should be trained to find, treat (chemically or using field expedients), and use natural water sources. (See FM 3-05.70 for ways the unit can supply its own water, if needed.)

8-71. When water is not scarce, leaders should urge Soldiers to drink water even when they are not thirsty. The body's thirst mechanism does not keep pace with the loss of water through normal daily activity. The rate at which dehydration occurs depends on the weather conditions and the level of physical exertion.

8-72. If water is in short supply, Soldiers should use it sparing for hygiene purposes. Water used for coffee or tea might be counterproductive since both increase the flow of urine. Soups, however, are an efficient means of getting both water and nutrition when water is scarce. This is especially true in cold weather when heated food is desirable. When in short supply, water should not be used to heat MREs. A centralized heating point can be used to conserve water yet provide warmed MREs.

TRANSPORTATION

8-73. Movement of supplies, equipment, and personnel with limited vehicle assets requires careful planning and execution. Dismounted reconnaissance troop units have limited organic transportation for resupply operations. The squadron or forward supply company provides vehicle assets for troop resupply operations.

8-74. When extra vehicles are provided to the troop, the troop employs them to capitalize on their capability to execute the mission requirement. They also return them for follow-on troop or parent-unit missions. Transportation assets are scarce, often resulting in trade-offs. For example, they are used to upload increased quantities of ammunition and less water, or carry unit rucksacks and remain unavailable for resupply. The DRT commander ensures the asset accomplishes the most important mission. Because time is critical, the troop must reduce on-station time so that all troop requirements can be met. Leaders must ensure that drivers know where they are going and how to get there. Land navigation training, marked routes, and strip maps referenced to landmarks are all ways to keep drivers from getting lost.

SECTION V – OTHER OPERATIONS

8-75. Other sustainment operations include reorganization and replacements, enemy prisoners of war, and FHP.

REORGANIZATION

8-76. To maintain effective, consistent combat power, the troop must have specific plans and procedures that allow each element to quickly integrate replacement personnel and equipment. Unit TACSOP defines how Soldiers and equipment are prepared for combat, including areas such as uploading, load plans, precombat inspections, and in-briefings.

REPLACEMENTS AND CROSS-LEVELING OF PERSONNEL

8-77. Replacements for wounded, killed, or missing personnel are requested through the squadron S1. Returning or replacement personnel arriving with the LOGPAC should have already been issued all TA-50 equipment, mission-oriented protective posture (MOPP) gear, and other items, including personal weapons. Within the troop, each PL cross-levels personnel among his crews, with the 1SG controlling cross-leveling from platoon to platoon.

8-78. Integrating replacements into a troop is important. A new arrival on the battlefield might be scared and disoriented as well as unfamiliar with local TACSOP and the theater of operations. The following procedures help integrate new arrivals into a troop:

- The DRT commander meets new arrivals and welcomes them to the unit, normally through a brief interview. The commander has a TACSOP for reception and integration of newly assigned Soldiers.
- The PL and PSG welcome the new arrivals, describe unit standards, and introduce section leaders.
- The section leader introduces everyone to their teams and briefs them on duty positions. He also ensures that each replacement has a serviceable, zeroed weapon, as well as ammunition, MOPP gear, and other essential equipment. His in-briefing covers the section and platoon's recent and planned activities.
- Troop leaders also tell new Soldiers about important TACSOP, and give them a paper copy of information about special issues concerning the AOs. Leaders also give new arrivals a form letter to send to their next of kin. The letter states where to mail letters and packages, explains how to use the Red Cross in emergencies, and lists the chain of command.

FORCE HEALTH PROTECTION

8-79. Effective timely medical care is an essential factor in sustaining the troop's combat power during continuous operations. The DRT commander ensures that troop leaders and medical personnel know how to keep Soldiers healthy, save their lives if they are wounded or injured, and care for them after injuries or illnesses.

HEALTH AND HYGIENE

8-80. The DRT commander and leaders, along with the troop senior trauma specialist and field sanitation team, emphasize and enforce high standards of health and hygiene This preventive-medicine approach covers all aspects of Soldiers' health and well being, including:

- Daily shaving to ensure proper fit of the protective mask when threatened by a CBRN attack.
- Regular bathing and changing of clothes as often as the situation permits.
- Preventing weather-related problems, including frostbite, trench foot, immersion foot, and wind chill that can occur in cold weather and heat exhaustion and heat stroke that are common in hot weather. Soldiers also learn the effects of sunburn, which can occur at any time.
- Preventing diseases, including insect-borne diseases such as malaria and Lyme disease. They learn that diarrhea diseases can be prevented with effective field sanitation measures, including unit waste control, water purification, rodent control, and insect repellents.
- Combating operational stress control, preventing fatigue, and implementing a strict unit sleep plan.
- Preventing fatigue, including strict implementation of the unit sleep plan.

CASUALTY RESPONSE PERSONNEL

8-81. Casualty response consists of a variety of tiered medical and leadership response personnel for medical care and assistance.

First Response

8-82. First response is defined as the initial, essential, stabilizing medical care rendered to wounded, injured, or ill Soldiers at the point of initial injury or illness. The first responder is the first individual to reach a casualty and provide first aid, enhanced first aid, or emergency medical treatment. First aid can be performed by the casualty (self-aid) or another individual (buddy-aid), while enhanced first aid is provided by the CLS. The individual who has medical military occupational specialty training is the combat medic (trauma specialist). He provides emergency medical treatment for life threatening trauma and stabilizes and prioritizes (triages) wounded for evacuation to the SAS. At the SAS, wounded Soldiers receive advanced trauma medicine by the treatment team composed of the surgeon, physician's assistant, and a senior trauma specialist.

Combat Lifesaver

8-83. The CLS is a nonmedical Soldier trained to provide advanced first aid/lifesaving procedures beyond the level of self-aid or buddy-aid. The CLS is not intended to take the place of medical personnel, but to slow deterioration of a wounded Soldier's condition until treatment by medical personnel is possible. Each certified CLS is issued a CLS aid bag. Whenever possible, the troop commander ensures there is at least one combat lifesaver in each fire team. An emerging *"first responder"* program expands CLS trauma treatment with increased emphasis on combat and away from training injuries.

8-84. Combat lifesavers are section members trained in emergency medical techniques. They are the *"911"* medical assets for the section until a medic or another more qualified medical person becomes available. Because combat lifesaving is an organic capability, the platoon and troop should make it a training priority. The combat lifesaver ensures the section CLS bag is packed, all IVs are present, and litters are properly packed, and identifies Class VIII shortages to the platoon medic. He participates in all casualty treatment and litter carry drills. The combat lifesaver must know the location of the CCP and the TACSOP for establishing them. He has a laminated quick reference nine-line MEDEVAC card.

Senior Trauma Specialist

8-85. The senior trauma specialist (troop senior medic) is both the troop's primary medical treatment practitioner and the supervisor of all battlefield medical operations. The latter role encompasses numerous responsibilities. The senior trauma specialist works closely with the DRT commander to ensure all members of the troop understand what to do to provide and obtain medical treatment in combat situations. He oversees the training of combat lifesavers. Once combat begins, he manages the troop CCP, provides medical treatment, and prepares patients for MEDEVAC. He helps the 1SG arrange CASEVAC. The senior trauma specialist also monitors the paperwork that is part of the medical treatment and evacuation process, including:

- Ensuring that the casualty feeder report remains with each casualty until the Soldier reaches the squadron main aid station or field aid station.
- If a Soldier's remains cannot be recovered, completing DD Form 1380 (US Field Medical Card) and giving it to the 1SG for processing as soon as possible.

Platoon Medic or Trauma Specialist

8-86. Because platoon members commonly address their trauma specialist as *"doc"* or *"medic,"* shows his critical role in providing competent, life-saving care. During combat planning and preparation, he inspects platoon CLS bags, verifies that IVs are placed in litters, and fills Class VIII shortages. He recommends the location for the platoon CCPs and the TACSOP for establishing them. He rehearses casualty treatment and litter carries with all platoon members, not only aid and litter teams; and conducts CLS refresher training. Designated medical personnel collect the DA Form 1156 (Casualty Feeder Card) at the aid station. They forward the form to the S1 section for further processing through administrative channels in the squadron field trains.

Platoon Sergeant

8-87. Although unit TACSOP dictates specific responsibilities, the PSG typically ensures that wounded or injured personnel receive immediate first aid and informs the commander of casualties. During critical operations, or when the platoon takes a lot of casualties, the PSG normally oversees the platoon CCP. He coordinates with the 1SG and troop senior trauma specialist for ground evacuation. He ensures that casualty feeder card (DA Form 1156) and field medical card (DD Form 1380) forms are completed and routed to the proper channels. The PSG carries a laminated quick reference nine-line MEDEVAC card.

First Sergeant

8-88. The DRT 1SG oversees the operation of the troop CCP, particularly in critical operations or when casualties are high. He brings the full measure of his experience and authority to bear in the efficient treatment, collection, preparation, and transport of casualties. Successful CASEVAC depends on the 1SG's ability to anticipate, plan, and rehearse the CCP operation. METT-TC dictates the CCP site location, which must be accessible by both ground and air transport. The 1SG supervises and coordinates casualty operations, collects witness statements, and submits them to the squadron S1. He also submits the battle loss report to the squadron tactical operations center. These duties also relate to another important combat function of the 1SG: managing the troop's personnel status. As needed, the 1SG cross levels personnel to make up for shortages.

Commander

8-89. The DRT commander has overall responsibility for medical services. His primary task is to position medical personnel at the proper point on the battlefield to treat casualties or to evacuate those casualties properly. The troop commander designates the location for the troop's CCP and ensures that the location is recorded on the appropriate overlays. He also develops and implements appropriate TACSOP for CASEVAC. Two key planning considerations are as follows:

- The commander analyzes both fundamental categories of treatment and evacuation to determine if he must accept risk in one or the other and how he may mitigate identified risks. For example, where distances to available medical treatment facilities (MTFs) are excessive and transportation assets stretched, the commander might request more medics during an operation.
- Sites for casualty treatment and evacuation vary widely on the noncontiguous battlefield. The commander tries to identify, disseminate, and coordinate with all available MTFs accessible to his unit, including those outside his organization.

Squadron Medical Platoon

8-90. The medical platoon is the focal point of FHP for the squadron. It is organized to support the squadron CPs and troops; acquire, treat, and evacuate casualties; and coordinate further evacuation as necessary. This platoon establishes a treatment point or SAS. The S1, assisted by the S4 and field medical assistant, plans FHP.

Squadron Aid Station

8-91. As noted, the squadron medical platoon establishes and operates the SAS. The SAS provides trained personnel to stabilize patients for further evacuation, provides emergency lifesaving and limb-saving treatment, and treats minor wounds or illness to allow patients to RTD. The SAS is normally consolidated with the CTCP.

8-92. The SAS can operate two treatment teams for a limited time. Based on the mission, the SAS may operate a forward and a main aid station or consolidate under a single aid station. When echeloned, the aid stations are limited primarily to triage, stabilization, and preparation for evacuation, which is the normal configuration during combat operations. The aid stations may also position laterally to cover a large frontage. The main aid station is capable of manning a CBRN casualty aid station during CBRN operations. The field medical assistant and surgeon position themselves where they can best support FHP operations. The primary responsibility of the senior medical NCO is to coordinate and supervise MEDEVAC, resupply Class VIII, provide support for the aid stations, and assist in FHP tactical planning. He moves between the two aid stations, coordinating evacuation and movement of the aid stations. When not deployed, the aid station is normally consolidated with the CTCP.

Medical Evacuation Teams

8-93. Medical platoon ambulances provide MEDEVAC and enroute care from the Soldier's point of injury (POI) or the troop CCP to the squadron aid station. The ambulance team supporting the troop works in coordination with the combat medics supporting the platoons. Medical evacuation teams are habitually attached to troops. They support the troop with treatment and evacuation to the squadron aid station. Units with area support responsibility are included in the planning process, and additional assets are allocated to the area supporting medical company to compensate for the additional patient flow. Under normal circumstances, ambulance support is pushed forward with the field trains to assist in MEDEVAC. Maximum use of aerial evacuation (when available) for litter-urgent patients should be planned and exercised.

Combat Medic Section

8-94. Combat medics are allocated with one combat medic per platoon in the troop. The platoon combat medic normally locates with, or near, the PL or PSG. The senior troop combat medic normally collocates with the 1SG. When the DRT is engaged, he remains with the 1SG and provides medical advice as necessary. As the tactical situation allows, he manages the troop CCP, provides treatment, and prepares patients for evacuation.

EVACUATION OF WOUNDED PERSONNEL

8-95. Medical evacuation is not the same as CASEVAC. They are defined as follows:

- **Medical evacuation.** This is the movement of casualties using medical assets while providing en route medical care. Ideally, casualties are transferred from a CCP to a MEDEVAC asset.
- **Casualty transport.** Commonly called CASEVAC, this is the movement of casualties by nonmedical assets without specialized trauma care. Casualty transport or CASEVAC is what is done when moving casualties from the POI to the platoon CCP or troop CCP.

8-96. The two areas of medical support are treatment and evacuation. Effective CASEVAC has a positive impact on the morale of a unit. Casualties are cared for at the POI (or under nearby cover and concealment) and receive self- or buddy-aid, advanced first aid from the combat lifesaver, or emergency medical treatment from the trauma specialist (troop or platoon medic).

Location of Casualties

8-97. During the fight, casualties should remain under cover where they received initial treatment (self- or buddy-aid). As soon as the situation allows, casualties are moved to the platoon CCP. From the platoon area, casualties are normally evacuated to the DRT CCP and then back to the SAS. The unit TACSOP addresses this activity, to include the marking of casualties in limited visibility operations. Small, standard, or infrared chemical lights work well for this purpose. Once the casualties are collected, evaluated, and treated, they are prioritized for evacuation back to the troop CCP. Once they arrive at the troop CCP, the above process is repeated while awaiting their evacuation back to the SAS.

Evacuation Personnel

8-98. An effective technique, particularly during an attack, is to task organize a sustainment team under the 1SG. These Soldiers carry additional ammunition forward to the platoons and evacuate casualties to either the troop or the squadron CCP. The leader determines the size of the team during his estimate.

8-99. When the DRT is widely dispersed, the casualties might be evacuated directly from the platoon CCP by vehicle or helicopter. Helicopter evacuation might be restricted due to the threat of enemy ground-to-air small arms, and shoulder-fired or other air defense weapons. In some cases, the casualties must be moved to the troop CCP before evacuation. If the capacity of the squadron's organic ambulances is exceeded, unit leaders may task supply or other vehicles to backhaul or otherwise transport noncurrent casualties to the SAS. In other cases, the PSG may direct platoon litter teams to carry the casualties to the rear.

8-100. Leaders should minimize the number of Soldiers required to evacuate casualties. Casualties with minor wounds can walk or even assist with carrying the more seriously wounded. Soldiers can make field-expedient litters by cutting small trees and putting the poles through the sleeves of buttoned ACU blouses. A travois, or skid, can be used for CASEVAC. The wounded are strapped on this litter, and one person pulls it. It can be made locally from durable, rollable plastic and fastened with tie-down straps. In rough terrain, or on patrols, litter teams can evacuate casualties to the SAS. They are then carried with the unit either until transportation can reach them or until they are left at a position for later pickup.

Treatment and Evacuation Duties and Responsibilities

8-101. Unit TACSOP and OPORDs address casualty treatment and evacuation in detail. They cover the duties and responsibilities of key personnel, the evacuation of chemically contaminated casualties (on separate routes from uncontaminated casualties), and the priority for operating key weapons and positions. They specify preferred and alternate methods of evacuation and make provisions for retrieving and safeguarding the weapons, ammunition, and equipment of casualties. Slightly wounded personnel are treated and returned to duty by the lowest echelon possible. Platoon aid men evaluate sick Soldiers and treat or evacuate them as necessary. Casualty evacuation is rehearsed like any other critical part of an operation.

8-102. Procedures for using the casualty feeder report are found in DA Form 1156 and field medical card, DD Form 1380. Before casualties are evacuated to the CCP or beyond, leaders should remove all key operational or sensitive items and equipment, including COMSEC devices or SOIs, maps, and position location devices. Every unit should establish a TACSOP for handling the weapons and ammunition of its wounded in action. Protective masks must stay with the individual.

8-103. At the CCP, the senior trauma specialist conducts triage of all casualties, takes the necessary steps to stabilize their condition, and initiates the process of evacuating them to the rear for further treatment. He helps the 1SG arrange evacuation via ground or air ambulance, or by nonstandard means.

Evacuation Vehicles

8-104. When possible, the HHC medical platoon ambulances provide evacuation and enroute care from the Soldier's POI or the troop's CCP to the SAS. The ambulance team supporting the DRT works in coordination with the senior trauma specialist supporting the platoons. In mass casualty situations, nonmedical vehicles can be used to assist in CASEVAC as directed by the DRT commander. Plans for using nonmedical vehicles to perform CASEVAC should be included in the unit TACSOP. Ground ambulances from the brigade support medical company or supporting corps air ambulances evacuate patients from the SAS back to the brigade support medical company MTF located in the BSA.

Ambulance Requests

8-105. The DRT or its platoons contact the medical company on the medical company command frequency for all MEDEVAC requests if the assigned DRT ambulance is not available. If unable to contact the medical company on that frequency, the DRT unit should attempt to relay the request on the next higher command frequency.

Air Evacuation

8-106. For evacuation by air, the DRT uses the standard nine-line air evacuation request format (see Table 8-2). The medical company prioritizes the request with others it receives to determine if air evacuation is possible. In conducting the evacuation operation, the DRT accomplishes the following tasks:
- Prepares and secures a suitable PZ/LZ for the aircraft.
- Provides terminal guidance during the aircraft's approach to the PZ/LZ.

Table 8-2. Nine-line air evacuation request

Line Item	Explanation
1. Location of Pickup Site.	Encrypt grid coordinates. When using DRYAD Numeral Cipher, the same SET line is used to encrypt grid zone letters and coordinates. To preclude misunderstanding, a statement is made that grid zone letters are not included in the message (unless unit TSOP specifies its use at all times.)
2. Radio Frequency, Call Sign, Suffix.	Encrypt the frequency of the radio at the pickup site, not a relay frequency. The call sign (and suffix if used) of person to be contacted at the pickup site may be transmitted in the clear.
3. No. of Patients by Precedence.	Report only applicable info & encrypt brevity codes. A = Urgent, B = Urgent-Surgical, C = Priority, D = Routine, E = Convenience. (If two or more categories are reported in the same request, insert the word "break" between each category.)
4. Special Equipment.	Encrypt applicable brevity codes. A = None, B = Hoist, C = Extraction equipment, D = Ventilator.
5. No. of Patients by Type.	Report on applicable information and encrypt brevity code. If requesting MEDEVAC for both types, insert the word "break" between the litter entry and the ambulatory entry: L + # of Patients – Liter; A + # of Patients – Ambulatory (sitting).
6. Security Pickup Site (Wartime).	N = No enemy troops in area, P = Possibly enemy troops in area (approach with caution), E = Enemy troops in area (approach with caution), X = Enemy troops in area (armed escort required).
7. Number and Type of Wound, Injury, Illness (Peacetime).	Specific information regarding patient wounds by type (gunshot or shrapnel). Report serious bleeding, along with patient blood type, if known.
8. Method of Marking Pickup Site.	Encrypt the brevity codes. A = Panels, B = Pyrotechnic signal, C = Smoke signal, D = None, E = Other.
9. Patient Nationality and Status.	Number of patients in each category need not be transmitted. Encrypt only applicable brevity codes. A = US Military, B = US Civilian, C = Non-US Military, D = Non-US Civilian, E = EPW.
10. CBRN Contamination (Wartime).	Include this line only when applicable. Encrypt the applicable brevity codes. C = Chemical, B = Biological, R = Radiological, N = Nuclear.
11. Terrain Description (Peacetime).	Include details of terrain features in and around proposed landing site. If possible, describe the relationship of site to a prominent terrain feature (lake, mountain, and tower).

This page intentionally left blank.

Glossary

Acronym	Definition
A	
ACA	airspace coordination area
AGT	air-ground team
AO	area of operation
B	
BDA	battle damage assessment
BHL	battle handover line
BHO	battle handover
BLOS	beyond line of sight
BSA	brigade support area
C	
C2	command and control
CA	civil affairs
CAS	close air support
CASEVAC	casualty evacuation
CBRN	chemical, biological, radiological, and nuclear
CCA	close combat attack
CCIR	commander's critical information requirement
CCP	casualty collection point
CI	counterintelligence
CLS	combat lifesaver
COA	course of action
COIST	company intelligence support teams
COLT	combat observation and lasing team
COMSEC	communications security
COP	common operating picture
CP	command post
CTCP	combat trains command post
D	
DRT	dismounted reconnaissance troop
DZ	drop zone
E	
EA	engagement area
EEFI	elements of friendly information
EOD	explosive ordnance disposal
EPW	enemy prisoner of war
ERT	engineer reconnaissance teams
F	
1SG	first sergeant
FA	field artillery
FARP	forward arming and refueling point
FBCB2	Force XXI battle command brigade and below
FEBA	forward edge of the battle area
FFP	final firing position

FHP	force health protection
FIST	fire support team
FLOT	forward line of own troops
FM	frequency modulation
FO	forward observer
FPF	final protective fires
FRAGO	fragmentary order
FRIES	fast rope insertion/extraction system
FS	fire support
FSCM	fire support coordination measure
FSO	fire support officer
FTCP	field trains command post

G

GCM	graphic control measure

H

HCT	HUMINT collection team
HE	high explosive
helocast	helicopter cast and recovery
HF	high frequency
HF-ALE	high frequency automatic link establishment
HHT	headquarters and headquarters troop
HPT	high-payoff target
HPTL	high-payoff target list
HUMINT	human intelligence

I

IBCT	Infantry brigade combat team
IAW	In accordance with
ID	identification
IE	information engagement
IED	improvised explosive device
IP	Internet protocol
IPB	intelligence preparation of the battlespace

J

JFO	joint fires observer
JTAC	joint terminal attack controller

L

LC	line of contact
LD	line of departure
LNO	liaison officers
LOA	limit of advance
LOC	lines of communication
LOGPAC	logistics package
LOS	line of sight
LRP	logistics release point
LZ	landing zone

M

M/CM/S	mobility, countermobility, and survivability
MCoE	Maneuver Center of Excellence
MDMP	military decision-making process
MEDEVAC	medical evacuation

METT-TC	mission, enemy, terrain, weather, troops, and support available, time available, and civil considerations
MICO	military intelligence company
MISO	military information support operations
MOPP	mission-oriented protective posture
MRE	meals ready to eat
MSR	main supply route
MTF	medical treatment facility

N

NAI	named area of interest
NCO	noncommissioned officer
NCS	net control station
NFA	no fire area
NGO	non-governmental organization
NVD	night vision devices

O

OAKOC	observation and fields of fire, avenues of approach, key terrain, obstacles, and cover and concealment.
OBSTINTEL	obstacle intelligence
OE	operational environment
OIC	officer in charge
OP	observation post
OPCON	operational control
OPLAN	operation plan
OPORD	operation order
OPSEC	operation security
ORP	objective rally point

P

PIR	priority intelligence requirement
PL	platoon leader
POI	point of injury
PSG	platoon sergeant
PZ	pick-up zone

Q

QRF	quick reaction forces

R

RHO	reconnaissance handover
ROE	rules of engagement
RP	release point
RPM	revolutions per minute
RTD	return to duty
RTO	radio-telephone operators

S

SA	situational awareness
SAS	squadron aid station
SEAD	suppression of enemy air defense
SINCGARS	single channel ground/airborne radio system
SITREP	situation report

SITTEMP	situation template
SOI	signal operation instruction
SOP	standard operating procedure
SP	start point
SPIES	special patrol infiltration/exfiltration system
SPOTREP	spot report
SU	situational understanding
SUAS	small unmanned aircraft system

T

TAC CP	tactical command post
TACSAT	tactical satellite
TACSOP	tactical standing operating procedures
TAI	target area of interest
TLP	troop-leading procedures
TOT	time on target
TRP	target reference point

U

UHF	ultrahigh frequency
UMCP	unit maintenance collection point
UO	urban operations
UXO	unexploded ordnance

V

VHF	very high frequency

W

WARNO	warning order
WP	white phosphorus

X

XO	executive officer

References

SOURCES USED

These are the sources quoted or paraphrased in this publication.

CENTER FOR ARMY LESSONS LEARNED (CALL)

CALL Handbook No. 09-49, *IED-Defeat Leader's Handbook*, September 2009.

FIELD MANUALS

FM 2-01.3, *Intelligence Preparation of the Battlefield/Battlespace*, 15 October 2009.

FM 2-22.3, *Human Intelligence Collector Operations*, 6 September 2006.

FM 3-0, *Operations*, 27 February 2008.

FM 3-05.210, *Special Forces Air Operations*, 27 February 2009.

FM 3-05.70, *Survival*, 17 May 2002.

FM 3-06.11, *Combined Arms Operations in Urban Terrain*, 28 February 2002.

FM 3-07, *Stability Operations*, 6 October 2008.

FM 3-09.32, *Multi-Service Tactics, Techniques, and Procedures for the Joint Application of Firepower*, 20 December 2007.

FM 3-20.96, *Reconnaissance and Cavalry Squadron*, 12 March 2010.

FM 3-20.971, *Reconnaissance and Cavalry Troop*, 4 August 2009.

FM 3-20.98, *Reconnaissance and Scout Platoon*, 3 August 2009.

FM 3-21.10, *The Infantry Rifle Company*, 27 July 2006.

FM 3-21.8, *The Infantry Platoon and Squad*, 28 March 2007.

FM 3-22.10, *Sniper Training and Operations*, 19 October 2009.

FM 3-34, *Engineer Operations*, 2 April 2009.

FM 3-34.2, *Combined-Arms Breaching Operations*, 31 August 2000.

FM 3-34.22, *Engineer Operations-Brigade Combat Team and Below*, 11 February 2009.

FM 3-34.170, *Engineer Reconnaissance*, 25 March 2008.

FM 3-50.1, *Army Personnel Recovery*, 10 August 2005.

FM 3-50.3, *Multi-Service Tactics, Techniques, and Procedures for Survival, Evasion, and Recovery*, 20 March 2007.

FM 3-55.93, *Long-Range Surveillance Unit Operations*, 23 June 2009.

FM 3-90, *Tactics*, 4 July 2001.

FM 3-90.6, *Brigade Combat Team*, 14 September 2010.

FM 3-90.119, *Combined Arms Improvised Explosive Device Defeat Operations*, 21 September 2007.

FM 4-0, *Sustainment*, 30 April 2009.

FM 5-0, *The Operations Process*, 26 March 2010.

FM 6-0, *Mission Command: Command and Control of Army Forces*, 11 August 2003.

FM 6-02.74, *Multi-Service Tactics, Techniques, and Procedures for the High Frequency-Automatic Link Establishment (HF-ALE) Radios*, 20 November 2007.

FM 90-4, *Air Assault Operations*, 16 March 1987.

JOINT PUBLICATIONS

JP 3-0, *Joint Operations*, 17 September 2006.

JP 3-09.3, *Close Air Support*, 8 July 2009

JP 3-50, *Personnel Recovery*, 5 January 2007.

TRAINING CIRCULAR

TC 9-64, *Communications-Electronics Fundamentals: Wave Propagation Transmission Lines, and Antennas*, 15 July 2004.

FORMS PRESCRIBED

N/A

FORMS NEEDED

These forms must be available to the intended users of this publication.

DA Form 1156, Casualty Feeder Card.

DA Form 1594, Daily Staff Journal or Duty Officer's Log.

DA Form 2028, Recommended Changes to Publications and Blank Forms.

DD Form 1380, U.S. Field Medical Card.

INTERNET WEBSITES

Reimer Digital Library, https://atiam.train.army.mil/

Army Publishing Directorate, http://www.apd.army mil/

Index

This page intentionally left blank.

By order of the Secretary of the Army:

GEORGE W. CASEY, JR.
General, United States Army
Chief of Staff

Official:

JOYCE E. MORROW
Administrative Assistant to the
Secretary of the Army
1029901

DISTRIBUTION:

Active Army, Army National Guard, and U.S. Army Reserve: To be distributed in accordance with the initial distribution number (IDN) 115890, requirements for ATTP 3-20.97.

www.ingramcontent.com/pod-product-compliance
Lightning Source LLC
Chambersburg PA
CBHW080017280326
41934CB00015B/3373